PROLETPEN

PROLETPEN

America's Rebel Yiddish Poets

EDITED BY
Amelia Glaser and David Weintraub

TRANSLATED BY
Amelia Glaser

WITH ILLUSTRATIONS BY
Dana Craft

SPECIAL EDITORIAL ASSISTANCE FROM
Yankl Salant

THE UNIVERSITY OF WISCONSIN PRESS
Dora Teitelboim Center for Yiddish Culture

The University of Wisconsin Press
1930 Monroe Street
Madison, Wisconsin 53711

www.wisc.edu/wisconsinpress/

3 Henrietta Street
London WC2E 8LU, England

Printed in the United States of America

Library of Congress Cataloging-in-Publication Data
Proletpen : America's rebel Yiddish poets / edited by Amelia Glaser and
David Weintraub ; translated from the Yiddish by Amelia Glaser ;
illustrations by Dana Craft ; special editorial assistance from Yankl Salant.
p. cm. "A Dora Teitelboim Center for Yiddish Culture publication."
Includes bibliographical references.
ISBN 0-299-20800-1 (hardcover : alk. paper)
1. Yiddish poetry—United States—Translations into English.
2. Yiddish poetry—20th century—Translations into English.
3. Yiddish poetry—United States—History and criticism.
I. Glaser, Amelia.
PJ5191.E3P76   2005
839´.113080973—dc22   2004025729

Contents

Preface

Dora Teitelboim was an internationally renowned Yiddish poet whose fiery social motifs sang and wept joys and sorrows and above all, the love of mankind. Ms. Teitelboim, the poet for whom "the wind itself speaks Yiddish," had a dream of establishing an organization that would promote Yiddish poetry and prose to a new generation of Americans by making Yiddish works more accessible to the American public, thereby cultivating a new harvest of Yiddish educators, writers, speakers, and performers.

The Dora Teitelboim Center for Yiddish Culture, the initiator of this volume, continues the dream of its namesake by publishing high quality translations of Yiddish literature, running an annual writing contest, promoting the rich texture and beauty of Jewish culture through lectures and events, developing Yiddish educational programming and children's activities, and producing documentary film and radio programming. To date, the Center has published eight highly acclaimed volumes for adults and children including *All My Yesterdays Were Steps, The Last Lullaby: Poetry from the Holocaust, The Four Butterflies, The Little House, The Witness Trees, The New Country, The Jewish Book of Fables: The Selected Works of Eliezer Shtaynbarg,* and *Sereena's Secret, Searching for Home.*

Yiddish has, for one thousand years, been the language of the troubadour, poet, sweatshop toiler, revolutionary, and dreamer. Yiddish became a vital expression of secular Jewish life, giving a solid footing to a people without a territory of their own. Although Yiddish fell victim to an unnatural death as a result of the Holocaust, it is experiencing a renaissance not seen for many years. This book is part of a series unearthing the beauty of Yiddish literature and demonstrating that Yiddish poetry and prose rivals the best of American literature. Since its founding, the Center has been determined to put a considerable number of unjustly ignored New York poets of the interwar years back on the map of Yiddish literature, both in the original Yiddish and in English translation. We feel certain that this volume will be the first of a number that will explore the magnificent creativity of so many American Yiddish poets who remain unknown to new generations of Yiddish students and enthusiasts, while ever more books and articles appear about the same few writers who now dominate the canon.

It must be said at once that politics has always been a driving force in Yiddish culture. The fact is that glaringly absent from nearly all Yiddish anthologies were some of the greatest poets of the twentieth century, all of whom were, at one time or another, affiliated with the Proletpen. In fact, so striking was their absence that the great Yiddish translator, Aaron Kramer, edited and published an entire book, *A Century of Yiddish Poetry*, dedicated to putting back into Yiddish literary history, in his words, "those who were utterly ignored or dismissed in a half-sentence."

In the twenty-first century it is hoped that rather than reviving the sectarianism that too often has divided Yiddish culture by "revising history" through false notions of quality control and outdated political litmus tests, thereby throwing out a significant part of Yiddish cultural history, that we knock down the walls that have divided us to work for the revival of our beloved culture and the study of its many internal diversities.

From this volume, we hope that finally we can grasp the wisdom gained from the Holocaust and set aside our lifelong political biases so that we can share another thousand years of Yiddish culture.

David Weintraub
Executive Director
Dora Teitelboim Center for Yiddish Culture
www.yiddishculture.org

Translator's Acknowledgments

I hope that in years to come I will be able to repay my colleagues, family, and friends for the literary and personal support they have shown me throughout my work on this volume. Of the many people deserving of thanks, I would like to name three in particular: Dovid Katz of the University of Vilnius, Lithuania, first introduced me to Yiddish and to the idea for this collection, offered translation advice, and supplied background information and poetry by his father, Menke Katz. Dov-Ber Kerler of Indiana University advised me at Oxford, where this book began as a master's thesis in Yiddish Studies. Itche Goldberg of the Zhitlovsky Foundation and *Yidishe kultur* has donated hours to my understanding of Yiddish poetry in America and to shaping the volume at many stages along the way.

Many thanks also go to several individuals whose comments and editing led to significant changes in the text. Among these are Shoshana Balaban-Wolkowicz, Gabriella Safran, Kathryn Hellerstein, Vera Szabo, Bernard Gowers, Joel Berkowitz, Marc and Beatrice Caplan, Jeremy Grant, Steven Zipperstein, Gregory Freidin, Monika Greenleaf, Eddie Portnoy, Yankl Salant, Ken Moss, Marci Shore, my parents, John and Carol Glaser, and my grandmother, Barbara Glaser. For their help specifically with my English verse, I am grateful to John Felstiner, David Goldstein, Barbara Harshav, Kerry Sean Keys, Ronald Bush, Bob McGill, Max Rankenburg, and Melisse Lafrance. I would also like to express my gratitude to Zachary Baker, Judaica curator at Stanford University, who has given me advice and help at many stages in this project, to Brad Sabin-Hill, Leo Greenbaum,

Yeshaye Metal, and many others at YIVO for help in locating sources for this book, and to Betsy and Don Landis and Nancy Burson, who generously opened their homes to me during my research trips to New York. The late Sonia Pomerantz of Grodno gave me insight into the life and work of her brother Alexander, and into her own experiences of the proletarian epoch. Finally, warm thanks to David Weintraub of the Dora Teitelboim Center for Yiddish Culture for bringing this project to life.

Though these people are not responsible for any of the book's shortcomings, their generosity with time and resources have allowed it to materialize. To my family, which has shaped my ideals, and to these poets, whose ideals have helped to shape history, I dedicate these translations.

A Note on Orthography

Where Yiddish words appear in these translations, I generally adhere to the YIVO system of orthography. In the case of several names, however, such as Chaim Schwartz (rather than Khayim Shvarts) and Alexander Pomerantz (rather than Aleksander Pomerants), I have bowed to the writer's preferred English spelling of his or her own name. The following sounds, according to the YIVO transliteration system, should be read as such:

Ay	as in "eye"
Ey	as in "Oy, v*ey*"
Oy	as in "*Oy*, vey"
I	as in "m*e*"
U	as in "*you*"
E	as in "*e*nter"
A	as in "c*a*ll"
Y	as in "*y*ou"
Kh	as in "*ch*allah"
Tsh	as in "*chi*cken"

The Yiddish poems that appear in this volume have been typeset to match the authors' own spelling and punctuation. While some writers choose to spell Hebrew words, for example, in the traditional way, many opt for the phonetic Soviet spelling. This generally reflects the time and place in which the poems were written.

Chronology

1880–1915 Immigration of approximately 2 million Jewish people from Eastern Europe to America.

1886 Chicago, May Day: Workers killed in Haymarket massacre during a demonstration demanding an eight-hour work day.
New York: Major strike of Jewish tailors.

1892 New York: Opening of Ellis Island center to deal with massive immigration.

1897 Basel: First World Zionist Congress.
Czarist Russia: Organization of the Jewish Labor Bund.

1907–8 New York: Foundation of *Di yunge* writers movement.

1911 New York: 146 female workers die in fire at Triangle Shirtwaist Company factory.

1912 April: More than fifteen hundred people die, including many impoverished immigrants, when *Titanic* sinks.

1914 August: Outbreak of First World War. Continues until 1918.

1917 Russia, November: Bolsheviks seize power in October Revolution. Civil war until 1920.

1918 Soviet Union: Formation of Proletkult, organization for proletarian culture.

1919   Berlin, January: Suppression of "Spartacist" communist
       revolt and murder of Polish Jewish Spartacist leader Rosa
       Luxemburg.
       Moscow, March: Communist International (Comintern)
       founded.
       U.S.: Foundation of Communist Party.
       New York: Publication of *In Nyu York* by Moyshe-Leyb
       Halpern.

1920   Moscow: Second Congress of Comintern denounces Zionism
       as "utopian and reformist."

1921   America: Establishment of Jewish federation of Communist
       Party.

1922   New York: Establishment of leftist Yiddish newspaper the
       Frayhayt, edited by Moyshe Olgin and S. Epstein.
       Moyshe-Leyb Halpern contributes poetry. (It later
       becomes *Morgn frayhayt*.)

1924   New York: Publication of *Yung kuznye*, edited by Alexander
       Pomerantz.
       New York: Formation of Yunger arbeter shrayber farayn
       (Young Workers Writers Union), first Yiddish proletarian
       writers' group.

1925   New York: Visit of Russian poet Vladimir Mayakovsky.
       New York: Publication of only edition of *Spartak*, in Russian,
       Yiddish and English.
       Soviet Union: Suicide of Russian poet Sergei Yesenin

1927   America: Execution of Sacco and Vanzetti, immigrant Italian
       anarchists, for alleged murder.

1928   New York: Formation of Yunyon skver (Union Square)
       Yiddish proletarian writers group. Publication of anthology
       by the same name.
       Soviet Union, May: Stalin securely established in power.

1929   New York: Formation of Frayhayt shrayber-farayn, the
        Frayhayt writers' union.
        Hebron, August: Riots involving Arabs.
        New York, September–December: Formation of Proletpen.
        New York, October: Wall Street stock exchange crash initiates
        Great Depression.

1930   Soviet Union: Suicide of Russian poet Vladimir
        Mayakovsky

1932   Scottsboro: Trial of eight African American males for alleged
        rape of two white women. Continues until 1937.
        Moscow: Stalin abolishes the Russian Association of
        Proletarian Writers, ending official proletarian literary
        movements in the Soviet Union.

1933   Germany, January: Nazi regime comes to power.

1934   Soviet Union: Establishment of Birobidjan as a Jewish
        Autonomous Region.

1935   Kiev: Publication of *Proletpen* by Alexander Pomerantz, based
        on the doctoral dissertation he wrote under Prof. Max
        Erik. Pomerantz returns to America.

1936   Spain, July: Fascist revolt begins Civil War. Nationalist
        victory in 1939.
        Soviet Union: Yiddish monthly *Farmest* (edited by Itzik
        Fefer) devotes an issue to Proletpen.

1937   Soviet Union: Purge of many Jewish intellectuals, including
        Max Erik.
        Paris, September 21: World Congress of Jewish Culture.
        New York: The leftist YKuF (Yidishe kultur farband [Yiddish
        Culture Union]) is founded.

1938   Publication of anthology *Khurbn Daytshland* (Catastrophy/
        Holocaust Germany) by Proletpen.

1939   New York: Death of Moyshe Olgin, editor of *Morgn frayhayt*.
        August: Molotov-Ribbentrop non-aggression pact between
            Soviet Union and Germany.
        September: Outbreak of Second World War. Germany
            invades Poland.

1941   June: Germany invades Soviet Union.
        December: United States joins war against Axis.

1943   Soviet Union: Dissolution of the Communist International.

1945   May: End of war in Europe.

1948   Tel Aviv: Declaration of the State of Israel.

1948–53 Soviet Union: Arrest and murder of most Yiddish writers.

1962   Buenos Aires: Publication of *Di sovetishe harugey-malkhus*
            (*The Jewish Writers Martyred by the Soviet*) by Alexander
            Pomerantz.

1969   New York: Publication of *A Treasury of Yiddish Poetry* edited
            by Irving Howe and Eliezer Greenberg.

1989   New York. Publication of *A Century of Yiddish Poetry*
            edited by Aaron Kramer, including a number of Proletpen
            writers.

PROLETPEN

Introduction

The Days of Proletpen
in American Yiddish Poetry

DOVID KATZ

History, they say, is written by the victors. That is the case not only for the military history of nation states. It can apply even within the heritage of stateless minority cultures and in the university study of their literatures, where there should be no losers on the basis of those external, political categories of winners and losers.

A half century ago, in the 1950s, Yiddish literature was beginning to win respect as a serious endeavor in an American Jewish society that had (and in many ways still has) a less than profound interest in the cultural and linguistic heritage of its recent East European ancestry. The grudging, piecemeal, and frequently superficial emergence of a recognition of Yiddish as the language of a serious modern literature came about in wider circles—in other words, beyond the limited and dwindling circles of the East European–born Yiddish cultural activists themselves—thanks to English translations that became fashionable in the fifties. Advances of the period include Irving Howe and Eliezer Greenberg's *A Treasury of Yiddish Stories* (1954) and the first major successes in translation enjoyed by Isaac Bashevis Singer. These include his novels *The Family Moskat* (1950) and *Satan in Goray* (1955; the original Yiddish appeared in the thirties). If some single literary event were needed as a symbolic turning point, it would be Saul Bellow's translation of Singer's "Gimpel the Fool," a short story, which appeared in 1952 in *Partisan Review*. Attention to Yiddish poetry was soon to follow, in expectedly smaller circles of readers.

And so it came to pass that Yiddish came out of the closet in America just as the McCarthy era was peaking and daily cultural ramifications of the Cold War were becoming omnipresent. In those years, Yiddish was also making its maiden appearance in American academia. By producing a sophisticated anthology, Howe and Greenberg did for the study of Yiddish literature what Uriel Weinreich's *College Yiddish*, which first appeared in 1949, had done to pioneer the study of the language at American universities some five years earlier.

Howe (1920–1993) and Greenberg (1896–1977), like all serious translator-anthologists, chose works they thought would work best in the target language (i.e., English). Nevertheless, there was, in those "revelation years" of serious Yiddish literature in America, a McCarthyesque political litmus test as well. This was an issue bound to arise under such circumstances, because many of the best Yiddish writers came from that part of the American Left that was the prime target of McCarthyism. It is no novelty in intellectual history that competing groups which are "close relatives" tend toward more mutual bitterness than those at vast conceptual distance (the classic instance is Judaism and Christianity vis-à-vis paganism in the early Christian centuries). Howe and Greenberg (who were to reveal themselves as fine anthologists of Yiddish poetry too) were both from the "socialist but anti-Soviet camp." Howe, who had cofounded the journal *Dissent* in 1953, was an old democratic socialist with Trotzkyist leanings (ergo, anti-Stalin from the start). Greenberg was in his earlier years a member of the Yiddish literary communist movement and had published in the movement's daily, the *Frayhayt* (*Freiheit*), and its monthly, *Hamer*, and like many others, later "switched sides."

And that takes us to the content of that political litmus test, which has, remarkably, remained a taboo topic in Yiddish literary studies to this day, a taboo this book aims to start taking down. The test, strange as it may strike readers today, was based not even on whether writers were *still* "among the communists" (none of *those* could be included, no matter how talented), but rather on *when* a writer "left the Left" to "join the Right." And here it is necessary to review some historical and cultural background and the vocabulary of the history of Yiddish culture in America before the thread of this narrative can be picked up.

∾

Modern Yiddish literature in all its branches is overwhelmingly a product of writers who were brought up in the traditional, religious, God-fearing, and strictly observant society of East European Ashkenazic Jewry. They became part of the minority segment of that society that underwent radical transformation from unquestioning religiosity to a western type openness to ideas, beliefs, doubt, and—action. These individuals had become part of a number of late-nineteenth- and early-twentieth-century movements that developed the use of Yiddish for modern genres, including the poem, story, novel, and play, as well as an extensive didactic and political literature and a vibrant press, all in the spirit of a rising Jewish modernism and a new attraction to the form and content of secular culture. The parent of all of these developments is the nineteenth-century East European *haskóle* (Haskalah), or "Enlightenment." Unlike its late-eighteenth-century German-Jewish "grandparent" (the Berlin Haskalah of Moses Mendelssohn), it did not, by and large, abandon the traditional languages of European Jewry. Instead, the Easterners recast and remolded both Hebrew and Yiddish into powerful media of expression for the modern literary and societal aims of East European Jewry.

By the late nineteenth century, when the anti-czarist movements in the Russian Empire were picking up momentum (especially after the assassination of Alexander II in 1881 and the pogroms that followed), the new Yiddish literary movement was emboldened by the various revolutionary tendencies. The most famous is the Jewish Labor Bund, founded in Vilna (now Vilnius) in 1897. But there were many more. By the early twentieth century, there were Yiddish journals published by anarchists, communists, social democrats, socialists (of various types and stripes), territorialists, Zionists, Zionist-socialists and more.

Emigré writers transplanted Yiddish literature to London's Whitechapel (the city's "East End") and to New York's Lower East Side (known simply as "the East Side" in Jewish cultural history and Yiddish literature). In both cities, the first major Yiddish poetry was closely linked with the labor movement. The immigrant sweatshop and its surrounding poverty and social injustice became a key theme. The pioneers of Yiddish poetry in the west were the "sweatshop poets," most famously Joseph Bovshover (1873–1915), Dovid Eydlshtat (1866–1892), Morris Rosenfeld (1862–1923), and Morris Winchevsky (1856–1932). Most spent some years in Whitechapel before continuing on to New York, where they established the first period of American Yiddish poetry. And, as is so often the case in the history of ideas and of literature, the pioneers set in motion a train of reactions and rebellions.

From around 1907, a group called Di yunge ("The Youngsters"—a name taken from their detractors) set out to write poetry that would not serve as the "rhyme department of the Jewish labor movement" (poems protesting exploitation of the workers and so forth), but would pursue art for the sake of art. They attracted writers who would come to be reckoned among the twentieth century giants of Yiddish verse, including Avrom-Moyshe Dillon (1883–1934), Mani Leyb (1883–1953), Moyshe-Leyb Halpern (1886–1932), Y. Y. Shvarts (1885–1971), and after his arrival in New York in 1913, H. Leivick (1886–1962). Nearly all were immersed in European literature.

A follow-on movement in New York Yiddish poetry came around 1919 with the launch of Inzikh ("In oneself" or introspectivism). The poets most associated with the movement, and its journal that began to appear in 1920, are Aaron Glantz-Leyeles (1889–1966), Yankev Glatshteyn (Jacob Gladstone, 1896–1971), N. B. Minkoff (1893–1958), and Yankev Stodolsky (1890–1962).

The period from around 1907 to the early 1920s, including both the Yúnge and the Inzikhístn (introspectivists), may be viewed as the second period of Yiddish poetry in America. The reaction against poetry for the sake of the labor movement, and the quest for genuine art, deep personal expression, and perfection of aesthetic form, went on to become part of most subsequent Yiddish poetry.

The third period, from the early 1920s to the years of the Second World War (and in many ways, beyond), was characterized by a new wave of immigration to New York that brought a lot of fresh young writers who would make their débuts in the early or mid-1920s, and by a new and different kind of politization. This was not a politization in the vein of the earlier sweatshop era ("the labor movement in general"), but a function of the acute new split *within* that movement. The starting point, around the time of the First World War and in its immediate aftermath, was that nearly all Yiddish writers in America published in newspapers and magazines affiliated with various socialist movements. This includes, by and large, even the maturing masters who were veterans of the Yúnge and the Inzikhístn. These "veterans" too were usually socialists, only socialists who believed in the freedom of literature from politics, including their own political affiliations.

These socialist movements underwent a bitter split in the years immediately following World War I and the rise of the Soviet Union. It was the split between those who supported or at least had high hopes for the daring new Soviet experiment and those who opposed it early on as a deceptive evil. By the mid-1920s, the two camps had coalesced around two daily Yiddish newspapers in New York City.

Opponents of the Soviet Union were led by Abe Cahan (1860–1951), founding editor of the *Forverts* (the *Jewish Daily Forward*). The pro-Soviets grouped around Moyshe Olgin (1878–1939), founding editor of the *Frayhayt*. The *Forverts* had been around since the spring of 1897. The *Frayhayt* arose a quarter century later, in the spring of 1922, as a specific enterprise of the pro-Soviet Yiddish movement, and had positive attitudes toward (and affiliations with) the American Communist Party (though most writers and the vast majority of readers were not members).

Both Cahan and Olgin sought to attract to their newspapers (and to their "satellite" literary journals) serious literary talent in addition to popular writers. Although somewhat of an oversimplification, Cahan was the clear winner in prose, having on his staff such giants of Yiddish fiction as Sholem Ash (1880–1957), Israel Joshua Singer (1893–1944), and Isaac Bashevis Singer (1904–1991). Olgin was the victor in attracting great poets, including Menachem Boraisho (1888–1949), Moyshe-Leyb Halpern (1886–1932), H. Leivick (1886–1962), and Avrom Reisin (1876–1953), as well as the classic prose humorist Moyshe Nadir (1885–1943) and the "poetic novelist" Isaac Raboy (1882–1944).

The literary quality of the Yiddish used and the sophistication of literary criticism were palpably higher in the *Frayhayt*. Unlike the *Forverts* and all the other Yiddish newspapers of New York, which stuck to the late-nineteenth- and early-twentieth-century Germanized spelling, the *Frayhayt* adopted the mainstream modern spelling used by nearly all leading American Yiddish writers of the twentieth century. The *Frayhayt* did not adopt the radical Soviet spelling, or its offshoot, the YIVO variant proposed in the late 1930s (and in their books of poetry, the affiliated poets adopted a uniquely American modernistic spelling of Yiddish). As in so many other things, the *Frayhayt* was manifestly American. And on the issue of Yiddish spelling, it is an almost eerie "coincidence" that a typical page of a 1930s issue of the *Frayhayt* is spelled almost identically to a number of orthodox publications today in the early twenty-first century. Rather than try to sell papers at the lowest common denominator through sensationalism, the *Frayhayt* taught tens of thousands of immigrant workers to appreciate the creativity of the most serious modern Yiddish culture. At the same time, its pages were full of lively advertisements for everything from kosher hotels to the latest movies to the best banks for working families. Despite the supposed "similar persuasion" of the *Frayhayt*, not one single page could ever be mistaken for one from a Soviet Yiddish newspaper.

The *Forverts* camp became known in Yiddish as Di Rékhte ("those of the Right"); the *Frayhayt* camp as Di Línke ("those of the Left"). That may sound strange today, given that both were so very proudly socialist and far to the left of the American center. Let it suffice to mention that the twin mottos on the front page of every day's *Forverts*, to either side of the name of the paper, were "Workers of the world unite!" and "Liberation of the workers depends on the workers themselves!" And that was the "right wing" paper!

As if to symbolize the "New Yorkness" of the scene, Lower Manhattan geographic concepts came to be signifiers of the camps: "East Broadway" was the symbol of the Rékhte, "Union Square" of the Línke. True, East Broadway was the home of a number of Yiddish newspapers, including religious and Zionist oriented papers, all of which were in some sense Rékhte, and true, Union Square was home to many American leftist and union institutions. Be it however cause or effect, it was the addresses of the two giants of the Yiddish daily press that came to be the "Temples of Jerusalem" for each camp: 175 East Broadway was the famed *Forverts* building and 35 East Twelfth Street (off Union Square), the premises of the *Frayhayt*.

This third period of American Yiddish poetry may be referred to as the "Left-Right Rift." The strife between the camps was its constant feature, and not infrequently its genuine inspiration. A sense of after-the-fact regret frequently accrues to that sharp divisiveness within Yiddish literature in America and all the "might have beens" about the differences unity could have made in the longer term. Who knows? A counter-argument is just as potent: The contentious spirit of the times, and the intense literary competitiveness engendered between the two camps, were a stimulation that spurred these circles in New York City to make the city a magnificent center (in both quality and quantity) of Yiddish literary output in the interbellum period.

But much of that output remains unknown today, even to the most serious students of Yiddish literature.

And the reason for that is to be found in politics and American Yiddish political correctness. Here we must turn to the history of the two camps against the backdrop of European and Middle Eastern history, both of which exerted powerful pressures on those happy-but-poor and war-free streets of New York.

In the early interbellum period, the successes of Yiddish in the Soviet Union were astounding. Here was a language, without a country or serious ambitions for becoming the national language of a nation-state, being given official status as one of a number of national languages in areas where it was widely spoken; where the government financed a system of education in Yiddish, from kindergarten through university-level institutes; where post offices and courts "spoke in Yiddish" in regions with dense Yiddish speaking populations; where Yiddish prose and poetry flourished and Yiddish writers were *paid* for their work (true paradise for the poets of, say, Delancey Street who worked in the garment industry, and other manual labor jobs, to keep themselves alive). This perception was not limited to the Línke of Union Square and the streets to its south. It took hold around the world. Two examples can make the point. The great Yiddish poet (and mystic prose writer) Moyshe Kulbak (1896–1940) migrated in 1928 from Vilna (then Wilno, in free Poland, a major international center of modern Yiddish culture) across the then Polish-Soviet border, eastward to Minsk. After various sojourns in Rumania, the Soviet Union, the United States, and Sweden, the famous novelist Dovid Bergelson (1884–1952), having "seen the choices," settled in the U.S.S.R. in 1934.

And then, history (or Stalin) mixed in and the Soviet paradise became hell on earth. To stick to our examples, Kulbak was arrested in 1937 and murdered soon thereafter, a fate that was to come upon Bergelson and many others in the later postwar purges. By the 1930s, there was extensive party meddling in the content and form of literature, and in the later years of the decade the Yiddish school systems were dismantled. The late 1920s Birobidjan experiment—establishment of a Jewish "homeland" in the Soviet Far East—was also ringing hollow by the later 1930s. During all this time, Jewish settlement in Palestine, by contrast, was succeeding ever more in building a viable state with the revived Hebrew-based language as its medium.

So it would be easy to argue that history happened to go Abe Cahan's way, not Moyshe Olgin's, especially as Cahan was prepared to shift on the

Zionism issue, while Olgin and the Communist Party were not. But things are never that simple. Within New York Yiddish culture, the *Frayhayt* took the lead in exposing Hitlerism for what it was from the first moment. Anti-Jewish laws and actions in Germany, even when directed against "capitalist Jewish institutions" were exposed in front page headlines. The unrelenting exposure of the Fascist threat was no mean feat in the early and mid-1930s. Still, the balance of a rapidly evolving history was tipping in the direction of the Rékhte, a tilt encouraged, at least in part, by a number of concrete events, each of which led to the defections of major writers from the Línke to the Rékhte.

First were the Arab riots in Hebron in 1929 which left sixty murdered and sixty-seven injured Jewish men, women, and children, many associated with the non-Zionist yeshiva community there (much of which had come from Lithuania to establish traditional Torah study in this ancient Jewish town). For the Rékhte, the need to support the Jewish cause in these circumstances was metamorphosing the whole attitude toward Zionism from negative to sympathetic. For Olgin and the Línke, whose cues on such matters came from the Party line, it was necessary to see the Arab perspective and not reach conclusions based on one's own race or religious background. After a first reaction, blaming Muslim fanatics, the *Frayhayt* reversed itself (catastrophically for its own interests) and adopted the Party line. This led to the first major spate of defections to the Rékhte, including the masters Boraisho, Leivick, Raboy, and Reisin. The leading periodical for serious literature, *Literarishe bleter* in Warsaw, published the declarations of all four in its September 27, 1929, issue. The fracas over Yiddishist reactions to the events in Hebron was not limited to New York and the writers around the *Frayhayt*. The editor of that prestigious Warsaw journal, Nakhmen Mayzl (1887–1966), devoted an editorial called "Nókhveyen" ("After-woes," October 11, 1929), begging Yiddish writers of all political stripes to disembark from the new internecine war of mutual destruction, boycotts, public disownings, and constant personal attacks in the press. A leftist himself, he noted with dismay how the Soviet press had suddenly turned the New York *Frayhayt* resigners into "enemies of the people" after years in which they had been "heroes of the people." Some of them, including Avrom Reisin, visited the new U.S.S.R. and their hometowns to a hero's welcome.

A decade later, in August of 1939, the Hitler-Stalin (Ribbentrop-Molotov) pact engendered analogous results in "Yiddish New York." Moyshe Nadir was among the literary luminaries who walked away from the Línke. But now the situation was more complex. Many saw the pact as a clever way to stop Hitler's eastward advance that would open an opportunity for escape for as many Jews as possible. After the dismemberment of Poland in September 1939, the humiliation and ghettoization of the Jews on the German-held side of the newly established border contrasted starkly with the Soviet-allotted territories to its east. Notwithstanding the dismantling of cultural and educational institutions in the religious, Hebrew, and mainstream Yiddish spheres, the Soviet side provided physical safety, the development of Soviet Yiddish culture, and for the first time in these regions, anti-racist laws which even imposed a fine for the use of racial slurs. For all the faults of the Soviet system, the situation was one of day-and-night contrast. With Hitlerist ghettoization, deportation, and imminent genocide looming to the west of the new line, life on the Soviet, eastern side of the line looked pretty good. And, after the Germans overran the Soviet areas in late June of 1941, in Operation Barbarossa, the Soviet communists became close allies of the Americans and British, and the *Frayhayt*'s stance was strengthened for some years.

There was another arena in which the *Frayhayt*'s hand was strong: domestic policy in the United States. Following the stock market crash of 1929 and throughout the Great Depression and beyond, the vast majority of the Yiddish reading Jewish immigrant masses in America suffered poverty. Today we justifiably remember the evils of the American Communist Party and its various "cultural affiliates," but that is somewhat anachronistic and therefore inevitably one-sided. For many simple, not particularly political people, these were the folks who came to put your furniture back in your tenement after you were evicted for being late with the rent one month. These were the people fighting for the rights of the poor, the unemployed, the disenfranchised, the victims of all sorts of prejudice, not least racial and religious. If these people also thought that something good was being built "way over there" in faraway Russia, so be it. In the twenties and thirties it wasn't particularly sensational. In those years, that was not the kind of issue of "loyalty to America" that it would become decades later during the Cold War.

The Holocaust was a devastating blow to all Yiddish writers, and it is hardly a surprise that many (by no means all) wrote much of their most original work before its full scope became widely known in the west. The calamitous realization that the civilization in which their language was native was totally destroyed in a mostly successful war of racial annihilation was, for the majority, demoralizing beyond description. But one moral issue hit the Línke harder than the Rékhte in the late 1940s and in the decades that followed. The age-old Jewish religious life in Eastern Europe, and all those rabbis, yeshivas, and God-fearing people which the Línke had rebelled against, had been savagely annihilated by the Nazis and their local collaborators. There could be little appetite for pursuing the old "anti-clericalist" line any longer.

Then came the Cold War and McCarthyism. The *Frayhayt* and its affiliate institutions, including the leftist Yiddish school system, faced constant harassment. And, the last major campaign of destruction against Yiddish culture by Stalin's government culminated in the murder of the leading Yiddish writers and Jewish intellectuals on August 12, 1952. When this became known in the United States, a significant group of younger generation writers (defined here, by and large, as those born in the early twentieth century) went over to the Rékhte. This third and most devastating wave of defections was the first to deprive the Línke of many of the very writers who had been the 1920s founders of the literary branch of the movement. Some of the best joined together in 1958 to move en masse to the *Forverts*-allied Workmen's Circle (Arbeter ring), where they established a (more or less) special branch for Línke-to-Rékhte-defectors. It was called the Dovid Bergelson Branch (no. 44) of the Workmen's Circle, named for one of the major writers murdered on August 12, 1952. This pivotal crossing over was trumpeted in a *Forverts* article of June 11, 1958, which has remained a sort of declaration of victory by the Rékhte. It reported: "Some two hundred people came to the inaugural meeting of the branch. It would appear that such a branch, an organization for the former Yiddish communists, who had been deceived by a false ideal, humiliated, bitterly disappointed, is very much a necessity." And so, victory was declared by the right in the *Yiddish* Cold War in New York, over thirty years before the disintegration of the Soviet Union.

Nevertheless, the Línke and their institutions continued to work tirelessly for modern Yiddish culture. The *Frayhayt* was published until 1988, and the Zhitlovsky Foundation continued to publish fine Yiddish books throughout the 1990s and to this day. The magazine *Yidishe kultur* (Yiddish

Culture), edited by the universally beloved, redoubtable Itche Goldberg, continues to be arguably the best Yiddish literary journal in the world. Goldberg, who celebrated his one hundredth birthday in 2004, denounced Stalin's crimes only slightly later than the Rékhte, but like many others, elected to continue leading and working for a distinct branch of secular Yiddish culture in America. And, he survived all the rest.

For their part, the Rékhte, or their heirs to be more precise, continue to publish the *Forverts*, now a weekly, with lavish subsidies from the Forward Association, as well as the magazine *Tsukunft* (The Future).

☙

Considering all that happened, it is not particularly surprising that those 1950s anthologists were petrified at the thought of including Línke writers who would be considered "disloyal" or "un-American." As they saw it, to do so would undermine the entire enterprise of winning acceptability for Yiddish in America. Moreover, they themselves were bitter enemies of those Línke, so they didn't really need much contemplation to decide to exclude their rivals.

But one problem was insurmountable. Like Eliezer Greenberg, one of the major anthologists, many of the fine anti-communist writers were themselves "former fellow travelers." The phenomenon is so important in the history of Yiddish culture in America that Yiddish developed a special ironic term for this category of person that inflects for gender and number: *gevézener* (literally "a former one"), feminine and plural *gevézene*. But irony aside, the word acquired the bitter aftertaste of a Cain-like stamp on the forehead.

In the mid-1950s, the Rékhte, in their own literary publications, particularly New York's *Tsukunft*, were applying unwritten rules that can be summarized with a simplicity that is so stark it is almost embarrassing, when applied to writers, many of whose writings had nothing to do with politics. In short: Whoever left the Línke for the Rékhte after the Hebron riots of 1929 was completely kosher. Whoever left after the Ribbentrop-Molotov pact of 1939 was sufficiently kosher. But those who waited until confirmation of the Moscow murders of the writers in 1952 were banished from the canon. And whoever hung around the Línke after that was not, heaven forefend, ever to be mentioned.

And so it came to pass that the canon of American Yiddish literature in English translation that thrives to this day was a creation, in part, of

1950s American political conformity. It is quite remarkable, when you think about it, that the book you are holding is the first serious attempt in English to *begin* the work of "constructively deconstructing" that sacred canon by outlining its political origins and, much more importantly, introducing a few of the poets who were at the core of one of the most exciting and creative milieus in Yiddish literary history: the Línke component of New York Yiddish literature in the interwar years.

But this is only the icebreaker. It cannot itself remedy the current situation in Yiddish literary studies, in which the same handful of authors get translated, anthologized, taught at universities, and endlessly analyzed in dissertations and conferences, while many *hundreds* of writers, many of them women, remain untouched and undiscovered, not in desert papyruses or manuscripts lost in war, but in printed journals and books that are easily found in major Yiddish collections.

∿

Who were these Línke writers? They were much the same as all the others. Yes, American Yiddish leftist writers walked, loved, worked, and did all the other things that other writers did. Since Yiddish writers were virtually all "leftists" in the sense of being politically far to the left of the American center, the positing of some "species differentiation" is a silly, spurious picture resulting from antiquated political correctness at worst, or anachronism at best. Before the factional splits traced to 1919 (when American communism officially got underway) or 1922 (when the *Frayhayt* was established), one would be hard pressed to find *any* difference. One is reminded of Shylock's speech: "Hath not a Jew eyes? Hath not a Jew hands?"

Dynamic young men and women, many still teenagers, came off the boats from the old country and underwent a sweeping metamorphosis that was in some cases initiated before migration, in many others on New York City streets. For them, the fervor of a received and ancient system of strict beliefs was replaced by (or "transmigrated" into) a secularist modernism that put high value on originality of the individual and on social and political movements to bring about a better world here and now. This gave way to a rapid throwing overboard of belief in the world to come, Godliness, and strict adherence to a multitude of laws that continued—and continues—to characterize the vibrant traditional Jewish religious culture. All of Jewish history, in fact, can be viewed as a permanent traditionalist religious trunk with sporadic, asymmetrical, creative secular outbranches that have brought magnificent cultural results without undoing the trunk, which continues apace with its own, sometimes imperceptibly slow, process of multi-millennial development. These outbranches include philosophy in medieval Spain, individuals like Spinoza in seventeenth-century Holland, and modern Yiddish literature.

Focusing in from these broader historic strokes to the streets of the Lower East Side in the years around World War I, it is clear that all of the modern Yiddish writers who settled in America and went on to build a literature centered in New York are part of the "same secular outburst" in Jewish history. It was a tiny matter of historic chance whether a young immigrant turned into a Yiddish writer after meeting people from "this" or from "that" circle. Once they were in one of the circles they enjoyed an environment of friends, lovers, and competitors, a vibrant café life, magazines and newspapers looking for new young talent, and an array of cultural institutions and clubs. This usually became the circle the writer stuck with. The overwhelming majority of these multitudes of young writers had little interest in party politics, but it was usually a politically oriented organization or movement that provided the infrastructure (and financial support) for Yiddish publications and events. After the Rékhte-Línke split of 1922 (if we date it to the founding of the *Frayhayt*), these young writers, of prose, poetry, drama, criticism, journalism, or educational materials "found themselves" in "one of two camps" as so often happens in the history of cultural movements and societies. It didn't matter whether their writing happened to concentrate on the old country or the new, on oneself, nature, love, life, death, or society, or on labor and class issues. There were myriad personal and literary inclinations.

One camp was aligned with a political movement (anti-Soviet socialism) that ended up—after a few decades—being a lot stronger than the other (pro-Soviet socialism) after the betrayals and crimes perpetrated by the Soviet Union became known (opinions differ on when to date the onset of those betrayals, and in the American scene, when evidence of them should have first been "believed"). Alas, both camps failed to viably transmit the language and its literature and culture to their children and grandchildren (the odd exceptions are so startling as to prove the rule). But that is another story.

The spotlight of this book is on the interwar period (with secondary attention granted the relevant postwar literary continuations). In the twenties and thirties, many of the most talented and original writers in New York were among the Línke. The group is perhaps best known by the name of its own writers' union, Proletpen, a Russian style Yiddish concoction abbreviated from *proletárishe pen* ("proletarian pen"). Nevertheless, the "formal" period of the actual union called Proletpen covers only the period from 1929, when it was formally set up (to help boost the Línke's literary output after the Hebron Riot defections that year), to 1938, when it was phased out upon creation of the YKuF, or Yidisher kultur farband, which became one of the leading forces for Yiddish culture in America during and after the war years. YKuF grew into a much more widely based and international secular Yiddish movement with branches in London, Paris, and other centers where secular Yiddish culture remained vibrant in the years after the Holocaust.

❧

The Yiddish literature of Proletpen did not come into being by party-related diktat in 1929, even if the name and the official status came into being in just that fashion on September 13 of that year. In real life, it became the new union into which a number of previous groups of Línke writers naturally streamed. Those earlier groups were often defined informally as those who "hung around the *Frayhayt* crowd." They included the Yunger arbeter shrayber fareyn (Young Workers Writers Union, called the Jewish Proletarian Writers Circle in English), set up in 1924, and the Frayhayt shrayber fareyn (The Frayhayt Writers Union, 1929). One of the most important organizations did not even have a literary name. That was the Daun-tauner Yidisher arbeter klub (Downtown Yiddish Workers Club), which provided premises for these young writers to meet and became a pioneering publishing house for Yiddish literature in 1920s New York.

The colorful proliferation of journals continued apace after that 1929 founding of Proletpen per se, and well after its demise. Among the best-known Línke publications that followed were *Yunyon-skver* (Union Square, 1930), *Signal* (1933–1936), the late 1940s *Yidish Amerike, Zamlungen* in the fifties and sixties, and of course, *Yidishe kultur* which continues to appear in New York today.

Throughout the interwar period, there were two streams among the Línke poets. There were those who believed in "art for the sake of art" including Zelik Dorfman (1905–1993), Yosl Grinshpan (1902–1934), Menke

Katz (1906–1991), Meir Shtiker (1905–1983), Abba Shtoltzenberg (1905–1941), and Leybele Sobrin (1907–1946). A second group believed in proletarian poetry "as such." Among them were Martin Birnbaum (1904–1986), Yosl Kohn (1897–1977), Aaron Kurtz (1891–1964), and in the 1930s, after her arrival in New York, Dora Teitelboim (1914–1992). Like all such classifications, this one too is flawed. Over the years, the poets within each of these literary tendencies experimented with verse from the "other" tendency, but usually the occasional crossovers within the two visions of poetry simply confirm where each poet's main strength and output were to be found on that particular axis.

Organizationally, the two major founders who helped put it all together in the 1920s were the union leader and prose writer Max Perlow (1902–1993) and the short story writer, educational author, and teacher Shloyme Davidman (1900–1975). In a memoir, Perlow recalled how it all started: "We used to meet at Shloyme Davidman's place over on Wise Avenue in the Bronx. He did everything calmly, slowly and modestly, and was incapable of antagonizing anybody." Perlow also reminisced about the motivation of most of the young writers in joining these organizations: "Their ambition was to write and to get published." Perlow and Davidman themselves produced a notable book of short stories, *Geknípte rítlakh* (Knotted Twigs), with alternating stories by each. The Downtown Yiddish Workers Club published it in 1928.

In many ways, Perlow and Davidman, middle ranking writers and first rate organizers, between them encapsulated much of the quintessence of the flavor of the Línke. Perlow brought from his native Dombrowitz, in the Ukraine, a background in Hebrew and Aramaic (he had studied at Lithuanian yeshivas before coming to America and switching to secularism). He became a major union organizer. Davidman was a laundry worker and baker of knishes in Brighton Beach. He worked for decades to qualify as a Yiddish teacher. After his *A Song to Yiddish* appeared in his later years, Deidre Carmody wrote him up in the *New York Times*. "Courage," her piece began, "can be a quiet quality when it breeds in the obscure and joyless corners of the city. For the most part it goes unheralded. But it can be found, if anyone tries hard enough. Shloime Davidman, 75, lives in Brighton Beach on $182 a month. He pays $143 a month for rent" (February 25, 1974).

From the literary point of view, the founder of the Línke Yiddish poets' groups in New York was Alexander (or Yeshia / Ishiye) Pomerantz (1901–1965), a talented young poet, inspirer, and editor. He came from a well-to-do big city family in Grodna (interwar Grodno, Poland; now in Belarus). He was the son of a faucet-maker who won a gold medal from the czar for inventing a sprouting tap for soldiers to drink from, obviating the need for producing cups. As a very young boy, Alexander excelled in Talmud and was sent to the famous yeshiva at Mir. As a teenager, he fell in love with Yiddish poetry and became the third and youngest member of the "Grodna threesome" of great Yiddish poets during the teens of the twentieth century, along with Leib Naidus (1890–1918) and Avrom Zak (1891–1980). The group disintegrated after Naidus's early death. Pomerantz immigrated to New York in 1920 where he rapidly became not only a stirring young poet, but also a magnet for talent. When he succeeded as editor too (even if his journals tended to be short-lived), it made for the rise of the group of writers, particularly the younger poets who were to become the core of Proletpen.

In the summer of 1924, Pomerantz founded the Yiddish literary magazine *Yung kuznye* (*kuznye* is Yiddish for smithy or a blacksmith's shop; *Young Forge* was the official English language title). Nearly all the participants "fed into" Proletpen some five years later, and it is therefore, intellectually as well as in terms of most of the personalities, the precursor of Proletpen. Pomerantz's own poem "New York" (see page <ooo> in this volume) ends with lines that are recognizably from the heyday of Línke Yiddish poetry of the period.

un shpéter—
(ven s'hiln di shotns fun nakht ayn fabríkn)
ze ikh tsegornte reyen bes-álmins,
ze ikh umendlakhe shures fun féntster,
shmol un lang—fentster-matséyves,
éydes—
af lebns fritsaytik farlórene:
(neshomes deózlin artilóyin)
bludne farvóglte neshómes — — —

and later—
(when shadows of night envelop factories)

I see rows of graveyards laid out vertically,
I see endless rows of windows,
thin and long—windows that graves are,
witnesses—
to lives lost before their time:
(souls that walk about nakedly)
stray, roaming souls — — —

What is, to use the cliché, "lost in the translation" is the virtuosity of the language-layers and imagery which come from the integrated parts of Yiddish that nevertheless evoke more than subtle consciousness of their origins that span thousands of years of Jewish history and language. Things start out with a contemporary proletarian bit of realia (a factory after dark), using the accepted formulas of contemporary Yiddish poetry. Sadness is introduced dramatically by the poet's radical reorganization of the "photographic scene" (tall buildings in New York City) to a vertical cemetery. The verticality is suggested by the newly minted Poetic Yiddish *tsegornt*, which is, for all its novelty, immediately comprehensible: divided up into the stories of a building, hence vertical and building-like. Of the various choices of word for "cemetery" Pomerantz passes up *besóylem*, the Yiddish term derived from the Hebrew, for the Aramaically formed *besálmin*. This serves as a signal for the much deeper Aramaic to come: the kabbalistic phrase, used in the poem as its entire penultimate line, *neshomes deózlin artilóyin* ("souls that walk about nakedly"). For much of the Yiddish readership of sophisticated poetry of the day (including, needless to say, the Yiddishist Línke of the time), the Aramaic line would evoke the kabbalistic image of its source, in the Zohar, the classic work of Jewish mysticism, where it occurs twice: once referring to souls that ramble from one world to another, and one time referring to souls that have been rambling since the six days of creation. But Pomerantz made one linguistic adjustment to the phrase: he replaced the Aramaic plural for "souls" from the Zohar, *nishmósin*, with the much more familiar Hebrew plural, *neshomoys*, which is graphically identical to the everyday plural in spoken Yiddish, *neshómes*, and which would be pronounced the Yiddish way by traditional East European scholars even when it occurs in a kabbalistic text. In other words, the poet has fused the most esoteric Aramaic with daily Yiddish, to evoke an ancient mystical image and apply it seamlessly to the streets of Manhattan.

The final line of the poem uses Slavic derived *blúdne* for "stray." It is a vivid shtetl term that would not infrequently be used of a stray dog or cat back in the old country. Having transported the reader of wherever and whenever to the new world metropolis seen through the ancient Kabbalah as it was distilled within the Jewish multilingual culture of Eastern Europe, the poet returns the reader safely to the warmth of that earthy shtetl term.

So there we have it, "the poetic world of a New York Communist Yiddish poet" in the poem that launched the literary movement, at the start of the first issue of its first major journal, *Yung kuznye*, in 1924. Nothing could be more different from the way Yiddish literature would develop in the Soviet Union, where the pressures of the Party and its law drove everything from the spelling and graphics of the Yiddish used to the topics permitted, and ultimately the poetic imagery itself, into the ever tightening Soviet stranglehold. Things were different over in New York City, where anyone who wanted could walk away and join another group. But most didn't want to "join another group" in the twenties and thirties, despite the fact that things were changing for the worst in the Soviet Union, because they were having a darned fine time among the Línke, whether or not their writing was politically oriented.

In 1925, this environment got a big moral boost from the visit to America of V. V. Mayakovsky (1893–1930), the leading poet of the Russian Revolution and the early Soviet period (the visit that led, incidentally, to his satiric *My Discovery of America*). He and Pomerantz teamed up to edit *Spartak*, a trilingual journal of revolutionary literature. Although only one issue appeared, in 1925, it remains a classic in Yiddish literary creativity.

The departure of some of the older generation of greats in 1929 had the curious side effect of leaving the poetic side of Proletpen to its youngest poets (who did not follow the masters out). It was as if, overnight, the young Línke poets had become the new Yúnge or "young ones" of the New York literary scene. When the renowned Vilna literary scholar Zalmen Reyzen (1887–1940?), compiler of the classic four-volume encyclopedia of Yiddish writers (known as "Reyzen's *Leksikón*," Vilna 1926–29), visited America in 1930, he, like other Europeans who were not in the thick of the New York polarizations of the previous year, took care to visit the different writers' circles. In an interview he gave to the Warsaw-based *Literárishe bléter* upon his return to Vilna, Reyzen remarked: "Recently the appearance of the monthly *Hamer* has been renewed, the journal around which the so-called 'Proletpenists' [Yiddish *proletpenístn*] group themselves, almost entirely young writers and people just starting out" (December 26, 1930). As ever, Reyzen's keen eye summed up a wide literary scene to the point to which it had evolved at the time of his observations.

It is fortuitous for future research into the interwar Línke Yiddish writers that the group's founder, Alexander Pomerantz, spent the years 1933 to 1935 in Kiev, capital of the Ukrainian S.S.R., where he worked with major Soviet Yiddish scholars, including Max Erik (Zalmen Merkin, 1898–1937). During that time he exchanged his writer's cap for that of the literary historian and wrote his thesis on Proletpen. He could hardly be objective about the chapter of American Yiddish literature that he co-founded. Moreover, the work suffers from all the trappings of Marxist prejudices generally, as well as the specific party line of those years. It is as if the earlier original Alexander Pomerantz (and luckily, the later one too!) became a Soviet hack for those years. Nevertheless, the thesis is invaluable as source material on Proletpen. It was published in Kiev in 1935 as *Proletpén. Etyudn un materyaln tsu der geshikhte fun dem kamf far proletarisher literatur in Amerike* (Proletpen: Studies and Materials on the History of the Struggle for Proletarian Literature in America). This 250-page volume includes chapters on the *Frayhayt*, the various writers' unions that fed into Proletpen, and the disputes of the journals of the Proletpen era itself with special attention to the role played by each of the journals of the time. There is a lively (if not impartial) encyclopedic section of biographies and bibliographies of the writers of Proletpen, statistics, and an array of facts that will prove invaluable when taken in context with other materials from the period. As if with an eye to the past, the future, and the west, Pomerantz's propaganda component, an inevitable feature of a thesis published in Kiev in 1935, is so constructed as to be straightforwardly separable from the vital data whose analysis and "English revelation" remain a necessity for Yiddish studies in the twenty-first century.

The life of Alexander Pomerantz is a microcosm of the whole of Línke Yiddish literature in America. The dynamic poet of World War I Grodna who founded those leftist Yiddish literary journals and circles in New York in the 1920s went on to write the history of the movement during a sojourn in Kiev in the 1930s. He returned to New York and to poetry but became increasingly disillusioned with the Soviet Union. When news of the Stalinist murders of the Yiddish writers and cultural leaders in the Soviet Union was confirmed, it was Pomerantz who teamed up with various of his old 1920s buddies, including William Abrams (1894–1969), Max Perlow, Menke Katz, and Chaim Plotkin (1910–1996), to break away from the Línke and form the special Dovid Bergelson Branch of the Workmen's Circle in 1958. Pomerantz's final major work is a masterly history and exposé of the tragic liquidation of Soviet Yiddish writers. As in that 1924 poem he used to launch the period of Línke Yiddish poetry in New York, he invoked a term from the ancient sources to symbolically close that period of Yiddish literature in New York. Pomerantz's five-hundred-page work, *Di sovetishe harugey malkhus,* derived its title from *harugey malkhus* ("people murdered by the government"), which originated in connection with the Roman murders of leading Jewish sages in the second century A.D. His book, which appeared in Buenos Aires in 1962, used the ancient untranslatable term to invoke the historic image from nearly two thousand years ago. And so, the same Alexander Pomerantz who founded, in the 1920s, the writers' group that was to become Proletpen, and wrote its history in the 1930s, also wrote the epitaph of its inspirational forces in the 1960s. It isn't many flourishing movements in world literature that get to be founded, chronicled, and lamented by one person. He was a fine poet himself all the way through.

~

It must be underscored that the impassioned literary debates within Proletpen are themselves an important chapter in the history of this era in Yiddish literature. The primary fault line lay in the very notion of "proletarian literature." Was it there to express the goals of the movements to bring about a better world, or could literature, and particularly poetry, be oblivious to the social goals inherent in the movements that created the infrastructure for Yiddish literature? In the case of Proletpen, it is characteristic that the inherent tolerance and pluralism of the American environment allowed fierce debates to play out on the pages of the movement's press, particularly the *Frayhayt* under Olgin. That level of debate, and perhaps of literary inspiration, came to an end with Olgin's death on November 22, 1939. His death was the emblematic end of the interwar era of the Yiddish poetry of the left, which is the primary focus of this anthology.

The debate about poetry within Proletpen circles went beyond the narrower question of whether poetry should serve the social and political aims of the leftists. It reached the universal question of whether poetry should serve *any* good purposes other than art for its own sake. I cannot claim objectivity here, as I grew up in New York hearing a lot about the debate from one of its key and most controversial protagonists, my father, poet Menke Katz.

The debate reached its climax over a controversy that erupted over Menke Katz's two-volume epic poem, *Brénendik shtetl* (*Burning Village*, New York 1938). Menke, as he was universally known in Yiddish poetry, had emigrated from Lithuania in 1920 at the age of thirteen and a half, and went on to become the most controversial poet in Proletpen. In 1932, he was expelled from the organization for publishing *Three Sisters* against the wishes of its leaders. It was a work steeped in mysticism and eroticism (poems from the book appear on pages 354 and 360). He was soon readmitted, however, and the debates over nonconformist poetry intensified.

In 1938, stalwarts of Proletpen launched a barrage of attacks against *Burning Village* for being steeped in the past, in the Jewish shtetl and ancient Jewish traditions, for not bringing happiness to working people and for ignoring the entire list of requirements for "constructive" poetry.

Menke replied on the pages of the *Frayhayt* on August 14, 1938, with his "Der braver pakhdn" ("The Brave Coward"), a defense of the independence of poetry. It comprised four poems, each of which answered one of the leftist complaints about poetry that does not serve good causes. The first, "Vegn freyd un umet" ("On Happiness and Sadness"), is a response to the notion that happiness can be "demanded" of poets. The second, "Vegn nekhtn, haynt un morgn" ("On Yesterday, Today and Tomorrow"), defends the poet's right to be passionately consumed with the past (which coincides, it so happens, with traditonalist Jewish culture). The third, "Un du bist umetik vi toyznt Kuni-Aylend zunen" ("And You Are as Sad as a Thousand Coney Island Suns"), is a broadside against faked happiness delivered up by poets as some kind of commodity. The final poem, "Di tfíle fun barabán" ("The Prayer of the Drum"), is an ode to the magnificence of true sadness in genuine poetry.

The most famous line in "The Brave Coward" is "I will not lead my poem into battle."

"The Brave Coward" led to a major debate on poetry on the literary pages of the *Frayhayt* in the late summer and fall of 1938. Nearly all the major poets participated. The majority were committed to poetry in the cause of the movement and roundly condemned "The Brave Coward." The polemics were colorful. Moyshe Katz's piece was called "Something Is Rotten in Denmark" (the *Frayhayt*, August 28, 1938). Aaron Kurtz called his "A Shot that Hits Its Shooter" (September 4, 1938). Martin Birnbaum's "A Libel-Sheet against Proletarian Literature" hit at Menke Katz for writing about everything in his *Burning Village* "from the purest poetic sadness to the weirdest spider, from Grandmother Toltse's shrouds to the wailing of hungry cats" (August 21, 1938).

This attack on the poet's beloved grandmother Mona (Yiddish Moyne), calling her "grandmother Toltse" (a disparaging Yiddish term for an elderly woman, a bit like "Aunt Tilly"), led Menke Katz to turn proletarian poetry on its head by coming back not with a polemic reply, but with an entire new book of poetry written "by" the poet's disparaged grandmother Mona, who had died before he was born. She appeared to him in his dreams in his Lower East Side tenement and dictated the book, which is an impassioned defense of shtetl life and values against the political bigwigs of downtown New York.

Menke Katz's *Grandmother Mona Takes the Floor* (New York 1939) made for a poignant end of the Proletpen era in Yiddish poetry. The book also contains a revised version of "The Brave Coward," which starts with the lines:

Ever will the coward
fear my proud Grandmother Mona—
fear, should the magic staff of Moses
wake her from her mossy sleep,
fear, should she return in purity from her ancient grave:
to deflect the tin grumble of his voice,
with her breath to blow away his overblown pride,
to blot with her blood that washed out red
and leave but the rattle of a rattler.

Acknowledgments

Sincerest thanks to the colleagues who provided generous help in the preparation of this introduction: Shoshana Balaban-Wolkowicz (associate editor, *Yidishe kultur*, New York); Amelia Glaser (Stanford University, California); Itche Goldberg (editor, *Yidishe kultur*, New York); Troim Handler (Cranbury, New Jersey); Ildi Kovacs (Central European University, Budapest, Hungary); Andrew Page (Vilnius); Professor Leonard Prager (Haifa University, Israel).

Many thanks to Harry Smith, publisher of The Smith (New York), who kindly allowed the use herein of materials researched for the introduction to *Menke, the Complete Yiddish Poems*, translated by Benjamin and Barbara Harshav, which appeared in early 2005. In many respects that volume directly complements this one. Harry Smith also provided valuable comments to earlier drafts of this preface.

David Weintraub, executive director of the Dora Teitelboim Center for Yiddish Culture, inspired the writing of this introduction and made valuable comments on earlier drafts.

Naturally, none of these colleagues bears any responsibility for the views expressed in this introduction or its shortcomings.

Urban Landscape

"New York! Monster-city," writes Alexander Pomerantz.

"The very best land is America," writes Beresh Vaynshteyn.

"Manhattan is distant luck and light," adds Esther Shumyatsher.

To the newly arrived immigrant, little could be more alluring and alienating than New York City. Home to most of Proletpen's members, New York was the literary address for all of them, embodying, in its size and diversity, all of the themes of class stratification, social interaction, political activism, labor, and the individual's struggle to survive, which were central to the movement. The immigrant's gateway between the old world and the new, New York was the relentless conveyor belt that took in the Eastern European Jew and transformed him into his American equivalent. Proletpen's reaction was to enter this new context as fully as possible, maintaining an ever-critical eye and verse.

All of the poems that make up this section take place on the street, each one offering a slightly different angle on the urban landscape. Pomerantz's three-part "New York" approaches the city from three different perspectives, beginning from the water, then moving into the architecture and infrastructure of the city, and finally settling into the city streets, where he finds an array of "stray, roaming souls." Proletpen's poets do not attempt to conceal their rage at the inequality decorating the American city street. From Martin Birnbaum's homeless man by the river to Avrom Victor's "shadows on each deaf-mute wall," poems of the streets reflect Proletpen's mixture of estrangement from and engagement with city life. They also place Proletpen's literary project firmly in an urban context and help to introduce the basic themes that will come up in all of their poetry. On the one hand, we see an appreciation of the positive aspects of city life—the combination of people, the mammoth architectural structures, and the music that emerges naturally from the cacophony of human life. On the other hand, we are confronted with the stark images of gaping wounds left by societal woes laid bare in city life—the idle wealthy class, the misery of poverty, and the isolation of the soul.

ניו יאָרק

.1

ניו יאָרק!
דו וואָנזיניגסטע ים־סירענע –
פֿאַרוואָרפֿן
האָסטו בריק־נעצן, שטריק־פֿעטליעם
איבער'ן האָדסאָן.
אָרומגערינגלט
האָסטו זיך מיט קייטן שוואַרצע בערג
און פֿאַליסאַדן –
דיינע מעכטיקע אַרמייען
צעשטעלט
האָסטו שומרים – ליכט־טורמס, טעלעגראַפֿן, פֿאָנען
לעבן אַלע ברעגן.
צעשיקט האָסטו שיף־פֿאָסטקעס, סאָבמאַרינס־מרגלים
איבער'ן אַטלאַנטיק,
איבער'ן פֿאַסיפֿיק
אין ווייטער, ווייט – – –
פֿאַרבונדן
מיט קונציק־פֿאַרצווייגטע סיסטעמען,–
דראָטן, קאַבלען,
קאַנאַלן, טונעלן –
אַלע ימ'ען, אַלע יבשה'ס פֿון דער וועלט . . .
דורך עראָ־מאַשינעם און ראַדיאָס
פֿאַרשפֿרייט
דעם כשוף פֿון דיין גאָלדענעם אוצר
אין גאָר דער וועלט – – –
ווערן הונדערטער שיפֿן מיט מענשן
טאָנטענלאַך פֿאַרשלונגען פֿון דיר;
פֿון מינוט צו מינוט
ווערן גרעסער די מחנות
פֿון דיינע קרבנות . . .

New York (1922)

〜 Alexander Pomerantz

New York!
Mad mermaid,
you've cast
bridge-nets and rope-nooses
across the Hudson,
surrounded
yourself with chains of black mountains
and palisades,
positioned
your mighty armies
as guards along all your shores:
lighthouses, telegraphs, flags.
You've sent ship-traps and submarine-spies
over the Atlantic,
over the Pacific,
into the faraway distance . . .
bound
all the oceans, all the continents
with clever network systems,
wires, cables,
canals, tunnels . . .
spread
the magic of your golden treasure
through airplanes and radios
to the whole wide world.
You swallow up
hundreds of shiploads of people a day,
the multitudes you sacrifice
grow greater
from minute to minute . . .

‏2.

‏ניו יָאָרק!
‏די מָאָנסטער־שטאָט ‏–
‏צעטראָטן
‏האָסטו די פעלדער;
‏די וועלדער אויסגעהאָקט ‏–
‏מיט אַספאַלט און שטיין און שטאָל
‏אַלץ באַדעקט.
‏אין דער לענג, אין דער הויך
‏צענאָרנט, צעטורמט, צעקעסטלט געבײדעם ‏–
‏אין הימל זיך אַרײננערײסן.
‏פאַבריקן, וואָלקנקראַצערס
‏אויפגענויט ‏–
‏צעפאַלמעסט דעם רוים ‏– ‏– ‏–
‏מיט ריזיקע טשוועקעס ‏–
‏פאַבריק־קומענס ‏–
‏צעלעכברט דעם הימל.
‏פאַרשטעלט מיט פינסטערע אײזן־פלאַטפאָרמעס
‏די זון ‏. ‏. ‏.
‏מיט קופער־דראָט ‏– שפינוועבס
‏פאַרוועבט
‏די בלוי פון הימל.
‏די מענשן אין תפיסות־פאַבריקן
‏געלאָזן:
‏(זײער מאַרך און בלוט אויסגעזויגן)
‏איז פון זײ הענט און פיס
‏געבליבן ‏– ‏– ‏–

‏3.

‏פיס ‏–
‏שלעפן פיס זיך צו די באַנען,
‏צו די „עלן", צו די „סאָבוויים" ‏–
‏ציען, יאָגן קאַטאָפאַלקן
‏צו פאַבריקן ‏. ‏. ‏.
‏הענט ‏–

2.

New York!
Monster-city,
you've trampled
the fields,
hacked down the woods
and covered it all
with asphalt, stone and steel.
You've ripped the heavens
up and crossways with
storied, towered, boxed up structures—
erected
factories and skyscrapers,
dissected space
with huge nails,
perforated the sky
with factory chimneys.
You've hidden the sun
with dark iron platforms . . .
and spun
copper wire spider webs
over the sky's blue.
You've left
people in factories—prisons
(their marrow and blood sucked out)
with nothing left
but hands and feet . . .

3.

Feet . . .
feet drag themselves to the trains,
to the Els, to the subways—
haul, chase catafalques
to factories . . .
Hands . . .

יאָגן הענט זיך לע׳ם מאַשינעס;

באָמבלען קעפּ זיך אום אויף אַקסלען;

שפּיזולען רויטע צאָרן־אויגן;

קריצן ציין . . .

פאַרנאַכט:

ווערן פול אַלע קאַמערן –

ברידער־קברים –

מיט בר־מינן׳ס: טעג, טרוימען, געדאַנקען –

שטיקער נשמות . . .

און שפּעטער –

(ווען ס׳הילן די שאָטנס פון נאַכט אײַן פאַבריקן)

זע איך צעגאָדנטע רייען בית־עלמינ׳ס.

זע איך אומענדלאָכע שורות פון פענסטער,

שמאָל און לאַנג – פענסטער־מצבות,

עדות –

אויף לעבנס פריציייטיק פאַרלאָרענע:

(נשמות דאָזלין ערטילאין)

בלודנע פאַרוואָגלטע נשמות – – –

hands hasten at machines,
heads bob on shoulders;
red angry eyes pierce,
teeth grind . . .
In the evening,
the halls fill up
like mass graves
with corpses: days, dreams, thoughts,
bits of souls . . .
and later,
(when night's shadows envelop factories)
I see rows of graveyards laid out vertically,
I see endless rows of windows,
thin and long—window gravestones,
witnesses
to lives lost before their time:
(souls that walk about nakedly)
stray, roaming souls — — —

מיין ניו־יאָרקער גאַס זינגט

אסתר שומיאַטשער ‎~

היינט האָט זיך די נויט אויף מיין גאַס צעזונגען,
מיט הונגער אין די קני, אויף ליפּן – אַ פאַרוואָנדיקט געשריי –
דאָס לעבן איז אויף צו פאַרדינגען
פאַר אַ העמד אויפן לייב, פאַר אַ לעפּל געקעכץ, פאַר אַ זופּ טיי.

עס רעדט דער הימל מיט בליי און מיט מאַנונג.
ווי אַ ווייט גליק שטייט מאַנהעטן פאַרטראַכט.
עס טראָגן הונגעריקע שאָטנס זייער דראָאונג –
עס צינדן זיך מיליאָנען אויגן – פייערדיקע פּרעגצייכנס אין דער נאַכט.

דער עלנט פון גראָז אויף דיינע סקווערן,
דאָס היימלאָזע נפש אויף דיין ברוק.
עס קוקן מדברדיק אַראָפּ די שטערן,
אַ מענטש פאַרגייט אין יעדן פיבערדיקן צוק.

איך גיי נײַ אום אין דיינע גאַסן מיט אַ יונגער קללה.
דאָס לעבן שפּאַנט מיט צעבלוטיקטע צײן –
רוקן שטופּט רוקן, לייב טרעט אויף לייב אין בהלה,
שאָטן יאָגט שאָטן, צעשיידט און אַליין.

דיין פרייילעכקייט שפּאַנט איבער פאַרפּייניקטע גופים.
מיט דאַקלאָון עלנט שניידט דער ווינט.
איך הער דעם בעטלער אויף זיין פידל רופן
און אויסלערן דאָס מידע האַרץ אויף דיינע גאַסן, בלינד.

דיינע ביימער, מאַנהעטן, מיט וואונדן בליען,
דיין אויסגעלײדיקטע ערד מיט אַ גרינעם געוויין.
היימלאָזע מחנות ציען
איבער דעם עלנט פון דיין שטאָק־און־שטיין.

דיינע גאַסן, מאַנהעטן, זיינען מיט רויש און מיט ווייסן פייער,
מיט אַ פאַרוויפּט פּנים ברענען דיינע נעכט –
באַצאָלן וועסטו, באַצאָלן טייער
פאַר דער שפלות און הונגער פון דיינע קנעכט . . .

36

My New York Street Sings

～ Esther Shumyatsher

Want sang and sang on my street today,
a torn cry on its lips, hunger on its knee.
This life is for hire for a shirt on my back,
for a spoonful of food, for a sip of tea.

The sky speaks with lead and dun.
Manhattan, like distant luck, is quiet.
Hungry shadows carry threats:
Millions' eyes ignite—fiery question marks at night.

The misery of grass on your squares,
the homeless soul on your pavement.
The arid stars look down at it all,
a human dies with every feverish movement.

I walk your streets with a young curse.
Its teeth dripping blood, life strides on—
spine thrusts spine. Body tramples body in chaos.
Shadows chase shadows, separate, alone.

Your happiness covers the suffering bodies.
With roofless futility, cuts the wind.
Emptying his weary heart on your streets,
I hear the blind beggar call on his violin.

Your trees, Manhattan, bloom with wounds,
your drained earth, with a green moan.
Homeless crowds stretch across
the misery of your stick and stone.

Your streets, Manhattan, are noise and white fire,
your nights burn up in drunkenness.
You will pay, and you'll pay dear
for your slaves' hunger and sunkenness.

בעריש וויינשטיין ⸾

פון "אמעריקע"

טראַכט מען אָבער צוריק אויף אַ רגע,
איז אַ וועלט נאָך אַלעמען נישט משוגע
צו זאָגן:
אַז ס׳בעסטע לאַנד איז אַמעריקע!
עס איז זיכערער דאָ די די ערד;
מען רייסט פון ייִדן נישט קיין בערד
און קענסט רואיק אויף בּאָנען פּאָרן;
זיך אויסלעבן דאָ דאָס ביסל יאָרן.

עדות דאַרויף איז פראַנקרייכס פרייהייטס־שטיין,
וואָס שטייט אינמיטן וואַסער ווי פון זיך אַליין:
מיט האָפערדיקע, פרויִשע אַקסלען
אין פּאַקלדיקן שאַר צו די הימלען.
ווי דורך שווערן בליי,
פאָרסטו די סטאַטוע פאַרביי
און עס ווייזט דיר די אויסגעהאַקטע האַנט,
אַמעריקעס לאַנד!
‒ ‒ ‒ ‒ ‒ ‒ ‒
אַ וועלט איז נאָכאַלעמען נישט משוגע
צו זאָגן:
אַז ס׳בעסטע לאַנד איז אַמעריקע!

38

from *America* (1955)

∾ Beresh Vaynshteyn

But when one stops to think back a moment . . .
Isn't the world, after all, a *meshugener*[1]
to say
that the very best land is America?
The ground is safer here;
no one rips the beards off Jews
and you can ride a train in peace,
live them out, your years, your few.

A witness, France's liberty-stone
stands in the water, as if on its own:
with confident, woman's shoulders,
torch reaching to the skies overhead,
as though through hard lead.
You travel beyond the statue
and it points, that chiseled hand,
to America's land!

A world, after all, isn't really *meshuge*
to say
that the very best land is America!

1. *Meshugener:* one who is crazy; *meshuge:* crazy.

שאָטענס

אב. וויקטאָר ๑๏

שוואַרץ־בלויע שאָטענס אויף ציגעל רויט־ברוינליכען.
טונקלען זיך שאָטענס אויף ווענט.
מאָרגען פריה. האַלבענטאָג. שעה'ן פארנאַכטיגע.
שאָטענס צו שאָטענס געוואַנדט.

שטויסען זיך, פלעכטען זיך, אָדער צעלויפען זיך,
מאַכען העװיות מיט העגט.
לאכען צי גענעצען, בענשען זיך, שילטען זיך,
שוואַרץ־בלויע שאָטענס אויף ווענט.

איך פון מיין פענסטער קוק, יענע – פון זייערען
שאָטענס מיט שאָטענס באַקענט.
ווייטער אין טאָג אריין, וואקסען אַלץ לענגער די
שאָטענס אויף טויב־שטומע ווענט.

Shadows (1922)

∾ Avrom Viktor

Black-blue shadows on red-brown bricks.
   The walls are dark with shadows.
Early morning, noontime, dusk,
   shadows turn to shadows.

Push each other, twist and race,
   gesture with their hands, fall,
laugh or yawn, curse or bless,
   black-blue shadows on every wall.

I look out the window. All
   the shadows know the other shadows.
Late in the day they grow long and tall,
   shadows on each deaf-mute wall.

פֿון „אויפֿ'ן האָדסאָן"

פֿיר מיך,
פֿיר מיך שיף
אױף די גרױע כװאַליעס פֿון דעם האָדסאָן
אַ גלױביקן
װאָס הערט זיך אײַן צו דײַן מאַשינגעזאַנג
פֿירסטו אַצינד.
פֿון ניו יאָרקער הפֿקר־שטאָטיב
האָב איך זיך אויפֿגעהױבן תּפֿילה טאָן!
טראָגן מיך,
טראָגן מיך שיף אױף די גרױע כװאַליעס...
מיר, דײַנע בױערס, גיבן זיך דיר הײַנט איבער
– פֿרוכט פֿון אונזער קראַפֿט –
פֿיר אונז...
. . . . . איך װיל תּפֿילה טאָן!...

42

from "On the Hudson" (1924)

~ Nokhem Vaysman

Sail me,
sail me ship
on the Hudson's gray waves.
A believer
who listens to your mechanical song—
that's who you're carrying now.
Out of New York's lawless dust,
I have raised myself to pray!
Carry me,
carry me, ship, on the waves of gray . . .
we, your builders, devote ourselves to you today
—born of our strength—
sail us . . .
. . . I want to pray! . . .

וועלף

י. א. ראָנטש ‎✍

וואָיען סטאָיעס וועלף אַף טראָטואַרן,
הונגער שטשירעט אויס די געלע ציין.
און צו רייצן אָפעטיטן בײַ אַ האַרן
שיסט פון פלעשער פרייילעכער שאַמפיין.

קינדערשע שוואַרצאַפלעך שטומע שטאַרן;
טשאָטען וועלף אַף בעסטן ביסן – ביין.
דאָמעם נייע פאַרנעענינגס נאַרן, –
אָנגעוואָרן האָט די וועלט איר ציין...

טאַנצן פאָלקעס אויסגעפוצטע נאַרן;
קינדער קעננען אַף די פיס ניט שטיין.
וואָיען סטאָיעס וועלף אַף טראָטואַרן,
הונגער שטשירעט אויס די געלע ציין.

44

Wolves (1936)

∿ Y. A. Rontsh

Packs of wolves howl on sidewalks,
hunger grinds through yellow teeth.
And champagne shoots from bottles,
for masters, an aperitif.

Children's pupils stare in silence,
wolves gnaw at the best bits—bone.
Ladies yearn for newfound pleasures.
The world has lost its charm . . .

Well-dressed dimwits dance the polka;
children can't stand on their feet.
Packs of wolves howl on sidewalks,
hunger grinds through yellow teeth.

By the River

ביים ריווער

מארטין בירנבוים ‎‮‬

אין פייכטן מערצ-ווינט גייט דער ווינטער אָפּ.
לעצטע קריעם שווימען לאַנגזאַמע מיט גראָען ריווער.
עס רוישט די לופט. די מעװועס פליען טיף
און ס'דאַכט זיך—אַלץ איז אויפגעלייזט
און דאַמפּט אַרוים פון זיך דעם לעצטן ווינטער-גליווער.

אַ באַרושע כריפּעט, שלעפּט זיך טונקל-שווער.
פאַראויס איר קומען, טרייבט דער ווינט איר אייגן רויך.
דער הימל קוועלט. אַן עראָפּלאַן אין בלויען רוים
שוועבט מיט אָדלער שטאָלץ, קרייזט גראָציעז
און רייסט מיט שאַרפּן אויפשוואונג זיך צו הויך.

דער אַלטער בערטער-פּיר איז פּוסט.
עס שמעקט מיט זאַלץ, מיט אויל און ברודיג וואַסער.
ביים שווערן סלופ, אויף ראַנד פון פּיר,
זיצט אָנגעשפּאַרט אַ מענטש אַזוי
און נייט—אַן איינגעהויקערטער אַ בלאַסער.

לעבן אים—אַ זעקל אויפגעראָלט.
מען זעט—זיין גאַנץ פאַרמעגן לינט דאָ אויפגעבונדן.
זיין אויבערגוף אַנטבלויזט, אַ ברודיג העמד אין שוים
און ס'שרייט זיין נאַקעטקייט אין פייכטן ווינט
מיט פיינלעכקייט פון נישט-פאַרהיילטע אויפגעריטע וואונדן.

ס'האָט די זון, די וואַרעמע, אים אַרויסגענעברײכט אהער
צו איינזאַמקייט פון בערטער-פּיר דעם אַלטן;
האָב איך זיין אויסבאַהאַלט אים דאָ צעשטערט—
איצט קוקט ער ביטער-בייז, פאַרשעמט אויף מיר
און פרואווט זיין נאַקעטקייט אין אַ לעבערדינג ראָק באַהאַלטן.

48

By the River (1938)

∽ Martin Birnbaum

The winter goes out in a humid March wind.
Last ice-floes float slowly with the gray stream.
Seagulls dip low. The sky rushes past.
And it seems to me, everything's melting. The last
winter numbness goes up with the steam.

A barge groans, dragging her dark heavy body.
The wind chases smoke round her smokestack.
The sky beams. A plane, with its eagle pride,
hangs in blue space, circles gracefully,
and sharply vanishes, tearing the heights.

The old planked pier is empty. It smells
of salt, of oil and filthy water.
Against the thick post at the edge of the pier,
a man sits, leaning, and sews,
his body, pale and hunched over.

Beside him a rolled up sack,
one sees all his belongings bound up in it,
filthy shirt in his lap, his torso bare.
His nakedness cries in the damp wind
from the pain of aggravated wounds.

The warm sun has brought him here
to the lonely, ancient pier;
I've interrupted his solitude,
and now he looks bitter, embarrassed,
takes a torn coat to cover his nakedness.

איך ווענדט מיך אָפּ מיט בושה־הָאסט,
פֿון שאַרפֿן בליק אין סאַמע טיפֿעניש געטראָפֿן.
דער הימל קװעלט. די מעװעס קװיטשען בייז.
אַ יאַכט־שיף, זון באַגאָסן, בלענדט פֿאַרביי
און לאָזט דעם ריװער הינטער זיך־אױלינג, גלייכגילטיג, פֿאַרשלאָפֿן.

I turn away, in shame and disgust,
from the gaze that has met me, sharp and deep.
The sky is beaming. Cruel seagulls shriek.
A sun-splattered yacht dazzles past us,
and leaves the river, oily and indifferent, to its sleep.

אויפ׳ן ראָג גאַס

מאַטעם ל.

אַ בעטלער אויפ׳ן ראָג – אַ בלינדער אײַנגעבױגן,
און אַ „פוינעל״ מיט שמייכלענדערופענדע אויגן
פאָכעט מיט פליגלען פון אָרימקייט
און זנות.
און אין אַ ווינקעל שטיל פאַררוקט
אַן אָרים־קינד מיט די אָקסלען צוקט,
ציטערט פון קעלט, פון הונגער און פון וועה.
און איבער זיי
קופאָלען הייליגע רופען מיט זייער גלאָקען־שטים
„קלינג־קלאַנג, קלינג־קלאַנג״
און צופרידענע קניהען,
שיקען צו גאָט אַ לויב־געזאַנג.

52

On the Street Corner (1922)

～ L. Mattes

A beggar on the corner is blind and bent over:
a *foygl* with smiling-summoning eyes.[2]
He flaps his wings of poverty
and depravity.
And sealed into a quiet corner,
a poor boy with twitching shoulders
shivers from cold, from hunger and pain,
and over them
sacred cupolas sing out in their bell-voices
"Ding-dong, ding-dong."
Contented kneelers
send God up a praise song.

2. *Foygl*: bird in the Yiddish; in addition, this word has the connotation of a pretty, or weak, fellow. It is sometimes used as a derogatory term for a homosexual.

מענער

אויף יעדן טראָט, אויף יעדן שפּאָן –
מאַן.
אַ מאָס,
אַ וואָג,
אַ מיקראָסקאָפּ,
ציען ס'לעצטע שטיקל קלייד פֿון מיר אַראָפּ
מעסטן,
וועגן, –
גרייט אינמיטן גאַס צעבייטן זיך
אויף נאַרנישט.
אויגן,
אויגן –
טיפֿע, ליידיקע טעפּ, וואָס קוקן אַרויס
פֿון אַ ניט־באַהייצטער קיך,
גייען נאָך,
בעטן זיך,
מאָנען,
גלעטן
יעדן פֿאַלד פֿון מיין קלייד.
טראָגן ווי אַ טשעק ביכל, זייער קאַלענדאַר,
און צאָלן פֿאַר יעדן גראָשנדיקן אָפּדאָכט
מיט טעג,
מיט יאָרן,
און יאָגן נאָך יעדע רגע וואָס גייט פֿון זיי אַוועק,
און שפּילן זיך מיט דער צייט,
ווי אַ קאַץ מיט איר אייגענעם
עק.

54

Men (1944)

᷒ Dora Teitelboim

Every step the sidewalks span:
man.
A gauge,
a scale,
a microscope,
stripping my dress to its last thread
measuring,
weighing;
ready for free-exchange,
mid-street.
Eyes,
eyes—
deep, hollow pots, gazing
from an unheated kitchen,
follow,
beg,
pet
each fold of my dress.
They carry calendars like checkbooks,
paying for their cheap nooks
with days,
and years,
and, chasing the moments they fail
to catch, they play with time
like a cat with its own
tail.

Being a "Greener"

The first section offered immigrant (or "green") poets' reactions to the new world. The poems in this section portray immigrant experiences and their attempt to settle into their American lives. The wave of Jewish immigration following World War I brought most of Proletpen's members to the United States. Around the same time, a number of Southern Italian immigrants arrived, settling in New York alongside Eastern European Jews. Many of the experiences of the Jewish immigrant in America were shared by the Italian immigrant. The proximity of these groups became, tragically, more intimate because of horrors like the 1911 Triangle factory fire, in which most of the workers trapped inside the burning building were Italian and Jewish immigrant women. The two groups would often find themselves working side by side in factories, frequenting the same locales, and sharing tenements, and the outcome was a mixture of conflict and solidarity. Yosl Grinshpan portrays an unfortunate Italian miner's family. Sarah Barkan's "Italian Masons" goes a step further by depicting a scenario in which Jewish and Italian immigrants are bonded by their common second language and shared workers' plight.

Two of the poems in this section address the infamous trial of Sacco and Vanzetti, two Italian anarchists who were executed in 1927 for alleged murder. What was widely viewed as an unfair trial that exploited the suspects' poor English underlined both the tenuous position of American radicals and immigrants' lack of power in the United States. For Sacco and Vanzetti, America was the opposite of what it promised. As Ber Grin writes "America is smoky days on blackened, rope-soled shoes." In Yosl

Grinshpan's tribute to the deceased, Vanzetti's ghost pays a visit to the presiding judge, Webster Thayer, finally able to take revenge on the judge for an outcome many believed was manifestly unjust.

Curiosity permeates Proletpen's poems of immigration and integration. It is with burning curiosity that Martin Birnbaum enters a Protestant church on Christmas Eve, only to leave again, opting to find inspiration in Lenin. The same Ber Grin who laments the Italian anarchists' rope-soled shoes celebrates the wanderings of his own shoes in "On Roads." This poem, in which the persona "travel[s] along broad paved roads," evokes some of the positive sides of being a greener. Resonant with the age-old tradition of the wanderer, Ber Grin's long poem leads his reader on a journey over new terrain. While the poem evokes a sense of great exploration, the poet plays with riddling anagrams. His references to the "green sea," "green houses," and "green dream," reflect both the gaze of the greener in the wanderer's new terrain and play upon the poet's own last name, Grin. In the line "Green bergs over blue valleys" there is no doubt that the author is placing himself directly into the changing landscape of his poem, a literary gesture that mirrors his integration into his vast new country.

אין דײַנע אױגן

דאָרע טײטלבױם ‎∽

אין דײַנע אױגן
אַזױ פֿיל
לענדער
און אין זיי
פֿון אַלע װעגן
פֿרעמדע
אַ פֿאַרגליװערטער
געשריי.

60

פֿון "צו מײַנע שטעטלדיקע יאָרן"

שטעטלדיקע יאָרן,
פֿלאַנטערט זיך ניט מער אין מײַן זיקאָרן –
אַן אַנדערער אינגאַנצן ווײַל איך וואָרן!
לאָזט מײַן האַרצן קלאַפֿן
צום טאַקט פֿון עלעקטרישע מאָטאָרן.
לאָזט דעם ריטעם פֿון מײַן בלוט פֿאַרמעסטן זיך
מיטן ריטעם פֿון די באַנען
אין נײַ יאָרקער אונטערערדישע אַרטעריעס
לאָזט צעוואָקסן זיך אין מיר
דעם דראַנג
פֿון פֿאַבריקדראָד און פֿאָס;
לאָזט אויפֿברויזן אין מיר
דאָס ליד
פֿון פּראָצעׁמעׁנטש בּאָם גראָבׁ און הײַבׁמאַשׁין –
איך זאָל
אין לעכער פֿינצטערע אַרײַן,
און אַרויף צו טויזנט רעשטאָוואָניעס
און העכסטע טורעםׁשפּיצן
קענען שלײַדערן
שטיקער זון און האָס.

from "To My Shtetl Years" (1931)

~ Yosl Grinshpan

Shtetl years,
quit wandering around my memory,
I want to be someone else completely!
Let my heart beat
the time with electric motors.
Let the rhythm of my blood race
the rhythm of the trains
in New York's underground arteries.
Let the pull
of factory wheel and belt
grow in me.
Let the song
of the worker by the excavator and crane
roar in me.
I must
submerge into dark holes,
and emerge to a thousand scaffolds.
The highest tower-tops
can fling down
bits of sun and wrath.

א ברכה איבער ברויט

דוד סעלצער ✍

– זאָג מיר, מאַמע, וואָס הייסט אַ ברכה?
צי איז אַ שטיקל הערינג אָרעמער פון פיש?
צי מאַכט מען נאָר אַן אַנדער ברכה,
ווען מען זעצט זיך צו צום רייכן טיש?

זע נאָר וויפל פלייִשן, וויפל ברויט
עס ליגן אָנגעלייגט און אָנגעוואָרפן,
ווען אין אונדזער הויף עס קלאַנגט די נויט
און קינדער גייען הונגעריקע שלאָפן?

– מיר זיינען, קינד מיינס, דאָ בלויז געסט,
קרובים אָרעמע פון הויף פון נויט.
אַ ברכה מאַכט מען ווען מען עסט
דאָס פאַרהאַרעוועטע אייגן שטיקל ברויט.

64

A Blessing Over Bread (1957)

∽ Dovid Seltzer

—Tell me, Mama, what's a blessing?
Is a bit of herring poorer than fish?
Does one say a different blessing
when he dines among the rich?

Have you seen how much meat and bread
is laid out and piled up high
when need's been crying in our shanty
and children lie hungry at night?

—My child, we're just guests here,
poor relatives from need's backyard.
One makes a blessing when he eats
his bit of bread that comes so hard.

איטאַליעגישע מוליערם

ساַרע באַרקאַן ~

עס זיצן זעקס מוליערם און ריידן.
מיר זיצן און הערן זיך איין.
זיי טריפן פון נאָר אַלטע באַטלעין
די לעצטינקע טראָפנדלעך וויין.

און יעטוווידער ווינקל – איקאָנעם.
עס קוקט אַף זיי מערי פאַרטראַכט.
זי מישט מיטן הילצערנעם לעפל
אַ פונט מאַקאַראָני פאַר אַכט.

די מוליערם זיי בײלן די פויסטן
און קוקן זיך איבער געטריי.
איך הער – און מיר דאַכט זיך: איך קוק
אין אַ קעסל מיט זודיקן בלײ.

זיי בעטן: סיניאָר, סיניאָריטאַ,
פאַרצײט אונזער אייגענע שפּראַך.
מיר ריידן פון אַרבעט און הונגער.
ס'איז פאַר אונז איצט אַ וויכטיקע זאַך.

מיר רוקן צו נאָענט די שטולן,
מען דריקט אונז ביז וויי טיק די הענט.
מען נעמט אונז אַריין אין דער מיטן,
ווי מ'וואָלט אונז פון יאָרן געקענט.

מיר הויבן אָן ריידן אַף ענגליש.
באַלד ווערט עס אַלעמענס שפּראַך.
מיר ברעכן און בויגן דעם ענגליש,
ביז קלאָר ווערט פאַר יעדן די זאַך.

אַז שולדיק – ניט מיר, נאָר די באָסעס,
און ענטפער איז – העלדישער קאַמף.
די אויגן – זיי פינקלען מיט גרייטקייט:
די הערצער – ווי קעסלען מיט דאַמף.

66

Italian Masons (1933)

⤳ Sarah Barkan

Six masons are sitting and talking.
We sit and listen in.
They drain the final drops
from ancient flasks of wine.

And in every corner—icons.
Mary looks at them, lost in thought.
She mixes macaroni
with a wooden spoon, for eight.

The masons pound their fists,
exchange loyal glances.
I suddenly realize I am staring
into a boiler of molten lead.

They plead: signor, signorita . . .
forgive us, we use our own tongue,
we're speaking of work and hunger,
for us a pressing thing.

We move our chairs closer to them,
they clasp our hands tightly in theirs.
They pat us and embrace us,
as if they'd known us years.

We start to speak in English,
suddenly the common tongue.
We break and bend the English
til it's clear to everyone

That we're not to blame, but the bosses,
and the answer's heroic fight.
Our eyes are sparkling, ready.
Our hearts are like steaming pots.

אײדעם – אַ לאָם אין אַ ווינקל
און צוויי פֿאַרצעמענטעטע שיך,
און מערי, אַ דאָרע, אַ שטילע,
וואָס זיצט אין אַ ווינקל אין קיד.

Witnesses: a crowbar in a corner,
a pair of shoes, caked with mortar,
and Mary, thin and quiet,
sitting in a kitchen corner.

די מײַנער-משפּחה

נ. גרינשפּאַן ❧

אַמאָל איז זי אַ שיינע געווען,
נאָר דאָס איז געווען אין סיציליע.
היינט איז זי אַ מײַנערס ווײַב
און אַ מאַמע פֿון אַ גרויסער פֿאַמיליע.

אַמאָל האָט זי איר מיידלשן חן
געוויקלט אין שוואַרצע וואָאַלן,
היינט שטראַלט פֿון איר פּנים צעקראַסטעט
די נויט פֿון איסט-סיידער קוואַרטאַלן.

דער מײַנער, איר מאַן, איז אַ ריז –
נאָר וואָס טויג ער, אַז ס'פֿעלן אים העַנט –
ער האָט זיי ערגעץ פֿאַרלאָרן אין גרוב,
זיצט ער און קוקט אַף די ווענט.

ס'ציטס אים צו טיף פֿון דער ערד,
צום שוואונג פֿון פֿאַרלאָרענע הענט,
צו ברידער, צום לעמפּל, וואָס האָט
ווי אַן אייגענע זון דאָרט געברענט.

לעבט איצט דער מײַנער אַזוי:
ער קוקט און ער רויכערט און ער שעלט –
און סע זינגען צוויי אַרבל אַ ליד
פֿון אַ חרוב געוואָרענער וועלט.

ער פֿאַרטראָגנט ניט די גרויסקייט פֿון ווענט,
פֿון הונגער – דעם קינדער-געוויין,
די קללה פֿון ווײַבעריש ברויט –
שעלט ער זיין אייגן געביין.

70

The Miner's Family (1929)

∾ Yosl Grinshpan

Once she was a beauty.
But that was in Sicilia.
Now she is a miner's wife,
mother of a big famiglia.

Once she wrapped her maiden grace
in black lace,
now East-Side poverty
beams from her unadorned face.

The miner, her husband, is giant,
but armless, what use is he at all?
He lost them somewhere in that pit.
Now he sits, watching the wall.

He yearns for the depths of the earth,
his missing arms swinging beside him,
for his brothers, for the lamp that burned,
a private sun to guide him.

And now the miner lives
to stare, to smoke, to curse.
Two empty sleeves sing a song
of a wasting universe.

He can't stand the gray of the walls,
the children crying, the hunger pains,
or the curse of the bread his wife has earned.
He curses his own remains.

צעטראָנט זי איר בראָך איבער גאַסן,
און זאַמלט דערפאַר שטיקלעך ברויט –
און אין שוואַרצן, אַף איסט־סיידער קוואַרטאַלן,
שפּאַנט אַרום אַ שטאָלצע, די נויט.

נױ־יאָרק, פֿעברואַר, 1929.

She spreads her misfortune through the streets,
gathers pieces of bread about town,
meanwhile in black, on the East Side,
need struts up and down.

סאַקאָ און וואַנזעטי

בער גרין ~

עס בליִען וואַזאָנע טוליפּן
און שוואַרצדרויטע רויזן
אין טויטןצעל,
און אויף צוויי וויאָלענדיקע גופים
וואַרט דער טויט ביים שוועל.
זיינע רויטע בלומען – פרישע גרוסן פון בלוטנדיקע פריינט
און דערמאָנען אין דאַנטעןם דעם זון,
אין לעצטן פאַרגיין און לעצטן היינט.

רויש פון עלעקטרישע מאַשינען אין די אויערן.
שלעסער־ציטער, טריט פון היטער, פולער מיט טהעיערן לויערן.
לייגט אַ שווערע האַנט אויף פּנים־פאַרמעט אַ טויטנשריפט,
בלייבן אויג העננען ערנעץ וויט, וויַט שטיל־פּאַרטיפט:
קינדהייט – באַרוועֿסע טעג, צעוואָקסן מיטן וויינשטאָק און אוילביברט־בוים,
און איטאַליעֿנישע נעכט העננעןֿאויס אויף יעדן צוויַיג אַ טרוים.
פּרימאַרגנם צעקלינגען זיך מיט געזאַנג און מיט קאָסע,
און שמעקן מיט גרינער לאַנקע, מיט אַפּריקאָסן און מיט ראָסע.
אמעריקע – רויכיקע טעג אויף זיך געשוואַרצט, אין שטעריק געוועבט,
און הייסע נעכט מיט פּלאַמיקן וואַרט צו מידע אַרבעטעֿרישע קעפּ.
און אָט: שטורמער אומעט פון גראָטעם טריננקט בלוט פון פּנים, פון העֿנט,
און זיבן יאָר, מאָנג־ביי־טאָג, אַז העֿנקער מאַרדעֿט לעֿבנס צווישן טויטע וועֿנט.
שלעסער־ציטער. שוואַרצע מיטער. אַ, הימעֿלן, ברידער, ראָזעטאָ!
אַש, אַש. פיעֿרדיקע זיילן: סאַקאָ און וואַנזעטי!

אויגוסט, 1930

Sacco and Vanzetti (1930)

∾ Ber Grin

Potted tulips
and black-red roses
bloom in a death-row cell,
and death waits at the threshold
for two wilted bodies.
His red flowers were fresh greetings from a bleeding friend,
reminders of Dante, his son:
the last today and the day's last end.

Electric machines clatter in his ears,
the watchman walks, locks rattle, Fuller and Thayer lie in wait.
A heavy hand pens a death-decree on face-parchment,
eyes hanging far away deepen with the silence;
childhood and their barefoot days,
grapevine and olive-tree, where they were raised,
and Italian nights hang a dream on each long
branch. Morning rings with sickle and song.
Scent of green meadows, of apricots and dew.
America is smoky days on blackened, rope-soled shoes,
and hot nights with flaming words on tired working heads.
This barred-window sadness drinks the blood from hand and face,
as the hangman kills every day for seven years in the deadened space.
Locks rattle. Black watchman. Oh, heavens, brothers, Rosetta!
Ashes, ashes. Flaming pillars: Sacco and Vanzetti!

וואָנזעטים געשפּענסט

יוסף גרינשפּאַן ✍

אין זיין פּאַלאַץ
אויף זיין גאָלדענעם בעט
ליגט טהעיער, דער ריכטער,
און רעדט
פון וואָנזין געשפּענסטפולע רייד.

אים דאַכט:
עס שטייט פאַר זיין בעט
וואָנזעטים פאַרברענטער סקעלעט,
פאַרהילט אין אַ פלאַמיקן קלייד.
זיין האַנט
לעשט דאָם לעמפּעלע אויס;
סע שווינדן די ווענט פונעם הויז
און,
ס׳פאַרגנייט זיך אין אַנגסטן די נאַכט . . .

און ווידער:
אין רויטן וואַקסט אויס –
– נאָר איצט אין גינאַנטישער גרויס –
וואָנזעטי.
עס הערט זיך אַ קראַך – – – –
– – – – – – – – –

ער שפּאַנט, וואָנזעטי,
און שפּאַנט
און ס׳פלאַטערט דער רויטער געוואַנט
און,
ס׳צינדט זיך די ערד אונטער אים.

און הינטער דעם רויטן סאַטאָן,
באַוועגט זיך
דער יענקישער קלאַן
און,

76

Vanzetti's Ghost (1929)

~ Yosl Grinshpan

In his palace
on his golden bed,
lies Thayer, the judge,
gone out of his head,
and talks a ghostly talk.

It seems:
Vanzetti's incinerated skeleton
is standing at his bed, he's come
shrouded in a flaming cloth.
His hand
puts out the light;
the walls disappear
and
the night goes out in fear . . .

And once again,
a red figure grows—
the now gigantically grandiose—
Vanzetti.
A crash resounds — — — — —
— — — — — — — — — —

Vanzetti walks the grounds
and walks,
and the red cloth flutters
and
the earth beneath him ignites.

And behind the red Satan stands,
the Yankee Klan,
swaying to and fro,
and

צעכוואָליעט פון שקלאָפן דעם הימן.
– – – – – – – – – – – – –
– – – – – – – – – – – – –

עס יאָמערט דער אַלטער פאַר שרעק,
ביז
ער פאַלט אין חלשות אַוועק
און ס׳וועקט אים
זיין הויזדאָקטאָר אויף,
מיט
אַן איינשפריץ
פון בלוט
אין זיין גוף.

(סעפטעמבער 1929)

the anthem swarms with slaves.
— —— —— —— —— —— —— ——
— —— —— —— —— —— —— ——

The frightened old man moans in fear,
until
he falls in a faint.
He regains
consciousness
when his house-doctor
injects
a little blood
into his veins.

Visiting Jesus

ביי יעזוס'ן צו גאַסט

מאַרטין בירנבוים ‎

כ'בין היינט געווען ביי יעזוס'ן צו גאַסט.
האָט זיין „פּראָמאָטער", אַ פּריסטער מיט אַ פּעון ברוסטיקול,
מיך האַרציג אויפגענומען:
. . . און דו, וואָס כ'האָב דיך לאַנג שוין ניט געזען.
מיין זינדיג לאַם, מיין שעפעלע–
ס'איז העכסטע צייט,
וואָס ביזט צו מיר, וואָס ביזט אין הויז מיינעם געקומען.

געזאַנגט האָט ער עס–
נישט צו מיר אַליין:
כ'בין געקומען מיט אַ טשערעדע פון תשובה־גרייטע,
יום־טוב'דינ פאַרפּוצטע לעמער . . .
צום געבורטסטאָג פון יעהאָווא'ס זון
האָבן מיר זיך זיאָוועט אין זיין ערדישן פּאַלאַץ–
אפשר וועט ער מוחל זיין די זינד . . .
ער וועט!– אַזוי פאַרזיכערט אונז דער פּריסטער
(פּאַסטוך רופט ער זיך אַליין דאָ אָן באַשיידן)
בעת ער רעדט צו אונז אַראָפּ
פון אַ פּרעכטיג, ליכט־צעפינקלטן באַלעמער.

מיר זיצן שטום.
די קעפּ אַנטבלויזטע.
ס'איז היינט די נאַכט פון היילינער געבורט,–
האָט דער פרומער פּאַסטוך אַנגעטאָן די שכינה אויף זיין פּנים
און מיט אַפּאָסטאָלד'פּסוקים
די נשמה אָנגענורט . . .

אָט דונערט ער מיט שטראָף־רייד פון אַ נביא–
אָט לאַטשעט ער אונז
מיט אַ זינגזאַנג קול, אַן אוילינג, געשמאַקן,–
ס'גלאַנצן אַזש נאַטפּפאַרכטיג זיינע באַקן,
בעת ער סטראָשעט אונז מיט גרויל,
מיט העלישן נשמה־מאַטער . . .

82

Visiting Jesus

∿ Martin Birnbaum

I visited Jesus today.
His "PR man," a preacher with a fat chest voice,
received me kindly:
. . . and you, we haven't seen you in a while.
My sinful sheep, my little lamb.
It's high time
you've come round to find me.

He wasn't talking
to me alone.
I came in with a flock, all ready to repent:
lambs dressed up in their holiday best
for Jehova's son's birthday.
So we all dropped by his earthly palace.
Maybe he'd forgive our sins . . .
He will! So the preacher assures us
(modestly referring to himself as "shepherd"),
speaking down to us
from his exquisite, lighted podium.

We sit in silence,
heads bare.
This is the night of the sacred birth.
The pious pastor has dressed his face in divine presence
and girded our souls
with the gospels.

He thunders a prophet's castigations
then pets us
in an unctuous, pleasing, sing-song voice,
until his cheeks radiate the fear of God,
and he fire-and-brimstones us,
threatening our souls with hellish torture.

נאָר אין גן־עדן׳ס געטלעכן טעאַטער—גאַראַנטירט ער—
װאָרטן אויף אונז הימלישדרײנע כאָרן:
װאָרט
די אײביגקײט . . .
און קענן איר—
װאָס מײנט דער קורצער לײדנסזוענג פון אַ מענטשנס ערדישע,
געצײלטע יאָרן . . .

יעזוס׳עס אומבאַפלעקטע מוטער
שמײכלט מיט אַן אומשולד־אויסדרוק פון אַן אויל־געמעל אַרונטער—
איר זון, װײזט אוים, איז נישט געװוזן קיין געזונטער—
מיט בלוט אויף דלאָניעם און מיט בלאַסקײט פון מאַרטירער,
האָט אים עמיץ צונעגנאָגלט אין אַ װינקל צו אַ צלם,
העננט ער דאָרטן אונטער ערעאָלן׳שײן
מיט גאָרנישט,
חוץ מיט די הײליגן געקרײציגט זײַן פאָרנומען . . .
און ס׳דאַכט זיך מיר—
ער לײדט דערפון
און שעמט זיך גאָר
צו העננגען דאָרטן אויף אַ טשװאָק,
מיט אַן אויסדרוק פון אַ היפּאָקריט אַ פרומען . . .

שפּעטער האָבן װײכע טענער זיך צעפּאָכעט איבער יעזוס׳ ערדישן פּאַלאַץ,
כװאָליענדינ און שטײנגדינ ביז פײערלעכן קלאַנגנ־טשאַד.—
לעבן מיר האָט זיך אַן אַלטיטשקע גע׳צלם׳ט;
איך האָב שטיל אין זיך אַרײַנגעענענצט—
מײן נשמה איז געװאָרן זאַט . . .
האָב איך דער אומשולדינ יונגפרוי—אויפ׳ן אויל־געמעל,
צוגעװאָרפן נאָך אַן אָפּשייד־בליק פון שװעל—
און בין אַרוים,
דאָס היטל אויפ׳ן קאָפּ אַ ביסל שיף,
שטראָפאָנדינ האָט מיך פאַרפאָלגט
דער פלינגל׳רויש פון הײליגן מאָטיװו.—

כ׳האָב אײנגעאָטעמט טיף די לופט.
אין אַ פענצטער פון אַן אָרים הויז
האָט אַ קריסטמעס׳בײמל מיט עלעקטרישע אײנגלעך אומעטינ געװאוונקען.

But on the holy stage of paradise, he guarantees,
heaven-cleansed choirs await us,
so does
eternity . . .
And what's a temporary sufferer have to lose
but earthly, mortal,
numbered years?

Jesus' unblemished mother
smiles down, guiltlessness painted in oil.
Her son, it appears, hasn't been so healthy.
Bloody palms, a martyr's pallor,
nailed up on a cross in a corner.
He hangs there under electric light
with nothing
to do but be crucified,
and it seems to me
he suffers it,
utterly ashamed
of hanging on a nail
with the mark of a pious hypocrite.

Later, tender tones were unleashed in Jesus' earthly palace.
Billowing and rising to a holy bellow.
Near me an old woman crossed herself.
I yawned softly to myself.
My soul had gotten full . . .
I cast the innocent young woman on the oil painting
a last look from the door,
and I'm outside,
my hat a little askew,
the rush of wings from the holy theme
reprimanding me.

I drew the air in deep.
In the window of a poor home
a Christmas tree blinked sad, electric eyes.

די נאַכט איז קלאָר געווען,
אין שטערן־פּראַכט צעשפּרענקלטער געטונקען:
איבער גאַסן שטיל־פֿאַרשלאָפֿענע בין איך געגאַנגען, לאַנגזאַם, אָן אַ ציל.
געטראַכט האָב איך—
פֿון לעבן׳ען:
פֿון מענטשן־ליבע . . .
פֿון יעווס׳ן געטראַכט – מיט רחמנות,
מיט טיפֿן, מיט פּאָעטישן געפֿיל . . .

The night was clear,
dunked in speckled star splendor.
I walked the quiet sleepy streets, slow and aimless.
I thought
of Lenin,
of human love,
I thought of Jesus with pity,
with deep, poetic sympathy.

אַף וועגן (פּאָעמע)

א. פרינץ (בער גרין)

כ'פאָר אַרום אַף ברײַטע געפלאַסטערטע וועגן –
אָ, וויפיל פיס פון דורות פאַרגאַנגענע און הײַנטיקע
האָבן געגלעט אָט די גלאַנציקע וועגן.
אַ גרינער ים.
רויטע דעכער טונקען זיך אין גרין.
טעלעגראַפישע סלופעס – בײַמער געוועזענע – הויבן זיך אַרויף, אַרויף
ווי מאַסטן אַפן ים.
בערגגרין איבער טאָלן בלוי.
אַ ים בלוי איבער טאָלן גרין.
אַ מאַראַנצענע זון בליט־פאַרבליט אַף גרינע שטיבעלעך,
אַף גאָלדיקע לײם־בערגלעך.   – – –

אַרום מיר שפּרייט זיך פעלד און פינצטער.
די פינצטער הילט אין דעם טאָל ביזן העלן פײַערל.
מײַנע אויגן נעמען אַרום די ברײַטע פינצטער.
ס'פײַערל זינגט צו מיר פונווייטנס.
כ'גלעט דאָס פײַערל, דאָס שטיבעלע.
אַרום פײַערל לויכטן מסתמא וואַרימע מענטשן.
נאָכן פײַערל ציט זיך פעלד און ס'פינקלען שטערן.
כ'באַהעפט זיך מיטן פעלד און מיט די שטערן.
די שטערן שפּילן זיך מיט די קײטן בערן:
אָ, ווי עלנט וואָלטן געווען די בערג אָן אָט־די ליכטיקע חברים.

פרײַלעכע ווינטעלעך פאַרטראָגן מיר אין די נאָזלעכער
אַזוינע זיסע קילע ריחות,
אַז ס'מעג מען קען שיכור ווערן.
ס'בליט דער גרינער חלום פון אַלטיוונגן וואַלד.
ס'צווייטן גאָרטן און פעלד.
ריחות פון קאָרן, ריחות פון טאַבאַק –
וועט זיין גענוג צום עסן און צום רויכערן.
צווישן פון פעלד און גאָרטן – שווייסיקע גליאיקע מי,
ריחות פון קאָרן און טאַבאַק – שווערע פויערשע טעג.
זיס און זעטיק זײַנען די ריחות פון לעבן. –

88

On Roads (1935)

❧ Ber Grin

I travel along broad paved roads,
oh, how many feet of how many generations
have come to stroke these gleaming roads.
A green sea.
Red roofs submerged in green.
Telegraph posts rise up, up, once trees,
like masts at sea.
Green bergs over blue valleys.
Sea blue over valleys of green.
An orange sun blooms in and out on little green houses,
on golden clay hills.

Field and darkness spread about me.
The darkness envelopes the valley's shining flames.
My eyes embrace the enormous darkness.
The distant flame sings to me.
I stroke the flame, the little house.
Warm people must be glowing round the fire.
When the fire dies down, fields stretch, stars sparkle.
I join the field and the stars,
the stars are playing with the mountain chains,
oh, how lonely the mountains would be without their shining friends.

My nostrils inhale happy breezes.
What sweet, cool odors are
intoxicating me.
The green dream of the old-young forest is blooming.
Garden and field are flowering.
Scent of rye, scent of tobacco,
plenty to eat and smoke.
The buds of field and garden are sweaty glowing toil,
rye and tobacco smell of heavy rustic days.
Sweet and filling are life's aromas.

געבענטשט זאָלן זיין די ערד און דער פויער
וואָס לאָדן אָן די ווינטעלעך מיט די ריחות פון לעבן.
היינט גליט דער טאָג מיט אַ ניהנום־היץ,
און איך שטרעק מיין האָלדז צו די קילע שאַרפן פון די ווינטעלעך,
און איך נויג מיין אויער צו זייערע וואָנדער־שיינע מעשה׳לעך.
היינט איז אַ יום־טוב פאַר מיינע אויגן און אויערן:
היינט שעפן זיי אָן אַזויפיל וואָנדער.
שיין און גרוים און ברייט און טיף איז – וועלט,
און מיט מיינע שטאַרקע הענט דריק איך זי צו מיין האַרצן.
כ׳וואַרף מיין לייב צו די טיפן און שיינקייטן פון וועלט. – – –
פאַר איך ווייטער. פאַר איך ווייטער.

קומען מיר פייער־פליגעלעך אַנטקעגן: באַגריסן און פאַרגייען.
– – ווי דער פייערצווייט פון יונגע יאָר, פון יונגע יאָר. – –
שטיבעלעך. שטיבעלעך. פאַר׳חלום׳טע.
אינעווייניק – מענטשן. חלומות. מאַן־ווייב־קינדער.
ביימער. ביימעלעך. לעבן אַ גרין לעבן.
קוקן מיר נאָך שטילע און פאַרגאַפטע.
שפרייטן צו מיר לאַנגע שלאַנקע הענט.
און ערגעץ – רוישט. רוישט. קוואַלן רוישן.
כ׳שעפ דעם רויש, כ׳שעפ דעם ריטם.
מיינע אויגן פאַלן אַף ווייסע וואַסערפאַלן.
טאַנצנדיקע וואַסערמיידלעך זינגען מיר אַ ליד.
כ׳טראָג אַוועק מיט זיך דאָס ליד – דאָס ליד פון טאָג.
אַ ברייטער טייך נעמט אַרום די ווייס־זווייסע מיידלעך.
פאַסן ליכט טונקען זיך אין טייך.
מיט ריחות פון טייך שווימען אין מיר אויף ריחות פון מיין קינדהייט,
כ׳דערזע מיין דניעסטער, דעם שיינעם טייך פון מיין קינדהייט. – – –

אין טונקלען אַרום שווימען פאַרביי פייערלעך – אויטאָם.
אינדערווייטנס – טראַבקעט. אַ צוג. פייער. רויך. פאַרביי. – – –
שווימט׳אויף אין מיר אַ גרוים פרייד;
צעגיסט זיך איבער אַלע ברעגעס;
צעוויג איך זי, צעוויג איך זי אַף קוליקולות –
קומען ווינטעלעך און צעטראָגן זי צו די בערג און צו די שטעט. – –
„טראָ׳טאַ׳טאַ!" – אַ מאָטאָר־שיפל גליטשט זיך שנעל אַוועק,
מיינע געדאַנקען שווימען נאָך,
יאָגן זיך מיטן שיפל ערגעץ אַהין, אין טונקעלע קוואַליעדיקע ווייטקייטן.

Blessed—the earth and farmer
who supply the breezes with scents of life.
Today the day glows hellish heat,
and I crane my neck to the wind's cool edges,
and I prick my ear to their glorious tales.
Today is a celebration for my eyes and ears,
today draws so much wonder in.
The world is beautiful and great, broad and deep,
and with strong hands I hold her to my heart.
I throw my body to the world's depth and beauty.
I travel further. I travel farther.

Fireflies come to me, greet me and fade.
Like the firebud of youth, of youth.
Little houses. Little houses. Dark. Dreamy.
Inside are people. Dreams. Man-wife-children.
Trees. Treelets. Green is life.
We look at them, quiet and amazed,
long tall arms reach out to me.
And somewhere rushes a rushing spring . . .
I inhale the rushing flow, I inhale the rhythm.
My eyes fall on white waterfalls.
Dancing water sprites sing me a song.
I carry the song away with me, the song of dance.
A wide river embraces the white, white girls.
Strips of light dip into the river.
The river odors evoke the odors of childhood,
I see my Dnestr, beautiful childhood river . . .

Firelets—cars—swim past in the dark.
Distant noises of a train, fire, smoke, riding past.
Enormous joy froths up in me,
and spills over every shore;
I rock it, sing it out in loud cries—
breezes come and carry it to the mountains and cities—
"Tra-ta-ta!" a motor boat skates quickly away,
my thoughts swim in its wake,
chase the boat somewhere off in the dark, billowy distance.

פייערן. פייערן. אַ שטאָט אין פייערן.

שיכורע, יובלדיקע טאַנצן פייערן אין די הויכן.

אין ריען, אין קרייזן, אין קאַדריליען. פייערן.

אַ פייער־דזשעז. טשאַרלסטאָן. בלעק־באָטאָם.

פייערלעך טאַנצן אויס אַמעריקע'ם טאַנץ.

טאַנצן פייערן אין טייך אַריין. שווימען אַפֿן טייך

אַ ליכט־קאַרניוואַל.

פייערלעך ציטערן־אויף,

פייערלעך טענצלען אַפֿן וואַסער.

אַ שפּיל פון שטאָט מיט טייך.

אַ ליכטיקע שטאָט באַהעפֿט זיך מיט אַ שפּיגלדיקן טייך.

מוירן. אַ פייער־שריפֿט איבער קעפּ פון מוירן.

ווער האָט אָנגעשריבן אָט די ליכטיקע פייערדיקע אותיות?

אַ, הייליקע פינגער. אַ, ליכטיקע הענט!

שטאָט. מוירן. טורעמס. קעפּ.

דורות גאַנצע אויסגענאָסן אין שטיין.

כ'באַהעפֿט זיך מיטן קאַלטן, פונדמענטש־באַוואָרימטן, שטיין,

כ'נעם אַרום די ליבע קעפּ,

כ'גלעט מיט מיין קאָפּ אָט די ליכטיקע באַלויכטענע קעפּ:

כ'באַגריס זייערע פרייַדיקע שמייכלענדיקע שטראַלן –

די שטראַלן פון גאַנצע הויפֿנס לעבנס פון די שטאָט־בויער.

איטאַליענער, נעגער – אַרבעטער: ווי אַ קרוין שיינט אייער מי

אַפֿ קעפּ פון מוירן, אַפֿ קאָפּ פון שטאָט.

קומענטס, קומענטס – האָבן אויסגעשטרעקט די העלדזער.

רויכן. רויכן. רויכיקע ריחות. ריחות פון לעבן.

רויכן דרייען זיך, דרייען, פאַרגייען.

טעען. יאָרן. דרייען זיך, דרייען, פאַרגייען.

ריחות פון פאַבריקן, ריחות פון ערד –

ריחות פון לעבן.

כ'פֿאָלג נאָך דעם גאַנג פון די רויכן –

כ'הער זייער געזאַנג פון רויכיקע לעבנס.

גלאַן! גלאַן! טראַמוואַיען. אויטאָבוסן. מיט־מענטשן־געפּאַקטע.

לעבעדיקע קלאַנגען. לעבעדיקע שטראָמען.

פון ערגיץ צו ערגיץ – די אייביקע פּראָצעסיע.

Flames. Flames. A city in flames.
Drunk, jubilant flames dance at the heights.
Flames in rows, in circles, in quadrilles,
a fire-jazz. Charleston. Black-Bottom.
Flames dance out America's dance.
Fires dance into the river, swim on the river.
A carnival of lights.
Flames quiver,
flames dance on the water.
A game between city and river.
A city of lights meets a looking-glass river.
Walls. Fire-script over heads and walls.
Who has written the fire-lettering?
Oh, holy fingers. Oh, hands of light!

City. Walls. Towers. Heads.
Generations poured in stone.
I become one with the cold, man-warmed stone,
embrace the beloved heads,
stroke these shining heads with mine,
I greet their joyous, smiling rays—
the rays of the heaps of lives of the ones who built the city . . .
Italians, Negroes—workers: your labor shines like a crown
on the heads of walls, the head of the city.

Chimneys, chimneys crane their necks.
Smoke. Smoke. Smoky odors. Odors of life.
Smoke coils, coils and vanishes.
Days. Years. Coil around, coil down.
Odors of factories, odors of earth—
odors of life.
I follow the path of smoke—
I listen to the steps of their smoky lives.

"Clang! Clang!" Trams. Buses. Packed with people.
Lively noises. Lively streams.
From somewhere to somewhere is an eternal procession.

אויך איך בין איך אין שטראָם. אין באָוועגלעכן שטראָם.—

אָט – אַ מאָנומענט. שפּאַרט אַריין מיט העלן קאָפּ אין הימל.

הויך און שטאָלץ: אַ ריז צווישן אַ מחנה קאַרליקעס.

שטערן רוען, שטערן נעכטיקן אַף זיין קאָפּ.

אונטן – טאָלן. ליכט צעוואָרפן אין די טאָלן.

ביימער קוקן אַרויף צום ריז מיט גליאיקע אויגן:

פײַערלעך האָבן זיך פֿאַרפּלאָכטן אין די ביימער-נעסטן.

לאָמטערנס האָבן זיך צעשטעלט ווי היטערס אַף די גאַסן.

צי ווייסט איר קאָטש, לאָמטערנס, ווער ס'האָט אייך אָנגעפֿילט מיט ליכט?

נאָך – מאָנומענטן. שווייגנדיקע ריזן.

אַ, וויפֿיל דורות אומבאַקאַנטע העלדן זיינען אין זיי פֿאַרשטיינערט.

און וויפֿיל דינאַמישע פֿילשפּראַכיקע רייד זיינען פֿאַרבאַרגן אין זייער שוויַיגן!

„קלינג! קלונג!" – דאָס קלינגען די גלעקלעך פֿון לעבן.

קלאַנגען-סימפֿאָניע. טענער שפּרינגען אַרום מיר. ראַדיאָ-פֿרייד.

לופֿט-כוואַליעם שפּילן אויס דעם מענטשנ'ס וואָרט.

סטענגנעם ליכט. ראַדיאָ-מוזיק. פֿאַרבן-כוואַליעם.

גלעקער קלינגען, קאָלירן טאַנצן. אַ שמחה.

די געסט זיינען פֿרעמדע. ניטאָ דער באַלעבאָם.

ליכטיק! ליכטיק! טעאַטערס, קראָמען, פּאַלאַצן, פֿאַבריקן –

וועלן צו אַלעמען געהערן, אַלעמען באַגליקן.

ווידער – קוימענס. קופּאָלן. טורעם-שפּיצן.

ווידער – פֿעלד. וואַלד. שטיבלעך.

ס'האָט וועלט פֿאַר מיר צעעפֿנט אירע הענט,

שטרעק איך מיינע אויגן, מיינע הענט –

צו נייע פֿעלדער, נייע ווענט.

I too am mid-stream. In the moving stream.
There stands a monument. Pushes its bright head into heaven.
High and proud: a giant amid a multitude of dwarves.
Stars rest, stars spend the night on its head.
Below are valleys. Light cast in the valleys.
Trees look up at the giant with glowing eyes:
flames nestle in the trees.
Lanterns stand guard along the streets.
Lanterns, have you any notion who filled you with light?

More monuments. Silent giants.
Oh, how many ages of unsung heroes, cast in stone?
How many dynamic languages are sealed into their silence?
"Cling! Clang!" The little bells of life are ringing.
Sound symphony. Tones jump about me. Radio joy.
Airwaves play the human word.
Ribbons of light. Radio music. Color waves.
Bells ring, colors dance. A party.
The guests are strangers. There is no host.
Light! Light! Theaters, stores, palaces, factories
will belong to everyone, make everyone happy.

Chimneys again. Cupolas. Spires.
Fields again. Woods. Little houses.
World has opened her arms to me.
I stretch my eyes, my arms
toward new fields, new walls.

Songs of the Shop

If Proletpen's home address is the diverse streets of New York City, its work address is decidedly the city's factories and shops. Whether or not a writer actually worked as a manual laborer is irrelevant. As the intellectual vanguard of the workers' movement, the writers, who often began their careers as teachers and scholars, aimed to both bring the proletariat to the center of literary discourse and to encourage more factory workers to take up the pen and write about their own experiences. Tools, factories, and machines symbolized the workers' party, and for Proletpen represented the production of poetry itself. Present in many of these poems is a rhythm borrowed from the factory. This is particularly true in the case of Kalman Hayzler's machine poems. Repeated phrases such as "at the machine, at the machine," and "she grows wild, she grows wild," suggest a poetry that comes naturally from the repeated sounds of factory labor.

First appearing in *Yung kuznye* in 1924, a journal that he edited himself, Alexander Pomerantz's "My Father the Foundryman" is an account of the poet's youth in his father's workshop. A brass foundryman by trade, Pomeranz's father, who spent a brief, unsuccessful period trying to establish himself in the United States, returned to Grodno where he received acclaim for creating a drinking fountain faucet, which was later used by the Red Army. The invention (or, perhaps, recreation) only briefly appears in Alexander's ballad.[1] Once in New York, Pomerantz was able to draw on

1. See Dovid Katz, introduction to this volume, page 18.

the working aspects of his family life, and on his own factory experience, in order to create the image, quite literally, of a proletarian mold.

Aaron Kurtz's "Two Songs of a Blacksmith" combines a country landscape with the smith's hammer to create a unique proletarian pastoral, tinged with the erotics of a man-made creation myth. Not only do the poets write about the workshop; they also offer songs about the retail shop. With strong tones of irony, Yosl Cutler rewrites the Song of Songs into a love song from a miserly shopkeeper to his customers, and Sam Liptsin evokes the terror of rising prices. Quite literally the trademark of the proletarian writer, shop poems exhibit a broad range of emotion, from excitement to hopelessness. The sad overtones of a world obsessed by commerce tempers the humor in these pieces. As Kurtz and Rapaport suggest, if the cruel market system does not lead the downtrodden worker to oblivion, it will lead him to rebellion.

Songs of the Shop

מיין טאַטע – דער מעשׁניסער

י. פֿאָמעראַנץ ‎⟨‎

(העלענען – מיט ליבע)

אַ מעשׁניסער איז מיין טאַטע,
כ'בין אַ קינד פֿון גרויסער שטאָט.
ס'איז פֿרעמד מיין בלוט די וועלט פֿון זאַטע,
ס'איז קאַמף מיין איינציקער געבאָט.

אַ פֿעסטונג און טאַבאַק־פֿאַבריקן –
מיין שטאָט אין ליטע מאַכן גרוים;
זי גרוימן אויך די אייזן־בריקן,
צעלייגטע אויפֿ'ן ניעמאַן־שוים.

עס האָט אַ ליבע, טרייע מאַמע
געבוירן מיך אין אַ וואָרשטאָט,
וואו ס'האָט באַגריסט מיך אַ דינאַמאַ,
פֿון גיסעריי דער קוילן־טשאַד.

דער ערשטער קלאַנג צו מיר געקומען
פֿון אונזער גרויסער שלייפֿשטיין־ראָד;
דאָס ערשטע ליד האָב איך פֿאַרנומען
פֿון אַ מאַשינען־קאַראָהאָד.

פֿאַרוויגט האָט מיך דער רויש פֿון גאַסן,
די האַמערקלעפֿ אין מעש און שטאָל;
די הודזשענדיקע לעדערפֿאַסן –
דערציילט מיר מעשות פֿון „אַמאָל"...

און אַנשטאָט פֿיעם – שטאָל־געשטעלן:
מיט זיי איז פֿול מיין קינדערוועלט;
געווען פֿון דלאָטעס, זענן, דרעלן,
מיין שפּילפֿאַרמען צענויפֿגעשטעלט.

My Father the Foundryman (1926)

∿ Alexander Pomerantz

For Helen, with love.

My father casts brass.
I'm a city boy, all right?
A stranger to the world of plenty,
my one commandment, "fight."

Fortress and tobacco factories
crown my Lithuanian town.
Massive iron bridges
arch across the river Nieman.[2]

A loving and devoted mother
delivered me in a foundry
to the welcoming engine
of the flaming furnace pounding.

Rocked to sleep by rushing streets,
hammer clap on brass and steel,
the first sound to reach me—
our giant whetstone wheel.

My first song came
from a machine's choral-dance.
The humming of the casting belt
told tales of ages past.

My childhood wonderland saw
steel scaffolds (not gray squirrels!).
I played to the surrounding cry
of chisels, saws and drills.

---

2. Nieman: a major river running through Grodno.

האָב מיט שרויבטאַקעם זיך גע׳חבר׳ט;
מאָדעלן פֿאַרביקע האָט מיך פֿאַרווירט.
מטבעות קופּערנע, פֿאַרזשאַווערט,
האָב איך געזאַמלט און פֿאָלירט.

געזען נאָר אַרבעטסזאַמע בינען
אין די טראַנסמיסיעם איינגעשטעפּט;
פֿון טאָקער, פֿרייזער, הויב־מאַשינען,
מיין קינדהייט־פֿרייד האָב איך געשעפּט.

געליבט אין פֿורעמען זיך אײַבן,
און אויסגיסן זיך שפּילעריי.
זכרונות מער פֿון אַלץ פֿאַרבליבן
איז מיר פֿון אונזער גיסעריי:

טשוגונגעראָמטע זאַמדןפֿורעמם,
ווי די סאָלדאַטן, ריי נאָך ריי;
די הרודעם מעש און קאָקס, ווי טורעמם,
ווי געל׳פֿאַרשוואַרצטע פּלאַכטעם שניי.

מיט צלמ׳לאָך די פֿונקען שיסן
אין גרויסן האַרן קנאָל נאָך קנאָל –
גענאַפּט צו זען מיין טאַטן גיסן
דאָס פֿייערדיק־צעגליט מעטאַל:

אָט שווינגט די הויבמאַשין דעם טיגל,
דער טאַטע רעגולירט די קייט –
מיר דוכט ער האָט באָקומען פֿליגל,
ער האָט באַזינט די שרעק פֿון טויט.

דעם טיגל שלים גרויסע רוננגען
אין שטאַרקע אײַזן־לאַפּעם אײַן;
פֿון הייסן מעש די פֿלאַמענצונגען –
זיי רייסן זיך אין לייב אַריין.

A slate became my playmate.
Colored models were my toys.
I used to gather up and polish
rusty copper coins.

I ladled childhood joy
from lathe, crane, capping machine.
In our playtime we would practice
the molding that we'd seen.

But my father's foundry
houses all my other memories.
Swept into the engine,
I still see worker bees.

Cast iron locked in sand-molds,
lined like soldiers, row by row:
clods of brass and lumps like towers,
like blackened yellow sheets of snow.

Dust of sparks like little crosses
in the giant horn, crack on crack.
Oh to see my father pouring
fire-flickering brass.

The lift wields the melting pot,
my father adjusts the casting belt.
It seems to me he sprouted wings . . .
The fear of death—he made it melt.

The melting pot is girded
by enormous rings.
Leaping from the brass
to lick at life are fire-tongues.

די ניסעריי איז העליש־ליכטיק,
פֿאַרגלאַנצט מיט גרינעם ערפֿאָרכטצער:
ס׳וואָלקנט רויך זיך ערנסט, וויכטיק,
ווי הייליק וויירויך ביים אַלטאַר.

ס׳דוכט דער טאַטע איז אַ פּריסטער,
ער ריכט דאָ איצט אַ מעסע אָפּ:
שטרענג פֿאַרזיכטיק אין פֿורעם גיסט ער
צעשמאָלצן מעש אַ טראָפּ נאָך טראָפּ.

און ס׳איז געשען דער גרויסער וואונדער,
ס׳האָט איינגעגעבן זיך דער גוס:
און ניינעבוירענער צילינדער –
שמייכלט, שיקט פֿון זאָמד אַ גרוס.

כ׳געדענק אויך גוט די שפּעטע שעה׳ן, –
דער טאַטע אַרבעט ביים וואַרשטאַט:
ער פּרואוװט צו מיר מיט פֿרייד פֿאַרטרויען
דעם פּלאַן פֿון זיינער־אויטאָמאַט.

פֿאַרפֿאַלגט דער גייסט אים פֿון דערפֿינדן,
ער פֿאַטענטירט אַ וואַסער־קראַן;
זיין אימפּעט וויל נאָר ניט פֿאַרשווינדן:
ער שרייבט מיר פֿון אַ נייעם פּלאַן. –

ער קלאָגט זיך נאָר: די שטאָט איז אָרים,
און אַרבעט איז ניטאָ קיין סך;
ס׳באַפֿאַלן זאָרגן אים, ווי ווערים,
און זויגן אויס דעם זאַפֿט פֿון מאַרך.

אויך מיר באַשערט געווען צו שפּינען
מיין טאַטנס פֿאָדים דאָ אין לאַנד:
בײַ שענדעליערס, שטאָל־מאַשינען
געהאַמערט לייכטער האָט מיין האַנט.

The foundry shines with bright light,
glowing green in anxious sorrow.
Smoke clouds up, important, somber
like holy incense by the altar.

Seems that Father is a priest
celebrating his mass.
Carefully he fills the mold,
drop by drop with molten brass.

And when metal submits to cast,
the miracle has come to pass.
Smiling greetings from the sand
is a newborn cylinder of brass.

And I well recall those late-night hours,
Father working in his shop.
Eyes full of joy, he shows me plans
for an automatic-clock.

Chased by the spirit of invention,
his water faucet patented;
impetus far from gone, he writes me
with another plan he's had.

His sole complaint: the city is poor,
and work is hard to find.
This eats away at him like worms
and sucks the nectar of his mind.

I too was destined to spin
father's thread in this distant land:
Under ceiling lights at steel machines
my hand hammered lamps.

אין קאַלטן לאָמפּן־גוף און טויטן
אַריינגעצווינג נעראָוון־דראָט:
עלעקטריע־שטראָם זאָל אים באַגלייטן
און אויפֿלויכטן זיין יעדן טראָט.

געמעשט, געקופֿערט און געזילבערט
די לאָמפּן־טיילן טאָג, ווי נאַכט;
געפֿיילט, געצירקלט און געעקבערט –
פֿאַר מענטשן ליכטיקייט געבראַכט.

און ליב איז מיר דער רעש פֿון אייזן,
פֿון מעש און שטאָל דער יום־טוב־קלאַנג;
דאָס לאַוואָ־אומרואיקע ברויזן
פֿון ריטמיש־בראַוו מאַשינגעזאַנג.

און כאָטש איך האָב געמוזט פֿאַרביַיטן
דעם האַמער אויף אַ פּען און טינט –
ביַינקט היַים מיַין בלוט נאָך יענע צייַטן,
ווען ס׳האָט מעטאַל מיַין ליד געשפּינט...

I pulled wiry nerves right through
the cold, dead figure of the lamp.
Electric current, light his way,
illuminate his every step.

In copper, silver and in brass,
I plated lamp parts, day and night.
Filed, compassed, perforated—
for the people, I brought light.

Dear to me the iron's racket,
brass and steel, their festive gong,
the row, the rough and restless roar
of the machine's brave, rhythmic song.

And though I've traded hammer in
for pen and ink, I long
with all my blood for days now gone
when metal spun my song.

צוויי לידער פון אַ שמיד

אַהרן קורץ ❧

1

אייִנגלווייַס בין איך
אַ פּאַסטוך געווען,
מיט שעפּסן און בעהיימעס געוואַקסן.
איצט שמיד איך
רעדער,
איצט שמיד איך פערד,
איצט האַמער איך אייַזערנע אַקסן.
געשלאָפֿן אַף
לאָנקעס, געברענט זיך
אַף פֿעלד.
איצט ברענט, איצטער פֿייערט,
איצט שייַערט די קאָזשניע
מייַן לעבן מיר אויס.
מייַן אַרבעט קלינגט איבערן פֿעלד.
מייַן אַרבעט האָט אַ נאָמען אין
די דערפֿער. מייַן אַרבעט און –
מייַן מויד.
זי זינגט אַף די זוניקע וועגן וואָס פֿירן צו מייַן קאָזשניע.
איך מיט די העלפֿער
קלינגען איר צו מיט די האַמערס.
און די אַרומיקע דערפֿער קען מען איר קאָל, אירע באַרוועסע פֿיס, איר הייזן,
רייפֿן לייַב אין דעם רויטן, בלומענדיקן קלייד.
זיינען מייַנע פֿרייד-ברייטע נעכט אונטערן דאָרף –
זיינען מייַנע זינגענדיקע טעג אין קאָזשניע – שפּילטערדיקע, שפּילנדיקע
פֿייערווערק.
רייִדן וועגן מיר
פּויערים אַפֿן קאָל און מיידלאַך – שטילערהייט
מייַן ליד און מייַן האַמער
האָבן פֿאַרשלאָפֿענע דערפֿער דערפֿרייט.

Two Songs of a Blacksmith

꩜ Aaron Kurtz

I.

When I was a boy
I was a shepherd,
grew up with the sheep and cows.
Now I cut
wheels.
Now I shoe horses.
Now I hammer iron axles.
I slept in
meadows, got
sunburnt on rocks.
Now the smithy burns and torches,
scouring my life.
My work rings out across the meadow.
My work is known
in villages.
My work and
my girl.
She sings along the sunny roads that lead her to my smithy.
My helpers and I
accompany her with our hammers.
They know her voice in the nearby towns, her bare feet, her hot,
ripe body in her red flowered dress.
Such are my joyful country nights,
such are my song-filled smithy days: flickering, playful
fireworks.
They talk about me—
peasants aloud and girls in whispers—
how my song and hammer
have brought joy to sleepy towns.

2

אינדערפרי איז דײַן ליבע אַ רואיקער, רײַפער אָראַנזש־בוים

צװישן אונזער שטיבל און

מײַן קוזיניע.

אינדערפרי

איז מײַן ליבע צו דיר

דער שעפעדיקער בוים מיט מאָראַנצן לעבן שטיבל, אונטער זון.

גייענדיק צו דער אַרבעט

קלײַם איך פון פלאַנצן

נאָנצע נאָכלעם אָראַנזש־בײַמער אַרום דאָרף.

נאָר ווען עם הײבן אָן זינגען די פײַערן, די האַמערם

איבער דער קאָוואַדלע

ווערט מײַן ליבע צו דיר דער אָנגעברענטער שמיד־אײַזן,

וואָם לאָזט זיך ניט אָפקילן.

ווערן מײַנע געדאַנקען ווען דיר ערשט־געשמידטע, ברײַטע, הײַסע שינעם

וואָם קײַקלען זיך באַרג אַרויף און

באַרג אַראָפ – צו דיר.

– איז מײַן ליבע צו דיר – די קוזיניע, אינמיטן באַטאָניקן אימפעט,

אינמיטן די

פרײַלאַכע פײַערן, דאָם קלאַנגיקע האַמערן

פון מיר און מײַנע העלפער.

ווען איך קלײַב צענויף מײַן געציַיג, פײַפנדיק אַ ליד

פון אַ ליבן טאָג אַרבעט און אָפרו,

לויפן פאָרויס פון מיר רונדע, רויטע רעדער איבער די בערג –

פון מיר צו דיר.

באַנאַכט איז אונזער ליבע אַ קוזיניע אין פלאַמען.

2.
Your love in the morning is a calm, ripe orange-tree
between our little house and
my smithy.
My morning
love for you is the bountiful citrus by the house, beneath the sun.
On my way to work
I dream of plants,
groves and groves of my oranges encircling the village.
But when the fire, the hammers on the anvil
start to sing,
my love for you is the red hot iron,
which won't grow cold.
My thoughts of you are the wide, newly forged
hot rails
that roll uphill and
down to you.
My love for you is the smithy, in my daytime impetus,
in the midst of
happy fires, the clanging hammers,
mine and my helpers'.
When I gather my tools, whistling the song
of a lovely day of work and rest,
round, red wheels run across the hills, from me,
from me to you.
At night our love is a smithy in flames.

ביים מאַשין

קלמן הייזלער ✺

אין אַ הייסער זומער-טאָג אין דרויסען
זעצען שטאָלצע ביימער גרינע ערגעץ דאָ –
בליהענדיגע.
קאָפעט, פאַלט אַ רעגען,
ווי אַ טוי פון הימעל,
איז וואויל צו די ביימער, צו די בליהענדיגע.
– – – – – – – –

גליט אַ קאַלד-אויווען ערגעץ וואו,
און מיין שטערן
איז אויסגעגליט פון דעם שווייס-געטראַנק
פון מיין אייגען לייב,
טרינקען מיינע ליפען
אַזוי אָט, טראָף נאָך טראָף.
פרעגעלט זיך מיין צונג און גומען
אין מיין שווייס-טייך.

בליהט אַזוי מיין שטערען-קאָפּ
ביים מאַשין
ביים מאַשין
אין אַ שעהנעם זומער-טאָג!

112

At the Machine (1922)

～ Kalman Hayzler

It's a hot summer day outside,
somewhere, proud trees are green
and blossoming.
Raindrops fall
like dew from heaven,
and please the trees in bloom.

— — —

A kiln is glowing somewhere,
and my forehead
glows with the salty sweat
of my own flesh,
and my lips drink it up
drop after drop.
My tongue and gums are sizzling
in my sweat stream.

This is how my brow blooms
at the machine
at the machine
on a beautiful summer afternoon.

די מאַשין

ביינאַכט איז זי
אַ רוהיגע, אַ שטילע,
אַ פאַרשלאָפענע!
אינדערפריה,
קיצלען מינע פיס דעם טרעטער.
װערט זי װילד, –
װערט זי װילד, –
װיינט, קרעכצט די מאַשין!
איך – אַ דערשראָקענער
ציטערען מינע הענט
װי אין קראַמף.
װאַרף איך אונטער
שטיקער זיידען צייג,
װערט עס צעשטאָכען
פון דער שפיציגער נאָדעל,
– װערט עס צעהאַקט
פון די שאַרפע ציין
פון דעם שיבער־שלעפער,
און ס'רייסט הוננגעריג
אין יענער זייט אַריין
דאָס זיידענצייג אַװעק פון מיר.
איך מוז איהר העלפען
איינשלינגען!
און ס'ציטערען מינע הענט
די שטילע נאַכט!
ביז ס'קומט די נאַכט –

114

The Machine (1922)

෨ Kalman Hayzler

At night she is
restful, quiet,
asleep!
In the morning
my feet tickle the treadle.
She grows wild,
she grows wild,
the machine cries and groans.
She frightens me.
My hands shake,
cramp.
I feed in
pieces of silk.
Her needle's point
pierces them,
her feeder's sharp teeth
cut them,
and hungrily she
pushes the silk out
the other side.
I have to help her
swallow!
And my hands shake
the quiet night!
Until night falls—

פינאַראַ

אַ. שטריקער

פינאַראַ אַהער, פינאַראַ אַהין.
אין הויזן רויטע ביז די קני,
אַהער, אַהין,
שנעלער ווי דער ראָדנגעדריי,
העבער ווי מאַשינגערויש,
זינגט ער: טראַלאַלאַלאַ, לאַלאַ, לאַלאַ
און לאַכט און שפילט און טאַנצט זיך צו.

אַהער, אַהין,
אַהין, אַהער,
מיר איז שווער
דער קאָפ וואָס זיצט
אַף מיינע דאָרע אַקסלען איצט...
אַהער, אַהין...

נו, שנעלער דריי זיך מיין מאַשין!
(פינאַראַ טאַנצט.)
אַהין, אַהער,
נאָך אַ דריי.
נאָך אַ גאַנג.
איינס און צוויי:
(פינאַראַ זינגט.)
האַלט זיך פעדים.
רייסט זיך ניט אינדערמיט!
(פינאַראַ לאַכט.)
כ׳שטריק
מלבושים אויפ׳ן שטיק...
(פינאַראַ שפילט.)

פינאַראַ, פינאַראַ,
אין הויזן רויטע ביז די קני:
שנעלער ווי דער ראָדנגעדריי

Figaro

꩜ A Shtriker

Figaro here, Figaro there.
Red knickers up to his knees,
   back and forth,
faster than wheels turn,
louder than rushing machines,
he sings: tra-la-la, la-la, la-la
and laughs and plays and dances along.

   Back and forth,
   back and forth.
   Heavy as boulders,
   this head that sits
   on my thin shoulders . . .
   here, there . . .

Well, spin faster my machine!
   (Figaro is dancing.)
   Back and forth,
   one more turn,
   one more row.
   Just like that.
   (Figaro sings.)
   Hold together, you threads.
Don't tear in the middle!
   (Figaro laughs.)
   I'm knitting
   piecework garments . . .
   (Figaro is playing.)

   Figaro, Figaro.
Red knickers up to his knees,
faster than turning wheels,

העכער ווי מאַשינגעזרויש,
זינגט ער: טראַלאַלאַ, לאַלאַ, לאַלאַ
און לאַכט און שפּילט און טאַנצט זיך צו.
אַהין, אַהער, אַהער, אַהין,
און דאָ, נאָר דאָ,
מיט מײַן מאַשין!

louder than rushing machines,
he sings: tra-la-la, la-la, la-la
and laughs and plays and dances along.
Back and forth, back and forth,
and here, only here
with my machine!

סטרייק

אהרן ראַפּאַפּאָרט ❧

די מאַשינען שטומען. מיט פֿאַרשטיקטער גװאָרע.
די שטילעניש שפּילט. אין הילעניש פֿון שװײגן – כאָלעם.
פֿון געהיים װינקט:
רעדער, צאָן אין צאָן פֿאַרביסן – זשאַװערן.
װי דער פֿאַרביסענער מױל, פֿון אַ נעװײלע אין גאָװערן...
האָמער טוליעט זיך צום אַמבאָס – שאָלעם:
הענט װאָס האָבן דאָ געשװאָונגען,
הענט װאָס האָבן דאָ געזונגען,
געצױמט װי אין אַ שטײג,
פֿױסטיקן אַ שטילעניש – שװײג!

Strike (1935)

∽ Aaron Rapoport

The machines keep quiet. Muffled might.
The silence plays. Under the cover of quiet is a dream.
Wheels beckon
from their hiding place; tooth rusts in tooth bit.
Like the clamped mouth of a carcass, foaming . . .
Hammer nestles against anvil. Peace.
Hands that swung here,
hands that sung here,
confined like in a cage,
clench the quiet. Silence!

דער רוף

אהרן קורץ ‎س‎

(צום דרעסמאַכער־סטרייק)

די שאַ,
דער רוף.
קלאָר דער קאָפּ און גרייט דער גוף.
אימפעטיקער צאָרן און געוואָנטער קאָל.
עס בוינט זיך אויס די גיננאָלד־שאָל – פון שאַרפן שטאָל
אין בלייכע לייבער.
די שאַ, דער רוף:
אַוועק פון ראָד!
שנײדער, שטעפּער, לויף און לאָד
מיט דײן אימפעט אָן די גאָסן, וואָס זעען אוים ווי אָנגעגליטע פאַסן
פון דײן ווייטיקדיקן לעבן. – גענוג,
גענוג געגנעבן
דער גאָס, דער שטאָט, דער וועלט;
די רעדער און דינאַמאָס אָפּגעשטעלט! פאַרשטילט!
אין רויטע ליכט־פּאָסן פאַרהילט
די קליידער־שעפּער און די קראָמען.
זאָל פינצטערן איבער פאַבריקן יעדער פינקלדיקער נאָמען,
וואָס איז פון אײער קנעכטשאַפט דער סימבאָל.
זאָל רוען אומרואיק און וואָקלדיק שפּאַצירן די גאַנצע שטאָט ניו יאָרק
פון אײער גאַנג און קאָל.
זאָל האָפערדיק גאַלאָפּירן
אפן פיקעטליין די פּאָליציי. – די זינער וועט איר זײן,
ניט זיי.

The Call (1933)

∾ Aaron Kurtz

For the dressmakers' strike

The hour,
the call.
Clear your head, prepare your flesh.
Daring voice and anger, rash.
Sharp steel bends the fine gold balance—
with flesh grown pale.
The hour, the call:
get away from the wheel!
Tailor, quilter, run and fill
them with your rashness, these streets with glowing rows
of your pained bodies—enough of it all,
enough giving
the street, the city, the world . . .
The wheels, the generators, stopped! Silenced!
The garment sweatshops and stores
enveloped in red light.
Darken the names over factories,
symbols of your slavery.
Let all of New York City rest restlessly, while stumbling along
from your voice and step.
Let the police
gallop, haughty, to the picket-line. You will be the victors,
not they.

שענדעליערס

יהושע גראָדנער ✍

זיי האָבן געלויכטן – – –
און האָבן מיין לעבן ניט ליכטיק געמאַכט.
א. ר.

שענדעליערס, לייכטער מאַכן מיר,
קונסט־לאַמפּן, עלעקטרישע לייכטער שאַפֿן מיר, –
אידן, נינערס, דייטשן, רוסן, גריכן, איטאַליענער –
חברים פֿון זעלבן פֿאַך.
און טאָג נאָך טאָג, און יאָר נאָך יאָר:
דער שניצט און גיסט דער פֿיילט און טאָקט,
פֿאַלירט און בויערט,
דער קופֿערט, מעשט, ניקלט, זילבערט און באַגאָלדט,
דער פֿאַרבט, בראָנזירט, לאַקירט און מאָלט,
און דער ציט דורך עלעקטרישע דראָטן –
די לעבנס־נערוון פֿון לאָמפּ. –
און אַזוי נאָכן דורכגיין זיבן און זיבעציק מענשלאַכע הענט
ווערט באַשאַפֿן אַ לאָמפּ.

Chandeliers (1924)

∽ Alexander Pomerantz

> They were lit,
> and didn't make my life any brighter.
> —AVROM REYZIN

Chandeliers: we make hanging lights.
Electric, or art lamps: we make 'em bright.
Jews, Negroes, Germans, Russians, Greeks, Italians,
comrades of a common skill.
And day after day, and year after year,
we cut and pour them, file and turn,
   clean and drill,
we copper, brass, nickel, silver, gold them,
we color, bronze, lacquer and paint them,
and trembling through electric wires,
living nerves fill the lamp.
Handled by seventy-seven hands,
a lamp becomes a lamp.

שיר ✿ אשיידים ✿ אַנשטער

ווי טויבן צוזוי
אַף גַמליבטערס טויס
זענסטו אום
ווען דו דערמיינגסט
מיט דיין באַשטערמטער
אין מיין כהראַם
פון טשיט־סקוירעב
זיך אַ נעמען
כאַסַננע קליידער

ווי זילבער־טוי
אַף גריבעם בלאָט
זעגט אויס דיין קומאָדער
אפּן דאַלעבער
ווען דו גיסט עס
מיר אין האַנט
קאַסטימער דו מיין

ווי רייפע טייטלען
זעגעגען דיינע ציסב
סטיילס טעבקסן
באַטאַמער
ווייל וועד קעגן ריידן
און וועד קעגן ציילן
טעקסן שמעקסן
אין אַ טיינעם
נערעוו פרילינג
נערעוו לעבן
נערעוו פריגל
לעבכא דורידי

ווי פינקל שטערן
אין אַ פרילינג נאַכט
איבער 2 פארליבטע
פאַסטענד־קינדער
פינקלען דיינע
דיימלענד
ווען דיין האַרץ
פארלאַנגט פון מיר
די וואוונדער־קונסט
פון טרימינגס
פאַר דיין זיידן העמד
פאַרדיין דאַמען־לייב

ווי סימפאָנייעס
פון בראַמס און מאַצאַרט
קלינגט מיין ניַיער
רעברזשעריסטער
נאָך יעדן
קערב דיקן סטייל
וואָס די מיין קאַסטימער
טוסטו
צו לעבין
געבן
מיר

האַל אַגען
מיין קאַסטימער
דען דו בינסט
אין מיין האַרץ
אין מיין זעל
פארוואַרבלט

פאַרוואַרבלט
ווי אַ לעכטיקער
נער טאַמיד
נער שטענדיק
נער אימער
אימער
דערגנרערמיד
קאַסטימער
דו מיין

האַל אַגען
מיין קאַסטימער.
דען דו דארפסט
קיין גוטער זיין
גאַסער. נאָמעם
מעגסט זיך זיין
ווי ביטער
מעגסט זיך זיין
ווי שלעכט
אפילב ווען
דו שפייסט
מיין פאַנס אַפּ
ביזטו מיין קאַסטימער
גערעבכט
ווייל דו נאָר
און נאָר דו
און שטענדיק דו
און טאַמעדו
ווענט זיין גערעבכט

קויל קויל קאַסן, קויל קויל. קויל קויל קאַלב, קויל
feelings
hard
האַל אַגען
no מיין קאַסטימער

פון די נאָך ניט פאַרעפנטלעכטע אַרבעטן פון יאָסל קאַטלער

Shir Asheydim Ansher[3]

‿ Yosl Cutler

You look
like two doves
on a lover's lap
when you and your
betrothed show up
in my shop
of dry goods
to get yourself
wedding clothes

Like silver-dew
on a green leaf
is your quarter
on the dollar
when you pour it
in my hand
customer o' mine

Like ripe dates
are your sweet
sales taxes
tasty, because
who can speak
and who can count
taxes shmakses
in a lovely
eve of spring
eve of life
eve of birdie
lekha doydi[5]

Like twinkling stars
on a spring night
over 2 lovers
shepherd children
your dimelets
shine
when your heart
demands of me
the wonder-art
of trimmings
for your silk shirt
for your dainty body

Like symphonies
of Brahms and Mozart
my new cash
register rings
every
solid fat purchase
that you, my customer,
make, to bring
me
income.

"Kol agen"[4]
my customer.
For you are
rooted
in my heart,
rooted

in my soul
a bright
eternal lamp
forever lamp
always lamp
always
feed me
customer
of mine

"Kol agen"
my customer.
For you need
not be good
Nossir. No ma'am.
you can be
as rude
you can be
as bad . . .
even when
you spit
in my face
you, my customer,
are right
because only you
and you alone
and you always
and forever—you
will be right.

Kol, Kol, bridegroom. Kol, kol, bride, kol, kol. . . "Kol-agen" my customer.

No   *Hard*   *Feelings*

3. "Shir Asheydim Ansher" is a playful takeoff on the Song of Songs, which begins, in Hebrew, "Shir HaShirim Asher." The changed pronunciation of the title reads as a Yiddish accented version of the original, which, in Cutler's cunning play on words, changes the meaning somewhat. "Shir asheydim" turns the "Song of Songs" into "Song of the Ghosts." Throughout the poem Cutler plays with a phonetic combination of Hebrew, Yiddish, and English, as a means of parodying capitalism and traditional Judaism.

4. "Kol agen": Cutler transliterates an accented English "Call again" in such a way that it looks like a Hebrew phrase, taken from the original Hebrew "kol" for voice.

5. *Lekha doydi*: song sung on the Sabbath eve, in which the Sabbath is greeted as a bride.

127

עם שטייגט!

סעם ליפצין ⤚

אין אלע גאַסן,
וואו איר גייט,
הערט איר אַלץ
די זעלבע רייד –
עם שטייגט!

מ'רייסט די הויטן
ביז'ן ביין,
אַנשטאָט סחורה –
קריגט איר שטיין...
און איר טאָרט
זיך ניט באַקלאָגן,
ס'איז ניט צו וויינען,
ניט צו זאָגן,
עם שטייגט? –
שווייגט!

סחורות לינן
גאַנצע בערגער,
נאָר מ'זאָגט:
ס'וועט זיין נאָך ערגער.
און זיי ווילן,
איר זאָלט גלויבן,
אַז פונעם רעדן –
נעמט זיך הויבן –
עם שטייגט!

איר זוכט אַ דירה,
קלאַפט אין טירן,
לאָזט מען אייך
אין נאָס קראַפירן.
ווילט איר שלאָפן
שוין אין דרויסן,

128

from "Going Up" (1969)

∾ Sam Liptsin

On every street
along your way
you hear it,
all the people say,
   going up!

They rip your skin
to bone.
Instead of merchandise,
you get stone,
and you dare not
complain,
what use are cries,
what use surmising,
will it rise?
Shut up!

Merchandise,
as a mountain, lies,
and they say
it'll just get worse,
and they want
you to believe
that talk will somehow
make it rise—
   it's going up!

You need a place to stay,
knock on doors, and they
leave you
to croak out in the street,
you're ready to sleep
outside, if you have to!

איז מען אייער
טובה אויסן...
און מ'נעמט אייך –
אין חדרגדיא...
דער ריכטער מאַכט דאָס
גאָר ניט טייער,
הייסט באַצאָלן
שטראָף אַ דרייער...
ווילט איר אָבער
זיך מאַכן קלערער...
זאָגט דער ריכטער:
ס'קאָסט שוין מערער! –
ס'קאָסט אים אַליין טייער...
עס שטייגט!

אין די קראָמען,
אוי די קראָמען,
פרייזן האָבן ניט
קיין נאָמען...
פּוטער, מילך,
ברויט אַ שטיקל,
פון אַ דאָלאַר –
ווערט אַ ניקל...
פון אַ ניקל
ווערט אַ פּעני –
פע, איר דינגט זיך, –
זאָגט ער, פּעני? –
עס שטייגט!

So they decide
on your behalf, to . . .
put you away.
The judge makes clear
that you needn't
pay dearer,
than the three-buck fine
they usually pay,
but if you
want it clearer,
the judge will say
that'll cost extra,
and costs him dearer, too . . .
   it's going up!

In the stores,
oh, the stores,
there isn't a name
for the prices . . .
butter, milk,
a piece of bread,
turns a dollar—
to a nickel,
and a nickel
to a penny—
Heh, then try to work for money,
he says, funny?
   It's going up!

Speaking of Scottsboro

The Scottsboro trial, inspired by the roundup of nine young African American men implicated in the alleged gang-rape of two white women, held the nation's attention throughout its duration from 1932 to 1937. One of the defendants was put to death shortly after the trial began. The remaining eight found their place in the national consciousness as America began to grapple with difficult issues of race and the scapegoating of African Americans. The trial ended only after one of the two women confessed to having invented the rape story. It took several more years before all of the defendants were released, and decades before they were formally pardoned.

Throughout the 1930s, left-wing groups actively supported the "Scottsboro Boys." The Yiddish daily *Frayhayt*, like other left-wing papers, featured regular articles, photographs, political cartoons, and poems, as well as excerpts from letters that the young defendants received and sent from the Scottsboro jail. Scottsboro quickly came to stand for "race" in Proletpen's poems.

Poems depicting the struggle of African Americans were already common in American Yiddish poetry, but Scottsboro prompted a series of new, and more contextualized responses to racism in America. Poets like Y. A. Rontsh, Betsalel Friedman, and Abraham Victor titled long poems "Scottsboro" as a means of immediately aligning their sympathies with the fight against racial injustice. In his essay "The African American in Yiddish Literature" Rontsh suggests that while some mention of Black protagonists can be found in Yiddish prose and poetry throughout early-twentieth-century American Yiddish literature, the most successful portrayals of African Americans are those of the Proletpen writers.[1] According to Rontsh, leftist writers, more than other Yiddish writers, made an effort to spend time in the South, where most of the racial turmoil originated.

Most of the poems in this section appeared during the Scottsboro trial. Others were written in its aftermath. Beresh Weinstein's "A Negro Dies" appeared in *Yidishe kultur* in December 1938. Betsalel Friedman's "Scottsboro" describes a parent's solution to the bias he finds in his son's education. When the protagonist's son tells him how Lincoln set the Black free, the former sends the latter to "Janitor Jim" (the title of another poem in Fridman's book) so that the Black man can tell the white boy about his life. Rontsh, in the lengthy prose poem "Done a Good Job," exposes racism by writing from the perspective of a lynch mob.

The idea of sharing the margins of American culture with African Americans had fascinated immigrant Yiddish writers long before the Scottsboro boys climbed onto a Southern Railway train in March of 1931. Sarah Barkan's "Negro Song" is only one example of many pieces that appeared in the twenties. These skin-deep accounts portray Black-Jewish relations that remained, for the most part, distant, while at the same time demonstrating a powerful desire to overcome racist violence, and disdain for the hypocrisy of the legendary "land of the free."

In my translations of this section I have made an effort to preserve the terminology around race that would have been used by a politically conscientious writer in the 1930s. In Yiddish, the appropriate term for a person of African descent is "Neger," whereas the word meaning "Black man," "Shvartser," is understood to be derogatory. Even in strongly ironic poems, such as Cutler's "Neckst" and Rontsh's "Done a Good Job," the poets tend to opt for the more generic "Neger" for the speech of their anglophone protagonists. In my translations I have chosen to use a combination of the terms Negro and black, which I hope reflects the writers' sensitivity to language without taking the English out of the context of the period.

---

1. Y. A. Rontsh, "The African American in Yiddish Literature," in *Amerike in der yidisher literatur: An interpretatsye* (New York: Marstin Press, 1945) 203–51.

נעגער־ליד

שרה באַרקאַן ✒

האַשעבבאַי־האַשעבבאַי, קליינקער קון.
באַשערט דיר צו ווערן אַ נעגערנס זון
מיט ציינדעלעך זילבער מיט ברוינדהויט אַ פּראַכט
פון רייכן פאַרמאַטערט, פון ווייסן פאַרלאַכט.

האַשעבבאַי־האַשעבבאַי, נעגערנס זון,
דיין מאַמעס האַרץ ציטערט, דו ווייסט ניט דערפון.
דיין פּאַ איז באַגינען צום ו ו י י ס ם ן אַוועק.
מיין קלייגקער זונעלע פילט ניט מיין שרעק.

האַשעבבאַי־האַשעבבאַי, ליבינקער קון,
פון בלומען דיין ווינל, דיין העמדל פון זון.
שווינג־אַלינג, שווינג־אַלינג – ווינקט דיר דער ווינט,
פּונקט ווי דו וואָלסט זיין אַ ווייסינקער קינד.

האַשעבבאַי־האַשעבבאַי, זון זיי געגרייט:
דער האַר האָט טונקעלע נעצן פאַרשפּרייט
פאַר נעגערלאַך שיינע מיט אויגעלאַך שוואַרץ
פּונקט ווי באַם ווייסן איז רויט אונזער האַרץ.

Negro Song (1929)

∽ Sarah Barkan

Hushaby, hushaby, wee little coon,
destined to live as a Negress's son,
with silvery teeth and brown skin, my delight,
tormented by rich, laughed at by whites.

Hushaby, hushaby, Negress's son,
your mother's heart trembles, you don't know such things.
At dawn your Pa leaves for the whites' from here.
My wee little baby, don't feel my fear.

Hushaby, hushaby, loveliest one,
your cradle's of flowers, your shirt's of the sun.
Swing-a-ling, swing-a-ling, wink in the wind,
just as if you were a white person's kin.

Hushaby-hushaby, son, be prepared:
the white man's spread out nets, everywhere
for the fine black children with the blackest of eyes.
Our heart is red, just like the whites'.

סקאַטסבאַראַ (פראַגמענט)

לינגער! איר דערצײלט די קינדער אונדזערע פֿון פֿרײהײט,
װען טעג און נעכט איר האַלט געשמידט אין קײטן און אין גראַטעס.
איר דערצײלט, אַז לינקאַלן באַפֿרײט האָט באָבעס, זײדעם,
און אױף בײמער װאַרגט איר איצט די קינדער און די טאַטעס...

ס'קומען קינדער פֿון קינאָ אַמאָל מיט פֿרײד אין אױגן,
אָפֿענאַרטע פֿונעם ליגן: „קעבין פֿון אָנקל טאָמען".
איר סמט דאָס מילך, װאָס קינדער האָבן קלײנערהײט געזױגן,
און גיסט אין הערצלעך שנאה־סם צו נעגערן מיליאָנען.

װי פֿאַרמאָרעט לײב, איז בלײך די פֿרײד אין שװאַרצע שטיבער;
פֿרײד, װען ס'װערט אַ קינד געבאָרן, דאַרפֿן זײ אױך קאָרגן –
– װער װײסט: דעם װײסן הערשער איז דאָס בלוט פֿון װעמען ליבער,
דעם שכנס זון װעט ער אױף דעם בױם דעם דערװאָרגן?

בלײך איז די לעגענדע פֿון אַמאָליקן מצרים:
קינדער פֿון די עברים צו דערטרינקען אין די טײכן –
ס'איז 1931 – בילבול אין סקאָטסבאַראַ –
שװער אין יאָר־נעשיכטע צו געפֿינען נאָך אַ גלײכן.

מאָמעס פֿון יינגלעך אין טױט־קאַמער,
מאָמעס אין שױדער פֿון טױט –
פֿאַר אײך און פֿאַר אונדז װײקט דער שׂונא
אין בלוט דאָס טאָג־טעגלעכע ברױט.

געלײענט דײן בריװ, מאַמע פֿאָועל,
געשריבן מיט פֿלײץ פֿון דײן בלוט.
שטאַרק זיך, פֿאַרצװײפֿלטע מאַמע,
יעדער חבר פֿאַר סקאָטסבאַראַ טױט.

138

Scottsboro (An Excerpt) (1931)

∼ Betsalel Friedman

Liar! You tell our children of freedom,
while day and night you lock them in chains and cells,
choke children on trees beside their fathers.
Lincoln freed grandmothers and grandfathers, you tell.

Children come out of the movies. Sometimes joy is in their eyes,
fooled by lies of *Uncle Tom's Cabin*.
You've poisoned the milk that little babies drink,
poured into little hearts hate for Negro millions.

The joy in Black homes is like starved flesh:
Even when a child is born, one spends joy sparingly.
Who knows where a white ruler draws his blood?
Will he choke the neighbor's son on a tree?

Pale is the tale of ancient Egypt
and the Hebrew children drowned in the river.
It's 1931, with a frame-up in Scottsboro . . .
nothing like it in the history of slavery.

∼

Mothers of boys in death-cells,
mothers shudder at the dead.
For you and for us, the enemy soaks
in blood our daily bread.

We read your letter, Mama Powell,
written with your gushing blood.
Keep strong, desperate mother,
every comrade works for Scottsboro's good.

געהערט, מאַמע רייט, דיך דערציילן:
דיינע, דיין טאָכטערלס רייד.
האָסט מיט אייגענע אויגן געזען –
יעדער חבר מיט בלוט דיך פֿאַרשטייט.

אומעטום, וואו מיר זאַמלען די כוחות,
אין לעצטער אַנטשיידענער שלאַכט –
שטעלט סקאָטסבאָראַ גרייט די חברים,
שטעלט סקאָטסבאָראַ קעמפֿער אויף וואַך.

ס׳בלוטיקן וואונדן אין פּיטסבורג,
צייט רייפֿט שוואס יאָרן פֿון גסיסה.
א י י ן פֿייער צינדט אָן אַלע קאַמפֿן
פֿון ניו־יאָרק ביז סקאָטסבאָראַער תּפֿיסה.

∽

אין טויט־שרעק אין בירמינגהאַם תּפֿיסה
ליגן נייַן יינגלעך פֿאַרגראַטעוועט –
צו דיר און צו מיר, צו אונדז אַלעמען
דאָס איינציקע וואָרט זייערס: ראַטעוועט!

פֿון שטיבער, צעפֿוילט און פֿאַרשימלט,
וואו שטראַלן, ווי חלב־ליכט, צאַנקען –
פֿאַר דיר און פֿאַר מיר, פֿאַר אונדז אַלעמען
סקאָטסבאָראַער מאַמעס געדאַנקען.

ערד פֿון וואולקאַנען צעריסענע –
מאַמעס שלאָף: – מיר׳ן ווידער אים גאָנצן...
אויגן, מיט טרערן פֿאַרלאָפֿענע, –
מיר׳ן ווידער זיי קלאָרן און גלאַנצן.
1931

We heard, Mama Wright, when you told us
what your little daughter said.
You've seen with your very own eyes
how you've moved every red-blooded comrade.

Everywhere we gather power
in the battle to win the war.
For Scottsboro the comrades stand ready.
For Scottsboro warriors stand guard.

Wounds are bleeding in Pittsburgh,
time ripens the enemy's years of travail.
One fire ignites all struggles
from New York to Scottsboro jail.

∾

In deathly fear in Birmingham jail,
nine young people lie behind bars.
Their single word, Help!, resonates
for you and me, and all of ours—

From rickety, decrepit homes,
like candle light, it radiates
toward you and me and all of ours,
the Scottsboro mothers' thoughts.

Earth from erupting volcanoes
is a mother's sleep: we'll help her rest again.
Eyes full of streaming tears:
we'll bring back their brilliance and shine.

סקאַטסבאַראַ

י. א. ראָנטש ⇜

איך האָב געזען די שװאַרצע מאַסע קניען
אין עקסטאַז פאַר יעזוסן דעם רעטער;
און אױגן גלאָציקע ניט אױפגעהערט צו גליען,
און הענט מאַזאָליסטע געשטערעקט זיך און געבעטן.

אַ, װיפל אונטערטעניקײט אַרױסגעזוננגען
האָט פון זײערע „ספיריטשועלס" די בלינדע;
אַזעלכע ברײטע פליצעם, באַסן־שטימען, ריזן־יונגען
האָבן זיך געשראָקן, װי קלײנע, קראַנקע קינדער.

איך האָב געזען דעם שװאַרצן – דזשעזן, טאַנצן,
פאַרװײלנדיק דאָס װײסע, פעטע באַלעבעסל;
דער שװאַרצער פײער אױסגעברענט איננאַנצן
האָט פאַר רײכן שיקער אין קאַבאַרעט־קעסל.

נאָר איצטער זע איך שװאַרצע ריזן־יונגען
רעװענדיק מיט װילדן אױפגעברױזטן צאָרן,
דאָס ליד פון סקאַטסבאַראַ, פון קאַמף מיט הונגער,
װאָס איז געװען פאַרשטיקט אין בלוט אַזױפיל יאָרן.

די װײסע גרױסע צײן ניט ציטערן פאַר בײטש־קאַנאַלן;
דער שװאַרצער דראָט זײן שטײפע פױסט דעם פײנט אין פּאָנעם.
ניט יעזוס־לאָרד, ניט „ספיריטשועלס", ניט קױרים פאַלן, –
נאָר סקאַטסבאַראַ־שאַל, דער אױפברױז־שאַל פון קאַמף מיט סאָנים.

Scottsboro (1936)

∼ Y. A. Rontsh

I've seen black masses on their knees,
ecstatic for Jesus the savior,
and glowing eyes' eternal gaze,
and calloused hands stretched out in prayer.

The blind have sung in spirituals
the servitude of a true believer.
How do young, broad-shouldered basses
cower like a child with a fever?

I've seen the black folk—jazzing, dancing,
indulging a chubby white boss,
wasting their black fire on
the wealthy drunks in cabaret halls.

But now I watch black sturdy youth
roar in spurts of rage the song
of Scottsboro, of struggling with hunger,
smothered in their blood so long.

Whips crack. Big white teeth won't chatter.
The black man shakes his fist in disgust.
Jesus, genuflection, spirituals won't matter.
Just Scottsboro and rage in the fight for the just.

א גוטן דושאב געמאכט

‏י. א. ראָנטש ‏&

מ׳האָט געלינטשט א נעגער היינט ביי אונז אין אלאבאמא.
ס׳איז ווערט געווען א טאָלער א בילעט
בייצואווינען דעם ספּעקטאַקל.
און ווער עס האָט געהאַט די זכיה
דערשטופן זיך צו א סואוועניר,
וועט האָבן צו באַרימען זיך פאַר קינדער׳ם קינדער.

געשען איז דאָם אזוי:
די דריי־און־אכצינ־יאָרינ אלטע מויד,
די פרומע נשמה, וואָם איז אודאי נאָך א בתולה,
האָט זיך צעקלאָנט, צעברומט אינמיטן העלן טאָנ,
אז א נעגער־יונג האָט זי געוואָלט באַמאנעגן.
מע זאָנט אפילו, אז זי איז היבשלעך „דאָסינ״
און רעדט צו זיך אליין די לעצטע צענדלינ יאָר...
נאָר וועמען אַרט עם?
ס׳איז לאָנג שוין שטיל געווען אין שטעטל
און נעגער־מאַלפּעס האָבן מיר דאָך – ליב דאָם לעבן!
בפרט נאָך איצט, ווען ס׳ווילט זיך דוקא זיי
ניט אנדערש. נאָר מיט וויסע ווערן גלייך.
מע זאָנט, אז זייער חוצפּה דערגרייט צו דעם,
אז זיי פאַרלאַנגען גלייכן ארבעט־לוין מיט וויסע...

נו, ס׳האָט א שמעק געטאָן אין לופט מיט לינטש־געבראָטנם.
מע האָט א לאָ געטאָן די שפּיר־הינט צו דער בתולה׳ם הויז,
נאָר זיי האָבן גאָרניט ניט געקענט דערגיין.
דער עולם האָט א לאָנגן זופ געטאָן דעם „בוז״
און יונג און אלט האָט האָפּערדין באַריכטעט:
ס׳וועט זיין א „נעקטאָי־פּאָרטי״ היינט אין שטעטל...
מיט ביקסן און מיט שטריק,
מיט גראַבליעם און מיט בייטשן,
האָט זיך דער וויסער עולם,
מיטן שעריף און מיט דער בתולה אין דער שפּיץ,
א לאָ געטאָן צו שוואַרצן שטאָט־טייל,
געפינען דאָרט א נעגער אף צו לינטשן.

Done a Good Job (1933)

~ Y. A. Rontsh

Today we lynched a Negro, here in Alabama.
It cost a buck a ticket
to get in to see the show.
And the ones that got the squatter's rights
to scramble for a souvenir
can boast about it to their children's children.

It happened like this:
the eighty-three-year-old spinster
pious soul (betcha still a virgin)
screamed and wailed in the light of day
that a Negro boy tried to make her.
    Some folks say she's not all there,
      that she's talked to herself a decade now.
But who cares?
Our little town's been too quiet,
and we *love* Negro monkeys so *much* . . .
especially now that they're startin'
to want to be treated like white folks.
Those Negroes have gotten so uppity,
now they want to be paid like whites.

Well, it's sent the scent of lynch-roast on the air.
They loosed the bloodhounds at the virgin's house.
But they couldn't find a trace.
The folks had a long sip of booze.
Haughty, young and old reported
    there'll be a "neck-tie" party in town today.
With rifles and ropes,
rakes and whips,
those white folks,
led by the sheriff and spinster,
rushed right into the black part of town
to find a Negro there to lynch.

גערעוועט האָבן זיי, די שוואַרצע מאַלפּעס,
ווי חזרים אינם שעכט־הויז.
מע האָט געטריבן און געטרײבערט זיי,
געבוכצעט און געשמיסן
און אונטערגעצונדן אַ אַוואַוינטע חורבה.
ביז ס'האָט די אַלטע מויד
אַרויסגעלאָזט אַ קווישט און אַנגעוויזן
אויף אַ יונגן נעגער, שוואַרץ ווי קויל,
וואָס האָט געציטערט, ווי אַ בלאַט אין ווינט.
„איך שווער ביים גוטן האַר יעזוס קריסטוס,
אַז כ'האָב קיינמאָל ניט באַרירט קיין פרוי".
נאָר ס'איז געווען גענוג.

דער שעריף האָט אַ ברום געטאָן:
„נעגער, דו קום מיט מיר אין דזשייל
און העננגען וועט מען דיך געוועצלעד".
אַזוי פאַדערט דאָס געזעץ פון לאַנד.
נאָר יעדער איינער האָט גע'חוזק'ט פון שעריף'ס רייד.
(און דער שעריף אַליין אויך, מסתמא).
מע דאַרף ניט פּטר'ן קיין שטײער־געלט פון שטאַט
צו העננגען אַ נעגער־הונט געוועצלעד...

עס האָט אַ שמעק געטאָן אין לופט מיט לינטשערײַ.
דער עולם האָט געטאָן אַ מורמל,
אינאַנהויב שטיל און העבער באַלד און שטאַרקער,
און ווי דער אויסברוך פון אַ שטורעם,
האָט זיך צעטראָגן קיקלדינג־געדונער:
לינטשט דעם נעגער!
לינטשט דעם נעגער!!

אַ שטופן זיך, אַ שטויסן זיך פאַרוים,
אַ הייס'אָטעמדיג געדראַנג
און יעדער פויסט
אויף נעגער'ם קאָפּ
און יעדנם שוך
אין נעגער'ם בויך.

Did they ever bellow, those black apes,
like pigs in the slaughterhouse.
They chased and beat them,
pounded and whipped them
and set their slums on fire.
'Til the old maid
squealed and pointed
at a young Negro, black as coal,
who shivered like a wind-blown leaf.
    "I swear by the good Lord Jesus Christ,
    I never touched any woman."
But it was enough.

The Sheriff growled,
    "Nigger, come on down to jail
    and they'll hang you legally."
That's how it's written in the law of the land.
But everyone was mocking the sheriff's speech.
(So was the sheriff, probably.)
One needn't waste taxpayers' money
hanging a nigger-dog lawfully . . .

You could taste lynching in the air.
The crowd let out a murmur,
quiet at first, then louder, then stronger,
like the breaking of a storm,
the thunder came rolling in:
    "Lynch the nigger!
    Lynch the nigger!!"

Pushing and pressing itself ahead,
a hot rush of breath
and every fist
on the Negro's head.
And every shoe
to the Negro's gut.

עס איז געוואָרן נאַכט.

און מיט שטאָרקאַצן ווי אין אַ וואַל־פאַראַד,

געבראַכט האָט מען דעם נעגער אויפן פרײַהייט־סקווער.

אַ שאָד געווען צו פטרן דעם אַלטן עלמ־בוים.

איינס און צוויי —

און ס'ווינט זיך נעגער אויפן שטריק. ווי אַן אומרו.

און ווער עס קען דערשטופן זיך צום בוים

מיט מעסערלעך, מיט שערלעך,

צי מיט די בלויז פינגער —

שנײַדט־אָפּ, רײַסט־אָפּ, צעפליקט

די אָווראָלס און שטיקלעך פלייש פון נעגער;

מע צילט דעם אבער זײַנעם אָפּצושנײַדן,

ס'וועט זײַן אַ סואוועניר פאַר קינד און קינדער'ס קינד.

עס פלאַמט אַ פייער שוין אַף דר'ערד

און פלאַמען קיצלען נעגער'ס פיאטעם.

מע ברענגט אַ קענדל געזאָלין

און פלאַמען סמאַליען נעגער־לײַב.

מע האַלט די קינדער הויך אַף פלייצעם,

זיי זאָלן זען דעם זעלטענעם ספּעקטאַקל.

עס בראָט זיך נעגער־פלייש

און פרוּוען די אַלטן צו די נעזער אײדעלע;

בײַ שוואַכע דרייט זיך קאָפּ פון דער געסראָאַכע.

ס'ווערט שפּעט. די פלאַמען צוקן שוין.

– אַ גוטע נאַכט, מיר טרעפן זיך אין קירך.

– איך קויף זיך מאָרגן אַ פּאָר שיך.

– לאָז גרוסן אַלע היימישע.

נאָר דער, וואָס האָט געדולד און וואַרט,

ביז נעגער־פלייש איז שוין פון פלאַם צעגריזשעט,–

באַקומט דעם בעסטן לוין.

מען לויפט צום רויכענדיגן קוילן־גוף,

מע האַקט אַרוים אַ ווײַסן גרויסן צאָן פון נעגער'ס מויל;

מע ברעכט די קרובלע קנאָכן אָפּ,

ווי צווײַגלעך פון אַ האַרבסט־בוים,

מע לויפט אַהיים מיט טײַערן סואוועניר.

Night fell,
and with torches lit like in an election parade,
they brought the Negro to Freedom Square.
A pity to waste the old elm-tree there.
In no time at all . . .
the Negro swung like a pendulum on the rope.
And whoever can push himself up to the tree
with pocket-knives, with shears,
or with his bare finger,
cuts off, tears off, plucks
the Negro's overalls and bits of flesh.
They're aiming to cut off his member,
a souvenir for kids and grandkids.

There's already a fire on the ground
and flames tickle Negro heels.
They bring a can of gasoline
and flames singe the Negro body.
Children sitting high on shoulders
get to see the special show.
Negro flesh is roasted.
Fine women hold fine noses;
the weak turn away from the stench.

It's late. The flames are dying down.
   "Good night, we'll meet again in church."
   "Tomorrow I'm going to buy new shoes."
   "My regards to the family."
But the ones who stay on
until Negro flesh is consumed by fire
get the best reward.
They run to the smoldering coal-body.
They hack a big, white tooth from the Negro's mouth;
they break off the brittle bones
like twigs from an autumn tree,
they run home with a precious souvenir.

מע וועט זיך טרעפן מארגן אפן מארק.
– דו האסט א שטיקל אָווערָאל, דאָם אליץ?
דערפאַר האָב איך א שאַקאָלאָדנעם אויער...
– און אים האָט אָפגענגליקט –
ער האָט געפּאַקט א צאָן!

א גוטן דזשאָב געמאַכט,
מיר שטעלן אונזער שטעטל אויף דער מאַפּע פון דער וועלט.
עס קלינגט מיט אונז דאָם לאַנד.
עס וועט אָן עולם קומען אונז באַקוקן
פון נאָנט און פון ווייט.
יעס, סער. א גוטן דזשאָב געמאַכט.

And tomorrow at the market,
   "All you got's a piece of overall?
   Well I got a chocolate ear . . ."
   "And he got lucky—
   made off with a tooth!"

Done a good job,
we're puttin' our town on the map of the world.
The whole country's talkin' about us.
Now folks'll come to look at us
from near and far.
Yessiree. Mighty good job.

Neckst

יאָסל קאָטלער ❧

עפשער האָט איר אַ ביסעלע צייט
און אייך ווילט זיך
אַ ביסעלע פֿאַרברענגען,
נעמט און הענגט עפּעס.
הענגט, הענגט,
שעמט זיך נישט.
אַ שטריק איז דאָ,
אַ בוים איז דאָ,
הענגט הענגט,
הענגט אַ נעגער־מענטש.
אַן אַלטן נעגער,
אַ יונגן נעגער,
אַ זיידענענער,
אַ באַבענענער,
אַ „בייבי"־נעגער –
אַלע שוואַרצכיינעוודיקע
און נעקרייזלט אַ כיעם,
אַ כיעם צו הענגען,
די נעגערס אַף טליעם.
הענגט, הענגט,
הענגט וואָס ניט איז.
אַ סאָדערן דזשענטלמען
דאַרף נישט זיין קיין איבערקלייבער,
אַבי אַ שוואַרצער קאָליר.
און אויב אַ ברוינער ווי ביר?
איז אויך נישקאָשע.
טויט נעגערלייט
און לעבט אַ טאָג.
נישקאָשע,
די אַרבעט וועט נישט זיין אומזיסט.

152

Neckst (1934)

∾ Yosl Cutler

Maybe you've got a little time
and don't know
how to spend it.
Take something and hang it.
Hang it, hang it,
don't be shy.
Here's a rope.
Here's a tree.
Hang, hang,
hang a Negro-man.
An old Negro,
a young Negro,
a grandpa Negro,
a granny Negro,
a baby Negro—
all of them, beautiful and black.
The curly pleasure,
a pleasure to hang
these Negroes on gallows.
Hang, hang,
hang whatever.
A *suthn* gentleman
oughtn't be particular,
long as the color is black.
And if he's brown like beer?
Also okay.
Kill black folks,
live it up!
Okay,
this work won't go unpaid.

אין טאָן פֿון דיזשוועכעשבן
וועט דער נעגער נישט מאַכן
קיין שום קונצן מיט אײך.
ער וועט זאָגן זײער פּאָשעט:

רעב דזשענטלמען,
דאָס העלדזל פֿליז!
היק־מיק ביק,
טענק יו, נעקסט!

רעב ריכטער פֿון אַלאַבאַמאַ,
זאַי־ – – – – –טשע מויכל,
אָהער דאָס העלדזל
אַף אײן מינוטקעלע!
היק־מיק־ביק!
טענק יו, נעקסט!

ס׳איז עמעס אַז איר זענט
זײער נישט אײנגעוואוינט
צו זײן אַ טויטער מאַן –
אָבער נישט געפֿערלעך
פֿאָנראָמשטשיקעס
זענען זײער נישט אײנגעוואוינט
אַז מע זאָל זײ פֿערזענלעך אויפֿהענגען,
אָבער די סאָוועטן־מאַכט
האָט זײ אויסגעלערנט הענגען,
און זײ הענגען גאַנץ גוט
ווי דערפֿאַרענע געהאַנגענע.

און מיט אײך,
דזשענטל־לינטשל־לײַט,
וועט זײן די אײגענע מאַיסע –
מע וועט אײך אײנמאָל אונטערהענגען
און נאָכאַמאָל

Come Judgment Day
the Negro won't go playing
any tricks on you.
He'll say real simple:

Reb Gentleman,[2]
your neck, please!
Ungh-urgh, ungh.
Thank you, next!

Reb Judge from Alabama,
So—so sorry,
pass the neck
for just a minute!
Ungh-urgh, ungh!
Thank you, neckst!

It's true that you are
very unaccustomed
to being a dead man—
but don't worry
pogromists
are quite unaccustomed
to being hanged, themselves,
but the Soviet-power
taught them to hang,
and they hang pretty good
like experienced hangees.

And with you,
gentle-lynch-folk,
it will be the same story—
they'll hang you a bit
and do it again

2. Reb: a Yiddish form of address, meaning "mister."

און ווידעראָמאָל

און אַזוי צו ביסלעך,

וועט איר זיך אײנגעוואוינען העגנגען

ווי די שײנע העגנגלייכטער.

אַזוי ווי אין יעדן ספּאָרט

האָט איר זײער ליב

צו זײן איבערשטײנגער,

אַזוי אויך אַף דער טליע

וועט איר ווײזן וואָס איר קענט,

און העגגגען

בעסער פון אַ נעגער,

שעגער פון אַ נעגער,

קולטורעלער פון אַ נעגער,

ווײל וואָס איז אַ נעגער?

משטײנס געזאָגט,

אויך מיר אַ העגנגער!

and one more time
and little by little,
you'll get used to hanging
like the pretty chandelier.
Just like every sport
you really love
to surpass the rest,
no different on the gallows
you'll give 'em what you got,
and hang
better than a Negro,
prettier than a Negro,
more cultured than a Negro.
Cause what's a Negro?
Good-for-nothing,
you call that a hanger?

באַנאַכט אין גרענד סענטראַל

ילה י. גרינשפּאַן

שוואַרצע ברידער מיינע,
טאַנצן אויס אין דער שטילקייט פון דער נאַכט,
אין דער רואיִנקייט פון מירמעלשטיין,
אַ טאַנץ פון שוואַרצער אַרבעט.

שוואַרצע ברידער מיינע–
ווי אַמאָל,
ווען זיי האָבן ניט צו זיך געהערט,
אונטער פלאַמען פון אַ פרעמדער זון
אויף דרומדיגע באָוול־פעלדער–
וואָגלען איצט אַרום
איבער אַ פעלד, וואָס גלאַנצט מיט ווייסער האַרטקייט.

שוואַרצע ברידער מיינע–
אין אַ שטיין, וואו ווייסע קאָלאָנעדריזן
שווינגען אויס אַ שטאָלץ צום קאַלטן נאָט פון ווייסע האַרן.
קריכן זיי איצט אום;
און שפּרייטן הענט באַקופּערטע;
און קניִען דאָ צום מירמלשטיין;
און פּרעפּלען אויס אין נאַכט אַריין
אַ ליד פון שוואַרצער אַרבעט.

שוואַרצע ברידער מיינע–
מיט עמער און מיט האַנטיכער,
מיט באַרשטן און מיט בעזימער–
שפּילן אויס אין נאַכט אַריין
אַ מאַרש צום רויטן מאָרגן.

Grand Central by Night (1930)

∿ Yosl Grinshpan

My black brothers
dance out—in the silence of the night,
in the calm of marble floors and walls—
a black labor dance.

My black brothers—
just as once
they didn't belong to themselves
under the flames of an alien sun
in Southern cotton fields,
wander now
over a field of sparkling white hardness.

My black brothers—
in a cage where white columns
silently prop up the white masters' cold god.
Now they crawl around,
spread bronzed arms,
kneel to the marble,
chant to the night
a black labor song.

My black brothers—
with pails and hand towels,
brushes and brooms,
play into the night
a march to tomorrow's red dawn.

דער ניגער אין סאָבוויי

מלכה לי ❧

אין אַ נאַכט אַזאַ בין איך געפֿאָרן אַהיים,
האָב איך אין באַן פֿאַרנומען אַ יאָמער־געוויין...
אַ יונגער נעגער מיט פֿאַרבראַכענע הענט
„אַ לאָרד, אַ, לאָרד, אַ העלף מיר, העלף!
זיי האָבן געלוויערט אויף אים ווי די וועלף,
פֿאַרוואָרפֿן אַ שטריק, ווי אויף אַ פֿערד אַ צוים,
און אים אויפֿגעהאַנגען אויף אַ סאָסנע בוים...
אַ לאָרד, וואָס האָסטו פֿאַרקויילט זײַן הויט?
פֿאַר זײַן שוואַרצן אָפּשטאַם צו ווערן געטויט...
אַ לאָרד, די מערדער גיב זיי דײַן שטראָף!
אויף אַ סאָסנע ווינט זיך מײַן ברודער'ס גוף“...

ער פֿאַטשט די הענט און בײַלט זיי ווילד.
אין יעדן מענטשן ער זעט דעם מערדער'ס בילד...

אין סאָבוויי פֿאָרן מענטשן אַ סך,
ניט פּלוצלינג דער נעגער זיך הויך אַ צעלאַך,
אַ פֿאַטש אין זײַן קני. „מײַן ברודער ער שפֿרײַזט
זײַן קאָפּ פֿאַרוואָרפֿן, זײַן גוף אויסגעלייזט“...
דער נעגער לאַכט, ער קײַקט און ער זינגט,
זוכט אין די טאַשן, דורך טראַרן ער ווינקט,
און ער ווינט זיך אום אויף די שיכורע פֿיס,
עס ווינט אויף אַ קול אַ טונקעלער ריז...
אַהין און צוריק דער נעגער ער שפֿאַנט
ווער עס פֿאָרט מיט, טראַנט די שאַנד –
„אַ לאָרד, אַ לאָרד, איך האָב געוואוונען די שלאַכט“.
צוויי שרעגעס צײַן שנײַדיג צעלאַכט...
„אַ, לאָרד, אַ לאָרד, אָט קוקט ער צוריק
אויף זײַן האַלז דער שלייף פֿון אַ ווײַסן שטריק...
מײַן ברודער'ס האַלז ווי אַ פֿידל דין,
אַנטשווינען אויף אייביג מײַן ברודער'ס שטים“...

Negro on the Subway (1933)

∽ Malka Lee

One night when I was traveling home
I took a train and heard the mournful moaning
of a young Negro who was wringing his hands,
"Oh Lord, oh, Lord. Oh help me, help!
They lurked in wait for him like wolves,
roped him like he was a horse,
then hung him from a pine.
Oh, why'd ya give him that coal-black face?
So he'd be murdered for his race?
Oh Lord, give the killers their just reward.
My brother's body's swinging from a pine . . ."

He clenches his fists, smacks his hands.
He sees the murderer's face in every man . . .

A lot of folks are traveling on the subway.
Suddenly the black man bursts out laughing.
He slaps his knee, "My brother's striding,
head held high, his body redeemed . . ."
The black man laughs, he gasps, and sings,
searches his pockets and winks through tears.
And he rocks himself on drunken feet,
weeping out loud, a dark giant . . .
Back and forth, he starts to pace.
The other passengers wear their disgrace.
"Oh, Lord, Oh Lord, I've won the battle."
Two lines of white teeth in a cutting laugh . . .
"Oh Lord, Oh Lord, he's looking back
at his throat in a loop of white rope.
My brother's throat is fiddle-thin,
my brother's voice, hushed up for good."

איך הער איצט אין ווינט זיין קינדערשן רוף.
אויף אַ סאָסנע ווינט זיך מיין ברודער'ס גוף...
ער הויבט זיין פויסט און בײלט זי ווילד!
אין יעדן ווײסן זעט ער דעם מערדער'ס בילד...

Now I hear his young cry on the wind,
"My brother's body's swinging from a pine."
He waves his wild fist, clenching tight.
He sees the murderer's picture in every white.

ווייסקייט

ווייסקייט!... ווייסקייט!...
ווײַסע בערג
און ווײַסע שווימענדיקע וואָלקענס.
מישען בערג און וואָלקענס זיך צוזאַמען.
ווייסקייט!... ווייסקייט!...
ערגעץ ווײַסעלט זיך אַ פּאַלאַץ –
ווײַסע ווענט,
און ווײַסע, גלאַנצינע קאָלאָנען.
זיצט אין אים אַ יונגער סולטאַן
אײַנגעהילט אין ווײַסע טיכער
און אַרום אים –
ברעכען זיך און ציהען...
פֿרויען לײַבער.
ווייסקייט!... ווייסקייט!...
עמיצער, אַ ווײַסער
האָט זיך איבער אונז פֿאַרצויגען
און מיר שוועבען אין אַ וועלט
פֿון ווייסקייט.

164

Whiteness (1921)

∽ Zishe Vaynper

Whiteness! Whiteness!
White peaks
and swimming white clouds.
Peaks and clouds mixed.
Whiteness! Whiteness!
Somewhere a palace whites away—
white walls,
and gleaming white columns.
There sits a young sultan
wrapped up in white cloths
and around him
women's bodies
twisting, stretching.
Whiteness! Whiteness!
Someone white
has spread out over us
and we are hovering in a world
of white.

א נעגער שטאַרבט

בעריש ווײנשטײן ⸕

א נעגער אין מיטן פעלד בלוטיקט אונטערן העלן מעסער;
שטאַרבט אין א תמוזטאָג פון א הייסן חלף.
אין דער שאַרף שפּיגלט זיך שפּיזזאָפּ אַלע גראָזן, אַלע צווייגן.
ווײבער, וואָס לינן גלוסטיק, גרינג אויף גרינלעכער ערד;
היימיש, פריש ווי אין די בעטן בײנאַכט –
שלאָגן זיך אויך אָפּ אינעם בלוט פון שטאָל.

פון א מעסער א פּרעכם פון א ווײסער האַנט,
פֿאַרגנײט א נעגערישער האַלדז אין קעלבערנע שחיטה:
בײזע שניטן ניסן זיך איבער זײן געזיכט
און זײן גוף זינקט מיט פֿאַרביסענע פויסטן אַראָפּ.
די צונג צווישן זײנע ברייטע ליפן פֿאַרהאַקט,
מאַכט ווילדער אויסזען דאָס צעגאָסענע שוואַרצע מת.

צעבלוטיקט, צעטריפט לינט דאָס לײב פון נעגער.
איבער זײנע טויטע, גרויסע אויגן ווינטלען בײמער
און פונעם טאָג ווערט ליקווײחמהדיקער האַרבסט.
נאָך א טויט אַזאַ ווערט אַפֿילו פון זומער – אַסיען:
בלעטער נעמען פֿאַלן טונקלער, געלער און געשווינדער
ווי דאָס בלוט פון שוואַרצן מת, פון קאַלטן מעסער.

די זון ציט אָפּ פונעם פעלד, פונעם הימל.
אויפֿן נעגער גלאַנצן נאָך די האָר פֿאַרקאַמט
און זײנע הענט גליווערן נאָכגעלאָזט און יונג.
אַזוי פיל לווײה שטומט אין זײן געזיכט;
אויף זײן לינדיקן, געלעמטן וואוקם ווײנט א פרוי;
א נעגערישע מאַמע אין זײנע אויגן פֿאַרגליוויט.

די שקיעה פֿאַרצערט דעם טאָג מיט שאַרלעכן בראַנד.
פייגל נידערן פֿאַרנאַכטיק צום נעגער נאָך פֿאַרציקונג אַראָפּ.
די נעגערישע מאַמע מים א זשמעניע גראָז רעדט צום מת;
ווישט דאָס בלוט פון זײן מויל, פון זײן האַלדז.
אַלע אירע פינגער קלאָמערן זיך אינעם טויטנם האָר
מיטצושטאַרבן אויפֿן קרייץ פון א נעגער.

A Negro Dies (1938)

∿ Beresh Vaynshteyn

A Negro, in the middle of the field, bleeds beneath a bright blade.
Killed, one Tammuz[3] day, by a hot slaughtering knife.
Every blade of grass, every branch glints spear-like off the sharp metal.
Appealing women, lying lightly on the green ground,
home-fresh as in their beds at night,
also cast their image on the bloody steel.

Dismissed by a white man's impudent knife,
a Negro neck is taken in a calf's massacre.
Cruel slashes spread across his face.
His body sinks beneath relentless fists.
Tongue, clamped between broad lips,
makes the drained corpse look stranger still.

The black man's body lies there, dripping blood.
Trees rustle over his dead, wide eyes.
Autumn eclipses the sun and the day grows dark.
Oh, after such a death, even summer turns to fall:
leaves start dropping, darker, yellower, faster,
like the blood from the black corpse, from the cold knife.

The sun deserts the field and sky.
And the Negro's combed hair still gleams.
And his arms stiffen, now calm and young.
So much funeral lies mute on his face.
And a woman weeps over his outstretched body . . .
A Negro mother's image is fixed in his glassy eyes.

The sunset devours the day in scarlet blazes.
Birds swoop low with the evening for leftover meat.
The Negro mother, her hand full of grass, is talking to the dead man,
wiping the blood from his mouth and from his neck.
And all her fingers cling tight to the corpse's hair,
to die along with him on a Negro cross.

3. Tammuz: the month on the Hebrew calendar, usually corresponding with July.

Jim the Janitor Is Dead

דושים דער דזשענעטער איז טויט

ל& דארע טייטלבוים

דושים דער דזשענעטער איז טויט.
זיצן אלע שטום ארום זיין בעט.
א נייער מאָנ האָט אין דרויסן זיך צעבלויט
און וועקט אים: דושים, שטיי אויף, ס'איז שפעט!

דושים! ס'וועט דיין באָס זיין בייז,
דושים, דער באָס וועט קריצן מיט די ציין –
ס'איז דאָס וואָסער נאָך ניט היים,
און די שטינן נאָך ניט ריין.

עס וואָרטן מיסט-קאָנען אין הויף,
און דער אויוון וואָרט אויף קוילן,
דושים, שטיי אויף און לויף –
עס טאָר א נענער זיך ניט פוילן.

נאָר דושים ליגט אויף ווייסער בעט –
מיט זיין נאָנצער מאָסע איינגעשלאָפן,
דאַכט זיך אז ער הערט, דאַכט זיך אז ער זעט,
ס'מויל פאַרמאַכט, נאָר די אויגן אָפן.

קוקן וויב און קינדער פאָרלאָרענע אויף אים.
פון קיינעמס מויל – קיין פאָרע.
נאָר דער קליינער וויינענדיקער דזשעק וועקט דעם טוטן דושים
מיט די הענטלעך – האַלאָוועשקעס דאָרע.

פּאַפּ – – ניך,
עס פאָרן שוין די סטריט-קלינערס אין דרויסן, –
האָסט צוגעזאָגט היינט קויפן שיך
און נאָנצע הויזן.

דושים דער דזשענעטער רוט.
ס'איז אים גערום אין בעט אַליין.
דושימען איז גוט –
ער הערט שוין מער ניט דזשעק'ס געוויין.

170

Jim the Janitor Is Dead (1944)

                                  ∾ Dora Teitelboim

Jim the janitor is dead.
All sit still around his bed.
A new day has bloomed outside
and wakes him: Jim, get up I said!

Jim! The boss will be upset,
Jim, the boss'll gnash his teeth—
the water isn't heated yet,
there's garbage in the yard to toss.

You've coal to haul—the ovens wait,
and stairs want sweeping.
Jim, get up and run—you're late,
a Negro shouldn't lie there sleeping.

But Jim upon a white bed dreams,
completely rested. Here he lies.
It seems he hears, he sees it seems,
his mouth closed, but with open eyes.

Wife and kids gaze, lost, at him.
Nobody's breath turns the air to steam.
But little Jack cries to wake dead Jim
with little arms and a frightened scream.

Pop—go!
The street sweepers are outside the houses—
you're buying shoes today, you know,
and trousers.

Jim the janitor rests.
It's roomy there in bed alone.
It feels good to Jim—
he's stopped hearing Jack's moan.

די פענצטער פוצט אַ טאָג אַ העלער
מיט די שטראַלן פון אַ נייעם מאַי,
נאָר ביי דזשימען איז דער טויט אין קעלער:
דזשים איז פריי.

דזשים איז טויט.
דזשים שווייגט.
ס'גאָנצע לעבן האָט ער אַלעמען געטרויט,
נאָר היינט האָט דזשים פאַרסטרייקט.

ווייסער היינט ווי שטענדיק איז זיין קישן,
ווייסער היינט ווי שטענדיק איז זיין הויט,
און היינט שלאָפט קיינער ניט צופיסנס —
בלויז דער טויט.

Death is in Jim's cellar today,
although the day shines splendidly
with the rays of newborn May,
Jim is free.

Jim has died
quiet-like.
He trusted everyone in life,
but today Jim went on strike.

Whiter than ever is the pillow at his head.
Whiter than ever, his skin,
and no one sleeps at the foot of the bed—
except for death, who's crept in.

Encounters with the Elements

With the workplace, streets, and political struggle at the center of the writers' daily lives, New York proletarian poetry seldom left the city. Still, a number of poets depict the natural world, primarily as it enters the daily life of the city.

Poems like Y. Nokhem's "The Fly" and "Hounds Howl at the Moon" need not show vast wildlife in order to bring perspective to a crowded world. It is enough to show, with Dickinsonian attention to detail, the fly that buzzes into the room reminding the speaker of a lover's grief. Likewise, the hound that comes out to howl at, presumably, a city moon brings to mind the human wildness innate to city life, such as whores laughing at night.

In the city, the elements are encountered through seasonal and temporal changes. Yuri Suhl, in "Winter," contrasts his own delight in the new season with "the ones who bundle up in newspaper shawls." In a poignant merging of society and nature, L. Miller describes a man who is out of work talking to his son about the colors of a sunset. The short poem makes space for nature within an urban environment. Miller shows the pride that a downtrodden man feels in knowing that he is still entitled to enjoy the glories of the natural world. "If the boss came here," he writes, "he'd take it all, then, somehow, use it / like a good profiteer . . ."

די פֿליג

נחום י. ־ב‎

פֿליהט אין חדר אום אַ פֿליג און זשומעט,
און באַטויבט.
אוי, די ווייסע פֿליגעל פֿון דײַן אומעט
זײַנען שוין פֿאַרשטויבט.

און דײַן צער איז מעהר ניט אײַנגעשלאָסען,
ניט געצאַמט.
האָסט דײַן שוימענדיגען ווײַן צעגאָסען
אויפֿ'ן הײַסען זאַמד.

טרוימען־פֿוינעל זײַנען זיך צעפֿלוינען
אין דער נאַכט,
דרעהט זיך אום די פֿליג פֿאַר מײַנע אויגען, –
דוכט זיך, אַז זי לאַכט...

176

The Fly

∽ Y. Nokhem

A fly, with a deafening buzz,
flies round the room.
How dusty they've grown—the white wings
of your gloom.

And grief is bound no longer,
unrestrained.
You've poured your sparkling wine out
on hot sand.

Last night the little dream-birds
flew off.
The fly circles before my eyes.
Seems to me it laughs . . .

וואויען הינט אויף דער לבנה

נחום י. ‎ﬞ

וואויען הינט אויף דער לבנה,
לאַכען זונות, שיכור, פרעך....
וואויען, קלאָגען שטומע הערצער,
לאַכען פנים'ער פון בלעך.

ציהט זיך, וויקעלט זיך דער פאָדים
פון דער אייביגקייט געשפינט....
לאַכען זונות אין די גאָסען,
וואויען, יאָמערען די הינט.

אַלעמען דער זעלבער אומזין
האָט אין וויסטעניש געבראַכט:
וואויען הינט אויף דער לבנה,
לאַכען זונות אין דער נאַכט.

178

Hounds Howl at the Moon (1922)

∽ Y. Nokhem

Hounds howl at the moon,
whores laugh, drunken, bold . . .
hearts howl, wailing silently,
tin faces laugh.

The thread of eternity
wraps round itself . . .
whores laugh in the streets,
hounds howl in lament.

The same senselessness
has brought everyone to desolation:
hounds howl at the moon,
whores laugh in the night.

Encounters with the Elements

חלום פון ערד

אסתר שומיאטשער

אין וואַסער־שאָטן,
צווישן ביימער פריי,
האָט זיך געבאָדן
אַ יונגער מאַי.

מיט גראָז אין די אויגן,
געוואַשן און קלאָר,
האָט זון אים געצווינן
ביי די בלאָנדע האָר.

מיט וואַסער־ריח
און זון אין די ציין
גרינט זיין כח
אין וואָרצל און שטיין.

אויף דער לבנה,
איבער דער בריק,
אין גאָלדענעם שאָטן
שווימט דאָס גליק.

מיט חלום פון ערד
אין איינגעוויד,
דורך רעגנבויגן
רעדט די פרייד.

זון אין די אויגן,
גאָלד אין די האָר –
דער זומער פאַרפלויגן
ווי יאָר נאָך יאָר.

לינגט זומער צעטראָטן
אין מאָכיקע צעפ,
און ס׳וויינט זיין שאָטן
אויף רויטע קעפ.

182

Earth Dream (1939)

⤳ Esther Shumyatsher

In water shadows,
a young free May
bathed between
the trees today.

With grass in his eyes
washed and clear,
the sun pulled playfully
at his blond hair.

Sun in his teeth,
and the odor of water,
his strength blooms
in roots and stones.

Over the bridge,
on the moon
in golden shadows
swims fortune.

In his belly
an earthly dream.
Joy, through rainbows,
speaks for him.

Sun in his eyes,
gold in his hair,
away summer flies
as year after year.

Trampled, the mossy-tressed
summer lies dying,
and over red heads
is its shadow, crying.

פֿון זון און גאָלד
אַ האַרבסטיקע שטריק;
אין זיינע אויגן
ווינט דאָס גליק.

אויף דער לבנה,
איבער דער בריק,
אָן אַ העמד אויפֿן לייב
פֿאַרנייט דאָס גליק.

Autumn's rope is spun
of gold and sun,
and in his eyes
luck cries on.

Over the bridge,
on the moon,
poor and shirtless,
luck goes down.

אָטעם פון פרילינג

שרה פעלייעלין ‎⤳

אָטעם פון פרילינג. פייכטע, צעגראָבענע בייטן.
אין באָדן צעוואָרעמטן, ערד־ווערים לוסטיקע טאַנצן.
ביים קאָשיקל זוימען, אַ מיידל מיט לאָקן צעוויטע,
הימל און זון אין די אויגן, ווי דימענטן גלאָנצן.

זי גלעט און צענגראַבלט דעם באָדן מיט אײדעלע פינגער,
אַליין, ווי אַ קוויט אַ צעבליטע, אין פאַרביק־צעבלימלטן קלייד.
ס׳ווערט אַלטיטשקע ערד פון באַריר איר שענער און יינגער –
זי ווערט בלימעלעך אויסטראָגן, בונטע ווי מיידלשע פרייד.

זי קניט צו דער ערד: זוימען רוען אין איטלעכער שורה –
איינס מיט צווייטן באַהעפט, איינס פון צווייטן צעשיידט,
יעדער שפּרייץ וועט איר ברענגען אַ דופטיקע בשורה,
אַז ס׳וועט שפע פון בליאונג באַציִרן איר בייט.

אַ מיידל האָט האָפענונג אין בייטן מיט ליבשאַפט פאַרפלאַנצט
און ס׳האָט דער אַרום זיך צעשמייכלט אַ פרישער, אַ יונגער –
פרילינגדיקגֿלויביק האָט זיך מיידל קינדיש צעטאָנצט,
מיט זון אין געמיט און רוי־ערד אויף אײדעלע פינגער.

Breath of Spring (1957)

∾ Sarah Fel-Yelin

Breath of Spring. Damp, dug up beds.
Cheerful earthworms dance, warmed in the soil.
By the basket rim, a girl with flyaway locks,
sky and sun in her eyes, like diamonds sparkle.

She strokes and scrapes the beds with slender fingers,
alone, like a blossom, in a colorful flowered dress.
Her touch makes old Mother Earth young and pretty,
she'll bring forth blossoms, sparkling like girlish happiness.

She kneels to the earth. Seeds rest in every row—
One united with another, one another separate.
Every sprout will bring her a fragrant announcement
when blossoming abounds to deck her garden bed.

A girl can hope for flowerbeds planted with love
and her surroundings smile, fresh and tender.
A spring-believing girl has danced like a child
with sun in her heart, raw earth on slender fingers.

Winter

Winter (1938)

∽ Yuri Suhl

Now winter's standing at the door,
face ablaze with frost
and upturned collar.
Any minute
the last leaf will fade,
fall's last day will dissolve.
But what awaits those
who make their home the open city
covering themselves with wind?
I love it when roofs exhibit their long icicle teeth,
when eaves freeze mid-trickle,
when, on windowpane canvas, winter paints a self-portrait
in frosty patterns.
But what awaits,
oh, what awaits
the ones who bundle up in newspaper shawls
and doze, standing, in unfamiliar corridors?

Now winter's standing at the door,
face ablaze with frost
and upturned collar.

דער הונגערטאַנץ

מעינקע קאַץ ⸻

קלעטערט אויף סירענעס אַ זונפֿאַרגייענדיקער ריז
און זוכט דעם העכסטן טורעמשפּיץ זיך צו הענגען –
ווינט דער טאָג זיך אַ געקוילעטער
אויף קעלערשויבן און אויף טורעמנעזער,
נאָלדיקט זיך יעדע נאַס ווי אַ היימלאָז בעט,
יאָגן רויטלעכע אויגן
ווי פֿון ווינט געטראָגן – פֿאַרבלוטיקטע קאַרעלן;
לויפֿן הינט מיט צעקאַרטשעטע פֿעלן
נאָך אייגענע שאָטנס ווי נאָך רייצנדיקן רויב,
און ריידן ווי שטומע מיט די פֿינגער,
און וויִען אויס ווי שטומע
דאָס ליד פֿון איבעריקע צינגער.

פֿאַר וועמען ס'איז די נאַס אַ היימלאָז בעט,
וועט באַלד ווי איך
מיט עלנט לייב – קאַרבן טרויעריקע רינגען
אויף וואַכע שטיינער פֿון פֿאַרקלערטע ראָנג,
און פֿאַרשטיין פֿאַרוואָס
געסעלעך צעקאַרבטע קענען אויך ווי מענטשן קלאָגן.

הערט דער פֿראָסט ניט אויף זיך דרייען
מיט היימלאָזע צינער אין דיִדין קאַראָהאָדן –
ווייזט דער טויט זיך אַזוי נאָענט און פֿראָסט,
ציִען ווי פֿון אוראַלטע קברים מתימדיקע רייען
און בלייבן ווי מצבות שטיין ביי יעזוזעס נשמות –
ווי פֿון ערגעץ וואָלט געטראָגן זיך אַ לעצטער רוף
און באַפֿעלט זיי אויפֿצולייִזן זיך אין פֿראָסט;
הערט דער פֿראָסט ניט אויף זיך דרייען
מיט היימלאָזע צינער אין דיִדין קאַראָהאָדן –
שפּילן ליפֿן ווי אויף פֿראָסטיקע דראָטן:

192

The Hungerdance (1932)

~ Menke Katz

A sunsetting giant climbs the sirens
and seeks the highest spire to hang himself—
the slaughtered day swings
from cellarpanes and towernoses,
every street grows golden like a homeless bed,
eyes grown red
chasing bloodied corals, carried, it seems, on the wind;
dogs with shriveled coats
run after their shadows—tempting prey,
and talk, like the mute, with their fingers,
and howl like silent singers,
the song of extra tongues.

He for whom the street is a homeless bed,
like me, with lonesome flesh,
will suddenly be notching gloomy rings
on the waking stones of pensive streetcorners,
and understand why it is
that notched streets can wail like people.

The frost will not stop whirling
with its homeless teeth in din-din dances—
Death appears so near and simple,
rows of corpses stretch, as if from ancient graves
and stop like tombstones at Jesus' souls—
as if from somewhere a final call had come
and commanded them to dissolve in the frost;
the frost will not stop whirling
with its homeless teeth in din-din dances—
lips play as though on frosty strings:

שטומער, שטומער, הונגער מיינער,
שטום אַרוים,
פֿון בלאָנדזשעניש פֿון אויגן און צער פֿון ביינער,
דו ביסט מיינער, מיינער, מיינער;
שפּילן ליפּן ווי אויף פּראָסטיקע דראָטן:

קרומער, קרומער וואָגן מיינער,
קרים זיך אויס
אין בלאָנדזשעניש פֿון אויגן און צער פֿון ביינער,
איך בין דיינער, דיינער, דיינער.

וואָלגערן זיך גאָסן ווי איך און דו
אין שטויב פֿון יעזוסן און ליד פֿון ווינט,
בין איך – אומרו
פֿון וואָגיניקע אויגן און צעביטשטטע הינט;
בין איך – אומרו
פֿון פֿאַרליבטע אָדלערס וואָס פֿאַלן פֿון הייכן –
פֿאַרלאָזטע מיילער חלומען פֿון זון און פֿלאַדן,
ווילן ערד און הימל זיך דערגרייכן,
רייסט זיך נאַכט און עלנט פֿון צונעפֿאָרעֶרענעם צעמענט,
שוואַרצט זיך אויף יעדער שטיין אַ גאָסנפֿנים,
האָבן נאַכט און עלנט זיך דערקענט –
האַלדזן זיך היימלאָזע שאָטנס
ווי לאַנגצעשיידטע וואַנדערער,
און פֿאַלן ווי אַ שטיין אַף אַ שטיין
איינער אַפֿן אַנדערן,
און בראָזגען אויס
אַ הונגערטאָנץ אַף אַקשאָנעסדיקן באָדן –
טאַנצן מיסימדיקע רייען
ווי צעראיעטער עלנט פֿון פֿאַרוואָרלאָזטע רואינעס,
און מאָנען
מיט בייסואילאָמדיקע גלידער
ב–ר–ו–י–ט!
דאַכט זיך אַז די טאַנצן ניט קיין ברידער,
נאָר טרויעריקע פֿאָנען,
וואָס דער טויט אַליין האָט אויסגעשיילט
פֿון קאַלטע הויטיקע פֿאָסן,

Oh my silent, silent hunger,
come mutely out,
from eyes with their wandering and bones with their sorrow,
you are mine, mine, mine;
lips play as though on frosty strings:

Oh, my twisted, twisted madness,
twist yourself out
from eyes with their wandering and bones with their sorrow,
I am yours, yours, yours.

Streets amble about, like me and you
in Jesus' dust and the song of the wind,
I am the restlessness
of mad eyes and whipped dogs;
I am the restlessness
of eagles in love, who fall from the heights—
neglected mouths dream of sun and fruitcake,
and heaven and earth long to reach each other,
night and loneliness are ripped from frozen cement,
on every stone lies a blackened street face.
They've recognized each other—loneliness and night.
Homeless shadows meet in an embrace
like wanderers, long parted
and fall like stone on stone
one on the other,
banging out
a hungerdance on the stubborn ground—
rows of corpses dance around
like loneliness, dug out of abandoned ruins,
demanding
with their graveyard limbs:
b-r-e-a-d!
It would appear that dancing here aren't brothers,
but gloomy flags,
which death itself has cut
from frozen strips of skin,

אָן צעװינט זיי דאָ
װי אַ געבעט פאַר דערפראָרענע נאָסן,
װאָס קאָרטשען זיך װי אין אַ פייערדיקן פויסט,
און רעװען מיט קוילעם פון אָטאָם און פון מענטשן:
ר–אַ–ט–ע–װו–ע–ט!

איבער שטאָט
װאַכט די לעװאָנע װי אַן אױפגעדרייטער שלאַנג,
און ס'דאַכט אַז באַלד –
און פון אַלץ װעט בלײבן נאָר אַ װײטער קלאַנג,
װאָס װעט באַם זונפאַרגאָנג אַמאָל נאָך קלאָגן;
און ס'דאַכט אַז באַלד,
װעלן שטײנער זיך צעברויזן – װעלן גאָסן זיך צעיאָגן.

and dangled here—
a prayer for frozen streets that twist
as though inside a fiery fist,
bellowing the outcries of autos and people:
h-e-l-p!

The moon
watches over the city like a coiled snake,
and it seems that soon—
and only a far-off noise will remain,
which will someday wail by the setting sun;
and it seems that soon,
stones will start to roar, streets will up and run.

דער אַרבעטלאָזער רעדט צום קינד וועגן זונפֿאַרגאַנג

‎‫~ ל. מילער

ווײ, ווי ס׳האָט דער הימל זיך צעברענט!
עס ברענט די אויגן.
פֿינקעלדינע פֿאַסמעס זון,
פֿאַרבן, צאַרטע, ווייכע,
הויפֿנס בליטן, בערג מיט בלומען...
וואָלט דער באָס אַהער דערגרייכן,
וואָלט ער אַלץ פֿאַר זיך גענומען
און געמאַכט פֿון דעם פּראָפֿיטן...

אַזוי פֿיל פֿרייד פֿאַר מענטשנ׳ס אויגן,
עס וועקט די בענקשאַפֿט אויף אין האַרצן
וויסט אַליין ניט וואָס זאָלסט גאָרן.
וויפֿל גאָלד און וויפֿל זילבער!
כאָטש מיט לאָפֿעטעס צו שאַרן.
נישט צום מעסטן, נישט צום ציילן,
ס׳וואָלט גענוג זיין יעדן איינעם
איינצוטיילן... – – –

פֿאַרבן רוישן...
קאָלירן קומען און פֿאַרגייען.
ווי זיי טוישן זיך און מיניען,
אַזש עס נעמט דער קאָפּ זיך דרייען.
אָט איז זייד, און דאָרטן ווייט איז סאַמעט.
פֿאַר יעדן הויז אַ פֿאַר גאַרדינען.
ווי שיין עס וואָלט געפּאַסט דער מאַמען
אַ קלייד פֿון יענעם זייד דעם גרינעם.
זי נייט און נייט און נייט,
און קען זיך ניט
קיין לייטיש קלייד פֿאַרגינען.

198

The Man Who Is Out of Work
Talks to His Son about the Sunset (1937)

∾ L. Miller

Oh . . . how the sky is in flame!
It dazzles the eyes.
Sparkling strips of sun,
delicate, tender colors,
mounds of blossoms, mountains of flowers . . .
If the boss came here,
he'd take it all, then somehow use it
like a good profiteer . . .

Such pleasure for the human eye,
it wakes the longing in your heart—
you don't know, yourself, what you should crave.
How much gold and how much silver!
Or simply spades to scrape at what's already there.
Measureless, countless,
there'd be enough to give everyone
to share . . .

Colors rush . . .
Colors come in and go out.
How they turn and change,
'til your head spins about.
That's silk, and satin over there.
A pair of drapes for every house.
How mother would look in
a dress of that green silk.
She sews and sews and sews,
and can't afford a decent dress.

באַלאַדע פון דער נאַכט

~ י. א. ראָנטש

אַ קינד האָט געוויינט אין דער פינצטער אַריין,
געכליפּעט אָן סיבה, אָן ציל.
די גאַס האָט געהערט און אַ קאַץ האָט געהאָרכט,
די נאַכט האָט געשושקעט זיך שטיל.

אַ מאַן האָט גע׳נוסס׳ט, די נאַכט האָט געוען,
געציטערט די וועלט האָט ביים בעט.
געבעטן האָט וויב זיך און קינדער: פאַרבליב.
די נאַכט מיט׳ן טויט האָט גערעדט.

אַ בחור געהאַלזט האָט זיין מיידל אין פּאַרק,
געבריט האָבן אויגן די נאַכט.
די ערד האָט געקילט און דאָס גראָז האָט געהיט,
די נאַכט האָט געקוקט און געלאַכט.

גע׳יום־טוב׳ט האָט נאַכט־קלוב מיט סווינג און מיט זויף,
מיט מיידעלעך נאַקעט—אַ פּראַכט.
לאַקייען, סאַרווירער, שאָפערן צום דינסט,
גע׳חבר׳ט מיט זיי האָט זיך נאַכט.

אַ פרוי האָט געשיירט אַ שטיינערנעם דיל,
אין טורעם, אויף צוואַנצינסטן שטאָק.
די גאַס האָט געוען און די נאַכט האָט געוואַכט,
די שטילקייט צעשטערט האָט אַ גלאָק.

דערמאָנונג פון גלאָק און אַ פייף פון אַ שיף
און פאַרהאַנגען שוואַרצע פאַרשאַרצט.
אַ רייטער בריגאַדע אַנטקעגן דער נאַכט
מיט שפּיזן מיט וויסע דורך האַרץ.

געוויין פון אַ קינד, פון אַ קוימען דער רויך.
און סודות׳דיג שווייגן פון נאַכט,
וואָס שלייכט פון געפאַר וי אַ קאַץ זיך אַרום,
אַנטקעגן דעם רייטער, וואָס לאַכט.

Ballad of the Night (1938)

~ Y. A. Rontsh

A child cried out in the darkness,
he sobbed without reason or aim,
the street listened, a cat heard.
From Night quiet whispering came.

A man was in agony. Night looked on.
The world trembled by his bed.
His sweet wife and children begged him to stay.
Night was conspiring with death.

A schoolboy embraced his girl in the park,
eyes searing the night.
The earth cooled down and the grass stood guard,
Night looked and laughed in delight.

A nightclub feasted on swing and swill,
with naked girls—what a sight!
Lackeys, waiters, and chauffeurs to serve;
their reliable friend was Night.

A woman scoured a masonry floor,
in a tower's vestibule.
The street noticed and Night kept watch,
a bell interrupted the still.

A pealing bell and a whistling ship,
black curtains drawn apart.
A team of horsemen charges Night,
and their white spears pierce her heart.

Child's cry, chimney smoke.
And mysterious silence from Night,
who slinks out of peril like a cat,
before the horseman, who laughs in delight.

רעגן

די זאַנגען־ליפּעלעך זײנען טרוקן פֿון דאָרשט,
און די ערד איז צעלײגט אַ פֿאַרשמאַכטע,
װי אַ שװאַנגערדיקע יונגע מאַמע.
דײנע אױגן – װי תפֿילות – גליען צו די װאָלקנס.
דײנע הענט – װי װאַנדערער אין מדבר –
שטרעקן זיך צום ערשטן טראָפּן.
שױן – ס׳טראָפּנט. ברכה טראָפּנט.

Rain

Ber Grin

The little ears of corn are parched,
and the earth is sprawled out and languishing
like a pregnant young mother.
Your eyes, like prayers, glow toward the clouds.
Your hands, like wanderers in the desert,
stretch to the first drops.
And now they drop. Blessing drops.

ווען די לבנה שײַנט ניט

∽ ל. מילער

1

עס בענקען די שטערן און פרעגן:
וואו איז די לבנה?
זיי קוקן ארונטער פֿאַרליבטע, באַטריבטע
און ווארטן אַנטוישטע און ליידן אַן שיעור —
אָט האָט שוין אַ שטערן דעם זינען פֿאַרלוירן
און פֿאַלט מיט אַ שמייכל אין פֿינצטערן רוים...

מיט בליקן פֿול אומעט און טרויער
באַגלייטן אים אַלע,
און, דאַכט זיך, עס וועלן די שטערן
באַלד איינס נאָכן צווייטן
זיך וואַרפֿן פֿאַרצווייפֿלט אין שוואַרצן תחום...

2

עס האָבן די ביימער פֿון וואַלד זיך געשראָקן
אַליין צו פֿאַרבלייבן אין פֿינצטערן סטעפּ.
האָט איינער ביים צווייטן דעם קאָפּ אויפֿן אַקסל
פֿאַרטוליעט, באַהאַלטן...
און האָבן זיך אײלנד אַ שלײער אַ שוואַרצן
פֿאַרצויגן אין אימה, אריבער די קעפּ...

זיי הערן זיך איינעט מיט אָטעם פֿאַרשטיקטן,
ווי ס׳טראַנט זיך אין פֿעלד אום אַ פֿאַרשטיקטער געוויין –
דאָס יאָמערן זשאַבעס, זיי ווײנען און קלאָגן, ווי קינדערלעך קליינע,
פֿון זינדיקע מאַמעס אין זומפּן פֿאַרטראָגן –
און דאָרטן געלאָזן אין חשך אַליין...

When the Moon Isn't Shining (1939)

∾ L. Miller

1
The yearning stars ask,
Where is the moon?
They gaze down, smitten and sad,
and wait, disillusioned, infinitely miserable.
Now and then a star loses its mind
and falls with a smile in dark outer space . . .

All of them follow it,
with lonely, sad gazes
and it seems the stars will
suddenly hurl themselves
one by one, desperately into the black abyss.

2
The trees in the woods are afraid
to be alone in the dark.
One has hidden, nestled his head
on another's shoulder . . .
And so they've hastily draped a black veil
in their dread, to cover their heads . . .

They listen intently with bated breath,
as a muffled cry travels the field.
It's the frogs' lament: crying and wailing like little children
carried off by sinful mothers to a bog
and left there, alone in the dark . . .

To a Butterfly

צו אַ פּלאַטערל

זע, דאָס
פּלאַטערל
גרייט זיך פאַרניין
ביים ערשטן גלי פון
געבאָרן ווערן. אוי,
אַזויפל שאָטנס אײלן
פאַרנאַכט אַן איינציק פּלאַטערל
באַפאַלן. דיין טאָג, דיין גרויס לעבן:
די וועלט קומט אום ביי דעם אָנקום פון דיין
אָוונט. אוי, פּלאַטערל, ביים סוף פון דיין טאָג
ווער איך, ווי דו, אַ וועלט אַזאַ וואו ס'איז ניטאָ
קיין הימל, קיין ערד, קיין לעבן, קיין טויט – אַ וועלט פון
נאָרנישניט. פּלאַטערל, מיר וועלן בלייבן ביידע אין
ווינט, נאָך אַ נעכטיקן טאָג זיך יאָגן. אויף אונדז וואָרט אַ נאַכט
אַזאַ, אַ בלינדע עקרה וואָס קען שוין ניט געבאָרן
קיין פאַרטאָג. פּלאַטערל, איך בין ווי דו אויפגעגאַנגען
אַזוי באַנעגדיק קלאָר. איך וועל ווי דו מיט העַנט,
ווי פאַרבענקטע פליגל ביי אַ פענצטער פאַרניין.
אָן דיר, אָן מיר וועט נאָך פינצטערער ווערן
די פינצטערניש. איך וועל ווי דו מיט דער
הויך פאַרצווילינגט ווערן, בלייבן וועט
מיין ליבע ביי אַ צעדערבוים
מיט די קושן פון מיין מויל
פון מיר טרוימען. איך וועל
זיין די ליכטיקסטע
טרער אין אירע
טויטפולע
אויגן.

To a Butterfly

Watch the[1]
butterfly
prepare to go
down in the first glow
of its morning hours. Oh,
so many shadows hasten
at dusk, to strike one butterfly.
Your day, your massive life: the world sets
at the coming of your evening—your dusk.
Oh, butterfly, when your day comes to an end
I too, like you, will turn into a world where there
is no heaven, no earth, no life and no death—a world
of nothing. Butterfly, we both will remain in the wind
to chase yet another yesterday. Such a night awaits us,
a blind and barren woman, no longer mother to any
dawn. Butterfly, I too, like you, have arisen, just as
clear as the break of dawn. And I too, like you, will set,
somewhere in a window, my hands like yearning wings.
Without you, without me, darkness will only
be darker. I, just like you, will be twinned
with the heights and all that will remain
shall be my love by a cedar
tree, with kisses from my mouth
dreamt down to her from me.
And I will be the
brightest tear in
her eyes full
of death.

1. The "Menke sonnet," a form developed by Menke Katz, contains fourteen lines, beginning with two syllables and increasing by one syllable per line until it reaches fifteen. This poem is a double-sonnet, in that the first half consists of fourteen lines of increasing syllables, and the second consists of the reverse.

Alexander Pomerantz, one of the founding poets of Proletpen.
(Menke Katz Collection)

Illustration accompanying Menke Katz's "The Hungerdance" in a 1933 issues of *Morgn frayhayt*. (Menke Katz Collection)

Woodcut of Yosl Grinshpan, one of the leaders of Proletpen.
(Menke Katz Collection)

January 1925 issue of *Yung kuznye*, an early Yiddish proletarian journal.
(Menke Katz Collection)

Union leader and prose writer Max Perlow, one of Proletpen's founders.
(Menke Katz Collection)

Cover for the 1925 issue of *Spartak*, a revolutionary Yiddish journal published in English, Yiddish, and Russian. (Menke Katz Collection)

June 1925 cover of *Yung kuznye*. (Menke Katz Collection)

Masthead for the January 1925 issue of *Yung kuznye*. (Menke Katz Collection)

United in Struggle

Crucial to understanding the political role of Proletpen is the emphasis they place on solidarity with other liberation struggles, both in the United States and abroad. Poems such as Ber Grin's "Strike of the Coal Miners," Sarah Barkan's "Bring Me Your Woes," and Shmuel Kreyter's "Vengeance" urged workers in America to unite in protest, to mutually support one another in the hardships of life as laborers, and to avenge themselves against the oppressive upper class. "Don't spare me," writes Barkan, "Speak of the factory, / your every word reddens my blood." Here, the poet portrays a listener who is at once compassionate, maternal, and ready to engage in class struggle.

Poems about communist leaders worldwide work to establish role models and educate the reader about international party figures. Yosl Grinshpan's "In Any Case" speaks about the murder of the Cuban communist leader Julio Melo. Nokhem Vaysman's "Anna Pauker" is addressed to the Rumanian-Jewish communist leader who would lead the country from 1947 to 1952. Vaysman compares the Rumanian activist to America's Ella May Wiggins (1900–1929), a Southern mill worker and single mother who fought for the right to unionize. Y. A. Rontsh's " Rosa Luxemburg" is a tribute to the Polish-born German-Jewish communist leader who was executed in 1919. The poets would often include their own explanatory notes when publishing a piece in the *Frayhayt*. I have preserved these in the translations.

ברײנג מיר דײן צער...

שרה באַרקאַן ～

(אַ מתנה נואַרק קאָונסיל 1,
צו איר צווײ יעריגן יוביליי)

ברײנג מיר דײן צער, וואָס דיר גיבן די טעג.
מיט טרײסט זײנען פאַרפוצט מײנע וועגט.
איך וויקל דײן צער אין האָפענונג זײד –
איך וואַרט יעדן טאָג מיט אָפענע הענט.

ניט זשאַלעווע מיר, דערצײל פון פאַבריק,
דײן יעטוועדער וואָרט מאַכט רויטער מײן בלוט.
פאַר טרערן דו שרעקסט זיך? אַ, דאָס וועט ניט זײן,
איך וועל גלעטן דײן קאָפ און רײדן פון מוט!

קום צו מיר, חבר, דײן שותף בין איך,
פאַר מיר איז אַ פרײד – פאַר מאַזאָלינע הענט,
די גרױקײט פאַרשווינדט אין מײן אָרימער קיך
מיט מוט און מיט ליכט – פאַרפוצט מײנע וועגט!

220

Bring Me Your Woes

~ Sarah Barkan

A gift to the Newark Council 1,
on the occasion of its second anniversary.

Bring me the woes your days have bestowed.
Solace drapes my walls.
I'll swaddle your woes with hope-spun silk.
I wait each day with open arms.

Don't spare me. Speak of the factory,
your every word reddens my blood.
Afraid to cry? Oh this needn't be,
I'll speak of courage and stroke your head.

Come to me, comrade, I'm your partner.
Callused hands are joy to me.
The grayness in my poor kitchen will vanish.
Drape my walls with light and bravery!

סטרייק פון קוילנגרעבער

א. פרינץ (בער גרין)

עס יאָגן זיך אַריין שפּיציגע געשרייען
אין פוסטע אונטערערדישע קאָרידאָרן
און האָקן שטומע וועגט מיט צעברענטן צאָרן.
מיט וואָכטעס אַרום די שאַכטעס
זיינען פול די שטויביגע שטייניגע שטעגן –
צעברעגענען זיך הייסע גליאיגע געשלעגן.
אין טויבע גריבער בלאַנדזשען טויטע קלאַנגען
פון שאַרפע העק און שווערע סאָושינע הענט,
צעהוידעט אף שוואַרצע טוכלע ווענט.
איצט יאָגן אַרום די קלאַנגען פון העק אַף ווען,
איצט צעוויין זיך העק קען וועט פון פאָליציי,
איצט צעברומט זיך קוילינע ערד מיט געשריי.
סטאַרטשען קוילן, ווי אָפגעהאַקטע קעפ בלוטיגע און רויטע.
יאָגן געשרייען, יאָגן ווינטן אין בלינדער הויל,
יאָגן מיינער שוואַרץ און האַרט ווי קויל,
יאָגן מיינער, לעמפּלעך אַף די קעפּ –
שוואַרץ דער צאָרן, ליכטיג דער וועג,
לעמפּלעך וואַרפן ליכט, לעמפּלעך וואָרפן שרעק.
מיט רויטע פינגער האָט הונגער
געציכנט: „קאַמף!" אַף קוילינע פלאַכטעס –
בלוט אַף שטויב, אַף קויל, אַרום שאַפטעס.
„קאַמף!" האָבן געציכנט קוילינע קערפערס אַף ווען –
איז ווער פון די קוילינע און לעמפּלדינע וועט אַצינד
בלייבן אין די טיפן, בלייבן בלינד?
איז ווער מיט מאַזאָלינע הענט און רויטן בלוט
וועט זיך שטעלן אין אַ זייט,
לאָזן הונגער פאַרמאַרען די ברידער אין שטרייט?

Strike of the Coal Miners (1931)

〜 A. Prints (Ber Grin)

Piercing shrieks race in
to hollow underground passageways
and break up silent walls with burning rage.
Guards around the mineshafts fill
the dusty rocky paths.
Fights flicker to flaming wrath.
In deaf pits
wander dead sounds of sharp picks
in hard sooty hands.
Now the hacking resounds down roads,
now pickaxes swing at the walls of jails,
now the coal earth roars, shrieks, wails.
Coals protrude like hacked-off heads, blood-red:
shrieks race the wind in blind caves,
race miners, black and hard like coal.
Race miners. Lamps on every head
light the way, black anger near.
Lamps casting light cast fear.
With reddened fingers, hunger has
written "Fight!" in coal on sheets . . .
Blood on dust, on coal, 'round shafts.
"Fight!" Coal bodies write on streets.
Which of the coal and lamp bearers present
will now stay below, stay blind?
And which of those with calloused hands and red blood
will desert the others,
leaving dispute to their starving brothers?

In Any Case

סיי־ווי־סיי

יאָסל גרינשפּאַן ⋐

(אפֿן טויט פֿון דערמאָרדעטן קובאַנישן
קאָמוניסטישן פֿירער, ח׳ כּוליאָ מעלאָ.)

סיי־ווי־סיי
צעצינדן מיר די וועלט!
און פֿאַלט אַוועק אין פֿעלד אַ רויטער העלד –
איז וואָס?
פֿלאַקערט אויף אין אונדז זײַן רוף,
ווײַנען מיר ניט נאָך זײַן גוף –
סיי־ווי־סיי
צעצינדן מיר די וועלט!

סיי־ווי־סיי
גייט אויף די ערד אין בראַנד!
און רײַסט אַרויס אַ העלד פֿון אונדזער רײַ די שוואַרצע האַנט –
איז וואָס?
ניט די ערד זיך אַ צעברויז,
וואָקסן טויזנט נײַע אוים –
סיי־ווי־סיי
גייט אויף די ערד אין בראַנד!

סיי־ווי־סיי
איז אונדזערע די זון!
און אַז מ׳רויבט פֿון אונדז אַ פֿונק איר –
איז וואָס?
מיט בלוט צו טריפֿן הייבט זי אָן,
ווערט נאָך רויטער אונדזער פֿאָן –
סיי־ווי־סיי
איז אונדזערע די זון!

In Any Case

～ Yosl Grinshpan

On the murder of Cuban Communist leader, Comrade Julio Melo.

In any case
we're setting the world on fire!
And on the battlefield, a red hero falls—
So what?
His call flames up in us.
We don't cry for his corpse.
In any case
we're setting the world on fire!

In any case
the earth goes up in flames!
And an evil hand rips a hero from our ranks—
So what?
The earth will soon reset its stage.
A thousand heroes will come of age.
In any case
the earth goes up in flames!

In any case
the sun is ours!
And if somebody robs us of a spark—
So what?
Now the sun is bleeding too,
our flag has turned a redder hue.
In any case
the sun is ours!

די אַלטע

די אַלטע זיצט אַף אַ צעבראָכענעם זייל
רויכערט אַ צינאָר, טראָגנט אַ צילינדער
אַרום איר שטייען אין ערפאָרכט
אירע געטרייע קינדער.

זי זיצט באַ אַ צעקרישלטע וועגנט.
באַ די זייטן – צוויי בלינדע יעוונונכן
זיי העקלען זאָקן מיט ליידיקע הענט
און זי – זאָגט שפרוכן.

אַ פעלדשלאַנג טראָגנט אַ זשאַבע אין מויל.
אַ קאָץ געהט צו קינד מיט קעצלאָך;
די אַלטע זיצט אַף אַ צעבראָכענעם זייל,
לעקט האָניק פון גאָלדענע טעצלאָך.

אָקטאָבערדיק מיין ליד

מ. א. סול ﬠ

וואָס פלאַטערט וווי אַ פאָן אין וווינט מיין האַרץ,
וואָס ציט אַזוי אין שטורעם מיין געמיט?
דאָס זינגט אין מיר דער אומרו פון אָקטאָבער,
זינג איך היינט אָקטאָבערדיק מיין ליד.

אַ לאַנד אַזאַ מיט באַוול און מיט קוילן,
מיט גאָלד און און זון, מיט ברויט און מיט גראַניט;
נאָר מיר די בויער – הונגעריק און באָרוועס;
זינג איך היינט אָקטאָבערדיק מיין ליד.

אַ לאַנד אַזאַ פון מוני און פון הוירנדאָן;
אַ צייט אַזאַ פון שלאַכטן אָנגעגליט.
וווי קאָן מען דען – וווי קאָן מען זינגען אַנדערש –
זינג איך היינט אָקטאָבערדיק מיין ליד.

איך בלעטער דורך דעם יערלעכן קאַלענדער:
כאַדאָשים זיינען היים פאַרטאָן אין קרין.
נאָר ס׳האַלט אַן אויג אַף יעדן פראָנט פון אַלע לענדער
דער קאָמאָנדיר – אָקטאָבער – באָלשעוויק.

און אַז דער טאָג בא אונדז וועט קומען אין דעצעמבער,
אין יאַנואַר, אין יולי, צי אין מאַי –
זיין וועט דאָס דער טאָג דער לאַנג׳געענאָרטער,
זיין וועט דאָס אָקטאָבער סיייווויײסיי.

My October Song (1935)

◡ Yuri Suhl

Why is my heart like a flag in the wind,
why is my spirit drawn to the storm this way?
October's restlessness sings in me,
I sing my October song today.

Such a country with cotton, with coal,
with gold and sun, with bread, with granite;
but we the builders are hungry and barefoot,
I sing my October song today.

Such a country of Mooney and Herndon,[1]
such a time of battles, may
we sing? Can we sing anything else?
I sing my October song today.

I leaf through the year's calendar:
months are spent in the heat of war.
But he keeps an eye on every front,
the commander: Bolshevik October.

And though our time may be December,
January, June or May.
It will come, the day we long for,
October's coming anyway.

---

1. Tom Mooney and Angelo Herndon: workers' heroes in the 1930s.

נקמה

א שמואל קרייטער

האָסט אין אַ זינד־צעגליטער נאַכט,
אין אונזערע ליבער אַרײנגענאָסן
אַ ברענענדיקן גיפט, וואָס פלאַמט
ווי אַ רויטער משוגעת,
און מיר לויפן אום, ווי פאַר'סמ'טע מײז,
צו זוכן הײלונג בײ פּראָסטיטוטקעס...
ניט הײלונג – נאָר אַ ווילדן צער
געפינען מיר בײ יעדן קער,
וואָס פליקט אונזערע לעבנס אויס...
און דו קײקסט פון לאַכן
בײ דעם שדים־קאַראָהאָד פון אונזערע נשמות,
דו זונה!
פון דעם אַש פון אונזערע לעבנס פאַרברענטע
וועט זיך אויפהײבן אַ נקמה־נעמענדיקע געשטאַלט:
וועמעס אויגן וועלן זיין פאַרהאָלטענע בליצן;
וועמעס שטים פאַרשעמען וועט די שטאַרקסטע דונערן;
וועמעס אָרעמס וועלן האָבן כוח בערג אַרויסצוריסן,
און אָנשטאָט פינגער וועט ער בלאַנקענדע פּאָניאַרדן האָבן;
זיין גאַנץ געשטאַלט וועט זיין אויסגענאָקנאַטן פון נקמה,
פאַר וועמעס גרוים די גאַנצע וועלט וועט זיין צו קליין...
דיין זונה'דיקער רייץ וועט פרעמד אים זיין, ווי דער טויט.
וועסט אים ניט קענען גובר זיין מיט דיין נאַקעטקייט...
ער וועט רייסן גליד נאָך גליד פון דיר,
ביז דו, אַ צעהאַקטע קופּע פלייש, וועסט געשענדעט ווערן
אין בלוט פון דיין אייגענער שאַנד...

Vengeance (1924)

∾ Shmuel Kreyter

Once on a night of sparkling sin,
you gave our flesh
a burning poison, the flames came in
like crimson madness,
we run around like poisoned mice
to seek a cure in prostitution . . .
no cure, but disillusion
we find at every turn
and so our lives are plucked and burn
out. You gasp from laughter
at the circle-demon-dance of our souls,
you whore!
May he rise up from the ash
of our burnt-out lives—an avenger:
he whose eyes are lightning streaks, delayed,
whose voice shames the strongest thunder,
arms with the strength to move mountains aside,
and instead of fingers he'll have gleaming daggers.
All his body will be kneaded out of vengeance
the world won't be big enough to hold him . . .
Your whorish flirtation foreign to him as death,
your nakedness won't conquer him.
He'll rip you open, limb from limb,
until you, a hacked-up pile of flesh,
will bleed from your own disgrace . . .

עװיקשאָנקאַמף

ג. ד. קאָרמאָן ❧

ס׳האָבן הײנט דאָ געפֿיבערט די שטײנער פֿון ברוק,
ס׳האָבן הײנט דאָ געשלאָגן די פֿױסטן; —
געװען איז באַלאַנגערט, דער בלאַק ביז זון ראַג;
ס׳איז מאָסע געקומען מיט פֿױסט און געזאַנג:

ס׳װעט כאָװער ניט װאוינען אינדרױסן!
האָט גאָרניט געהאָלפֿן באַפֿעל פֿון גריכט,
און מאַרשאַלס און גענגסטערס אָבלאַװע;
ס׳איז מאָסע געקומען מיט קעמפֿערשן פֿליכט,
באַשיצן אַ הײם פֿון אַ כאַװער.

האָט מאָסע צעװיגט די קנאַביקע הענט,
פֿאַליציי, זײערע דעמבענע שטעקנס. —
און בלוט איז גערונען פֿון קעפ און פֿון הענט;
און זאָלן די לענדלאָרדם זיך עקן.

דעם דאָלעם געדושװוינגעט צוריק אַף די טרעפ,
נאָר בלוט איז געבליבן אַף שטײנער; —
שרעקט ניט געזעץ, פּאָליציישע קלעפ,
װען הונגער מיט קאַמף איז פֿאַראײניקט.

דערנאָך האָבן שכינים געטײלט זיך מיט פֿרײד,
כאָטש ס׳האָבן געװײטיקט די גלידער,
ס׳האָט קאָונסיל (*) גערופֿן: כאָװערים זײט גרײט!
מיר גרײטן אַף מאָרגן זיך װידער!...
— — —

*) אַרבעטלאָזער קאָונסיל װאָס אָרגאַניזירט דעם
קאַמף קעגן עװיקשאָנס.

Eviction Fight

∾ N. D. Korman

The pavement here was feverish today
fists today were beating;
the block was under siege today,
masses came with fists to say:

A comrade won't live on the street!
What good is the law of the land,
the marshal's and gangster's raid;
masses have come to fight—to defend
out of duty—the home of a comrade.

Masses swung their gnarled hands,
police, their clubs of oak—
and blood, it flowed from head and hands;
just let the landlords croak.

Need was moved back to the stairway,
but blood remained on the stones;
neither law nor police blows frighten them
when hunger and struggle are one.

Afterwards neighbors shared their joy,
despite their bruised limbs,
the Council[2] called: comrades be prepared!
Tomorrow we plan to continue! . . .

2. The Council of the Unemployed, which organized the fight against eviction (Korman's footnote).

ראָזע לוקסעמבורג (פראַגמענט פון אַ דראַמאַטישער פּאָעמע)

י. א. ראָנטש ‎⋄

אַזוי אַ איז דער טויט פון קעמפּער־פירער;
זיי שטאַרבן העלדיש, קדושים און מאַרטירער;
און וויַיזן אונז דעם וועג פון ברעכער, בויער,
וואָס שפּאַנען שטאָלץ אין שטריַיט דורך בלוט און טרויער.

אַזוי האָט אויך געמוזט געשען מיט ראָזען.
האָט ווען אַ פרוי אַמאָל נאָך זיך געלאָזן
אַ ציל אַ שענערן, ווי ראָזעס נאָמען?!
פון אירע ריַיד און טאַטן וועלן זאָמען,
צעוואַקסן וואונדערבאַר זיך איבער וועלטן
און בענטשן זי... נאָר אויך מיט האָס פאַרשעלטן
אָט אַלע יענע רויבער־פּאַראַזיטן,
וואָס האָבן ראָזעס לעבנס־פרייד פאַרשניטן.

אַף ראָזע'ם קעמפּער־פּנים איז געלענן
דער צער פון אַלע ליַידנדע, וואָס פרעגן:
„אַ, ווען קומט אָן די בשורה פון דערלייזער?"

אין ראָזע'ם אויגן איז געווען דער ביַיזער
פון דורות הערצער צאָרניקע, וואָס פילן
דעם שמאַרץ פון הענט געקאָוועטע, און וויל[ן]
אַ וועלט פון נויט און שקלאַפעריַי באַפריַיען.

ס'איז ראָזע'ם בליק געווען צום ליכטיק נייעס,
און ס'גרויסע האַרץ געהאַט גענונ האָט ליבע
פאַר אַלע ליַידנדע אין ציַיטן טריבע.

און ס'איז איר טויט געווען דער קרבן
פאַר פריַיהייטס־צונונג, וואָס מיט בלוט דערוואָרבן
עס האָבן אונז'רע בראַווע רויטע רייען,
וואָס ניט דערלעבט האָט זי מיט זיך פריַיען.

Rosa Luxemburg (1926)

Y. A. Rontsh

Fragment from a dramatic poem.

Such is the death of struggle leaders,
holy and heroic martyrs,
they teach to break and build again,
strutting struggle through blood and pain.

Thus it must have been with Rosa.
What woman has left greater goals
than she? Her name and words and deeds
will grow to cover worlds like seeds,
blessing her, cursing the parasites
who stole the joy from Rosa's life.

Over Rosa's fighter mask
was all the sorrow of the wronged who ask,
"When will the savior's tidings arrive?"

Anger shone in Rosa's eyes,
generations of angry hearts, the pain
of hands that long to lose their chains
to free the world from slavery and need.

Rosa's glance was hope, indeed
besides, her ample heart had room
to love the wronged in times of gloom.

The sacrifice: her life, exchanged
for the blood-soaked freedom train
of our red ranks, and in the end
she didn't live to rejoice with them.

אַננאַ פּאָוקער*)

.1

ס'איז אָנהויב פֿרילינג דאָ ביי מיר אין לאַנד.
לינט אַזוי פֿיל זון צעגאַסן און שמייכלט אין מיין שויב...
ווילט זיך זינגען, ליד פֿון ערשט אַרויסגעשפּראָצטע בלומען,
ווילט זיך זינגען, ליד צו פֿעלדער דאָ אין גרין...

האָב איך באַקומען אָבער גרוסן פֿון מיין אַלטער היים:
אַז טורמעס פֿול מיט יונגע קעמפֿער...
איז ווי'זשע קאָן איך זינגען היינט פֿון ערשטע בלומען?
איז ווי'זשע קאָן איך זינגען איצט פֿון פֿעלד אין גרין?

זיי שרייבן מיר: "הויב אויף דיין קול! לאָז פֿאַלן דיין געשריי!
ס'איז אַ ‏נ ‏נ ‏אַ ‏פּ ‏אָ ‏ו ‏ק ‏ע ‏ר אויך דאָרט צווישן זיי!
איז רייסט מען שטיקערווייז די גלידער פֿון איר גוף!
העי, לאָזט הערן איצט אין מערץ, דעם קאָמונאַרן רוף!"...

ס'איז אָנהויב פֿרילינג דאָ ביי מיר אין לאַנד.
און אַזאָ זון לינט היינט צעגאַסן אויף מיין שויב:
איז ווי'זשע קאָן איך זינגען ליד פֿון ערשטע בלומען?
איז ווי'זשע קאָן איך זינגען ליד צו פֿעלדער דאָ אין גרין?

.2

איך האָב דיין נאָמען–אַננאַ פּאָוקער–קיינמאָל ניט געהערט–
ווי כ'האָב אַמאָל אויך ניט געהערט פֿון עללאַ מעי:
כ'בין צו יונג געווען, ווען כ'האָב מיין לאַנד פֿאַרלאָזט
און זיך געלאָזט אויף וואַנדערונגען גיין...

‏*) אַ ‏נ ‏נ ‏אַ ‏פּ ‏אָ ‏ו ‏ק ‏ע ‏ר , די מוטיקסטע פֿירערן פֿון די רומענישע
האַרעאַפּשענע מאַסן, די רומענישע עללאַ מעי וויינס, זיצט פֿאַרשפּאַרט אין דער
גרעסטער רומענישער טורמע.

238

Anna Pauker (1937)

⮩ Nochem Vaysman

1.

My country is at the break of Spring.
So much sun pours down and smiles in my window:
it wants to be sung, song of newly sprung flowers.
It wants to be sung, song to these fields of green . . .

But I've just got news from my former home,
that prisons are full of young strugglers.
So, today, how can I sing of first flowers?
How can I sing now of fields of green?

They write, "Lift your voice up! Let your cry fall!
Anna Pauker[3] is among them!
They're ripping the limbs from her, piece by piece!
Hey, this March let them hear the common cry! . . ."

My country is at the break of Spring.
Such sun today pours through my windowpane.
But how can I sing a song of first flowers?
However can I sing to these fields of green?

2.

Anna Pauker, I'd never heard your name,
as I'd once never heard of Ella May.
I was too young when I left my country.
I let myself go wandering away . . .

---

3. Anna Pauker served as prime minister of Rumania after World War II. In a footnote
to the poem, Vaysman writes, "Anna Pauker, the most courageous leader of the Rumanian
proletarian masses, the Rumanian Ella May Wiggins, sits in the biggest Rumanian jail."

כ׳האָב געוואוסט: דער פױער האָט קײן מאַמעלינע ניט–
פֿאַרקױפֿט איז ער צו פֿריץ׳ס פֿעלד און װאַלד:
כ׳האָב זײן קלאַנגנדינע „דײנע־ליד" ניט אײנמאָל דאָרט געהערט
אין ליד פֿון מײנע װײסע, רומענישע נעכט!....

אַ קינד בין איך געווען, ווען כ׳האָב געזען
אין רױטן פֿלאַם דעם פֿריץ׳ס װײצנלאַן:
כ׳האָב ניט פֿאַרשטאַנען (כ׳האָב נאָך ניט געקאָנט פֿאַרשטײן!)
אַז ס׳איז אין לאַנד אַן אױפֿשטאַנד פֿון צאָראַן!

װיפֿיל טורמעם װעלן זיך נאָך בױען?
װיפֿיל תפֿיסות דאָרט שױן אױפֿגעבױט?
װיפֿיל קעמפֿער פֿױלן אין די צעלן?
און צעשאָסן, װיפֿיל, פֿאַר׳ן מאָרגנדרױט?

.3

מײן ליד צו דיר, מײן שװעסטער–אַננאַ פֿאָוקער–
אַ מוטיגע דיך זע איך פֿאַר מײן אױג!
און ווען מען רײסט דאָס פֿלײש פֿון דײנע בײנער–
ניט בױג דײן שטאָלצן קאָפֿ, ניט בױג!....

כ׳װעל מיט אַ טשיזל אױסהאַקן דײן בילד
אױף שפּיץ פֿון העכסטן פֿעלזנשטײן!
אין װערטער פֿראָסטע, פּשוט׳ע, מאַסאָװע,
דער װעלט װעלט צו װיסן טאָן, פֿון דײן געבײן!....

I knew the farmer had no grits,
he was sold to the nobleman's field and forest:
more than once I heard his *doyna*[4] song there,
in the song of my white, Rumanian nights.

I was a child when I saw
the nobleman's wheat field red with flame.
I didn't understand (I couldn't yet have understood!)
that there was an uprising in the land!

How many more prisons will they build?
How many jails have already been built?
How many strugglers will rot in the cells?
How many shot until the red of dawn?

3.
My song to you, my sister, Anna Pauker,
I see you, courageous, before my eyes!
And when they tear the flesh from your bones,
don't bow your proud head, don't bow!

I'll carve your portrait with a chisel
on the tip of the highest stone!
In the simplest and plainest words for the masses,
the world should know of your bones! . . .

4. *Doyna*: a Rumanian folk dance.

מיר זיינען די יאָרשים

איזיק פּלאָטנער ‎ﭏ‎

פאַרשמורעט די אויגן, און הערט מיט אַ ציטער,
מיר זיינען די יאָרשים פון לעבן!
און זאָל זיך אייך פאַרדריסן – מיר קאָנען זיך הייבן,
און פליִען אויף פליגל פון דרייסטקייט, און גלויבן.
די װעגן פאַרשטויבן,
מיט אונזערע מאָקנעם.
איר פרואװוט צו אונז שרייַען –
האָט אפשי פאַר אַלטע,
פאַר אַלטע, װאָס װייסן!

–מיר, װעלן פאַרשפּיִען,
מיט װילן מיט היִסן,
מיט יונגן געלעכטער פאַרקלינגען,
פאַרשאַװוערטע טאָנעם פון אַלטע נאַראָנים,
װאָס ליגן צוזאַמען מיט נעכטנס געבונדן,
אין צייַטן װאָס זיינען פאַרשוװאונדן...
פאַרשמורעט די אויגן, און הערט מיט אַ ציטער,
עס קלאָפן די מוטיקע טריט פון די יונגע, –
די יאָרשים פון לעבן...

We Are the Heirs (1925)

～ Isaac Platner

Squint your eyes, listen and tremble,
we are the heirs of life!
And it ought to vex you that we can rise up,
and fly on wings of bravery and faith.
Our multitudes
cover the roads with dust.
You try to cry out to us,
"Honor the old,
the old ones who know!"

We will spit
our burning will,
our young laughter ringing
on the rusty complaints of old fools,
who lie bound up with yesterdays
in times that have disappeared . . .
Squint your eyes, listen and tremble,
the bold steps of youth resound,
the heirs of life . . .

נישקאַ

יאָסל קאָטלער &

טרעפּט־זשע ווער ער איז!
איר קענט נישט?
טאָ כאַפּט נישט,
ס'ברענט נישט.

פרעגט זיך אַ פראַגע
וואָס אי'דאָס פאַר אַ פיש?
וועל איך אייך דערקלערן
וואָס ער איז ניש.

ער איז נישקאַ סטאָליר,
ער איז נישקאַ פּויער,
ער איז נישקאַ שנײַדער,
ער איז נישקאַ בויער.

ער איז „נישקאַ"
און פּאַרטיק.

און כאָטש ער איז נישט
אָט די אַלע זאַכן,
פונדעסטוועגן קען ער
אייך אַלצדינג מאַכן.

ווען אַ פאָריער, לעמאָשל,
דאַרף מאַכן אַ פעליץ:
נעמט ער אַ פעלכל
און מאַכט עם.

ווען אָבער נישקאַ
דאַרף מאַכן אַ פעליץ:
נעמט ער אַ פעלכל
מיט אַ פאָריער
און מאַכט עם.

Not-a (1934)

∽ Yosl Cutler

Guess who we have here!
Don't know him?
Don't worry.
No hurry.

You ask yourself, what sort of fish
have we caught?
Well, let me explain
what he is not.

He's not-a carpenter
he's not-a farmer
he's not-a tailor
he's not-a builder.

He's "Not-a"
and that's all.

And though he's not
all of these things,
he can do for you
just about anything.

Let's say, a furrier
needs a fur:
he gets a pelt
and makes one.

But when Not-a
needs a fur,
he gets a pelt
and a furrier
and makes one.

ווען אַ שרײַבער װיל שרײַבן
אַן אָריגינעלע ליד:
נעמט ער אַ פּען
מיט אַ שטיקל פּאַפּיר
און מאַכט עם.

ווען נישקאַ װיל שרײַבן
אַן אָריגינעלע ליד:
נעמט ער אַ שטיקל פּאַפּיר
מיט אַ שטיקל שרײַבער
און מאַכט עם.

און װאָס מאַכט עם אױס
אַבי ער װערט גרױס.

ער ערגערט זיך דערפֿון
אַפֿילע קיין האָר נישט,
ער מאַכט אײך אַלצדינג
און קענען קען ער
נאָרנישט.

אַלײן גאָרנישט קענען
איז דאָך גאָרנישט שײן,
אָבער עסן, זאָגט מען,
קען ער אַלײן.

פֿרעגט זיך אַ פֿראַגע
װאָס איז ער פֿאָרט?
װאָס איז ער נישט?
ער איז װאָס אין דער קאָרט:

אַ יאָגער, אַ זױפֿער,
אַ לאַקבן, אַ קױפֿער,
אַ כאַפּער, אַ װיכער,
אַ נעמער, אַ קריכער,
אין דער רומענישער שול

If a writer wants to write
an original poem:
he takes a pen
and a piece of paper
and makes one.

If Not-a wants to write
an original poem:
he takes a little paper
and a little writer
and makes one.

Who gives a fig,
long as he gets big?

This harms him, you know
not even an inch,
he does it all for you
and can't do
zilch.

Nothing good in doing
nothing alone.
But eating, they say
he can eat on his own.

You ask yourself,
what is he, after all?
Well what isn't he?
He's the worst of it all:

A chaser, a guzzler,
a crook, a buyer,
a grabber, a shaker,
a snatcher, a dawdler.

איז ער אַ פּאָליטישן אַ שטיקל,
ער פֿאַרקויפֿט זיי
ריבוינעשעליילעמם
צוויי פֿאַר אַ ניקל.

ס׳גייט „נישקאָ״ן נישקאָשע,
עם לעבט זיך אים גלאָט,
ער איז גװאָלדיק צופֿרידן
װאָם די מאַמע האָט אים געהאָט.

He's some "politician"
in the Rumanian shul,[5]
sells 'em God-Almighties,
nickel for two.

Not-a gets on fine,
living's not-a problem.
He's awfully pleased
that his mother had him.

5. Shul: Yiddish term meaning synagogue.

Matters of the Heart

"I've never written a love poem before," writes Yuri Suhl in the final verse of his tender "Kh'hob Dikh Lib." Of all the topics Proletpen spans, arguably the most candid is love. Stepping away from world and national politics, strikes and gloomy city streets, even a devout proletarian writer like Suhl enters the realm of his own vulnerability. The love poems of Proletpen vary from descriptions of hurtful triangles to unlikely locations. Who would expect to find a love poem, such as Dora Teitelboim's "Your Arms," in the backseat of an old Chevy? In a second surprising love theme, Teitelboim compares herself to a young foal, tearing through the pasture of her lover's chest hair.

Suhl's "Kh'hob Dikh Lib" (I Love You), is a rare nonpolitical moment for him. The poem's occasionally rhyming meter echoes the unhurried, casual encounter that it describes. The youngest member of Proletpen, Suhl captures the innocence of a group of writers who have made a name for themselves by singing about blood, war, and a radical political coalition. In the group's idealized, collective poetic imagination everyone was a worker by day and an artist and lover by night.

These pieces also give a sense of the social life of the New York–based writer's movement. Most of the Proletpen poets were in their twenties or thirties. In addition to publishing their poetry, many of the members of Proletpen worked, at some point, on the editorial staff of the *Frayhayt* or on one of the smaller literary journals, such as *Yung kuznye*, *Hamer*, or *Yunyon skver*. Many also taught in the Yiddish schools that were run under the auspices of the YKuF (Yiddish Culture Union), also associated with the Left. Leftist Jewish summer camps such as Kinderland and Nit Gedayget drew the young writers as counselors and became the sites of passionate love affairs and equally passionate breakups. In short, Proletpen became a stage for the drama of everyday life just as much as it was a forum for international affairs. Love, jealousy, and personal conflict may not have been a conscious focus of their work, but these aspects of life occasionally penetrate their poetry, as it did their social sphere.

כ'האָב דיך ליב

יורי סול ‎⤸

...
אין אַ טאָג אַ פּראָסטן
(וואָס קאָן פּראָסטער זײַן ווי דאָנערשטיק באַטאָג)
האָב איך צעשויבערט דײַנע האָר, די רויט־צעלאָזטע,
און דערנאָך פאַרגלעטנדיק געזאָנגט:
כ'האָב דיך ליב.

די זון האָט זיך פאַרשפּילט אויף אונדזער בעט,
און איך האָב זיך פאַרשפּילט מיט דײַנע האָר
און האָב מיט זיי אַף גלעט־לאָשן גערעדט –
פון דײַנע קוים־קוים אַכצן יאָר.

דײַן פּאָנעם האָט מיט זומער־שפּרענקעלעך געבליט,
האָב איך מיט מײַנע ליפן זיי געציילט
און אַלע ווײַלע אָנגעהויבן פונדאָסניי.
די זון האָט מינאָסטאָמע זיך געאײַלט,
איז זי אַוועק און אונדזו געלאָזן זאַלבעצווײַט –
מיך און דיך און אָט די ווערטער דרײַ:
כ'האָב דיך ליב.

כ'האָב קיינמאָל נאָך קיין ליבע ליד געשריבן
כאָטש פאַרליבט בין איך פון טאָמיד אָן – פאַרוואָר,
נאָר ס'דאַכט זיך מיר, אַז כ'האָב צום ערשטן מאָל הײַנט אויפגעקליבן
אָט די ווערטער דרײַ אין דײַנע האָר:
כ'האָב דיך ליב.

254

Kh'hob dikh lib (1938)

~ Yuri Suhl

One day, a simple one
(as only a Thursday afternoon can be)
I mussed up your loose red hair
and then, caressing it, I said:
I love you. *Kh'hob dikh lib.*

The sun lolled, playing on our bed,
and I lolled, playing with your hair,
and I told it in a tongue of caresses
of your barely eighteen years.

Your face bloomed with summer freckles.
I counted them with my lips, one by one
and every time I lost my place I had to start afresh.
Apparently, the sun was in a rush.
It left the three of us alone,
me and you, and also those three words:
kh'hob dikh lib.

I've never written a love poem before,
though, yes, I am eternally in love.
But it seems to me, I picked them for the first time today,
those three words in your hair:
kh'hob dikh lib.

צו מיין געליבטן

ר. נ.קא. ‏✍

מיין ליבער,
צו וואָס די טויזנט שבועות
שוין פאַרשוואוכטע,
אַז איך וויים:
איך בין פאַר דיר
אַ בעכער גליענדער גענום
און זינד...
וואָס צינדט דיין ליידנשאַפט
ביז פלאַמיק הייסן גלוט,
און גליט ביז פייער אָן
דיין הייסעס בלוט.
איך וויים...
איך בין פאַר דיר אין העלע טעג
אַ העלער ליכט, אַ העל געשטאַלט.
איך בין פאַר דיר, ווי זונשיין
וואָס באַשטראַלט,
און ווי דער דונער,
וואָס ער קנאַלט
אין העלן בליץ.
איך וויים
איך בין פאַר דיר אין שווערע טעג,
דאָס נאַכטגעבעט, דאָס שטילע,
די רו, די אייביקע –
די זאַנפטע רו פון תפילה.
איך בין פאַר דיר
די אַלץ פאַרניבנדע,
די ליבנדע...
איך וויים...
כ'בין אויך פאַר דיר אַ כלי, דו באָנוצט
אויף אָפצוטאָן פון זיך די שמוץ –
די זינד,
און פאַר די צוקונפטיקע יאָרן
פאַרפלאַנצן זיך אַ קינד –
אַ דור.

To My Beloved (1923)

∽ R. G. Ka

My love,
for you the thousand oaths
were desecrated long ago.
Far as I know:
to you I am
a glass of glowing pleasure
and sin . . .
that ignites your passion
to a flaming hot desire
and brings to a boil
your hot blood.
I know . . .
to you, I am, in light days
white light, bright joy.
To you, I, like the sunshine,
spread my rays,
and like the thunder
crack in bright displays
of lightning.
I know
to you, I am, in your hard days,
night's soft prayer,
eternal rest—
the mild rest of prayer.
To you I am
the all-forgiving
the loving . . .
I know . . .
to you I am a vessel you use
to strip yourself of dirt,
and sin,
and for those years, in anticipation,
a child grows within . . .
a generation.

Triangle

ל. מילער ๑

איך האָב איר אַ ביכל צום לייענען געבראַכט.
זי האָט מיר אַ שמייכל געשאָנקען דערפאַר.
און ער האָט, פאַרשטיי איך, זיך דאָמאָלסט געטראַכט:
אַזוי קריגט דער הונט אַ גלעט פון זיין האַר...

זי האָט אַ פאַרטראַכטע געגלעט מיר די האַנט,
און ער האָט געשמייכלט פול אומעט און צער.
עס האָט מיר זיין שמייכל, דער טריבער, דערמאָנט:
דעם בליק פון אַ הונט, ווען עס שלאָגט אים זיין האַר.

זאָלבעדריט (טרייענגל)

דאָרע טײטלבוים ‎⤺‎

מיר זיצן אין מאַשין אין זאָלבעדריט.
זײַן אָטעם האָט מײַנע אויגן צוגעמאַכט.
מײַן האַרץ ווי אַ יונגער בוים אין צווײט
האָט מיט גליק צעעפנט די קנאָספן פֿון דער נאַכט.

די מאַשין לויפֿט. הערצער וועלן רעדער איבעריאָגן.
שטיל. ס'רעדט דער ציטער פֿון די שפּיץ פֿינגער.
טענער צו מײַנע אויערן זיך טראָגן –
אַ כאָר פֿון צען טויזנט זינגער.

ער האַלט מיט זיכערקייט די ראָד.
און ער – מײַן האַרץ אין זײַנע הענט.
ס'ווערט אָן אַלטע שעווי אַ נײַע וואונדער-שטאָט,
און זײַנע אויגן אין יעדן ציגל פֿון די ווענט.

מײַן קאָפּ ווערט פֿון פֿרייד מיר מיד,
און שפּאַרט זיך אָן אין הימל מיט די שטערן,
מײַן לײַב זינגט אַ שטילע סאָלאָ ליד.
שטיל. ס'זאָל די נאַכט מיך ניט דערהערן.

260

Threesome (1944)

～ Dora Teitelboim

We sit, a threesome in the car.
My eyes have closed under his breathing.
A youthful tree in bloom, my heart
has opened with joy the buds of evening.

The car speeds on. Hearts race with wheels.
Quiet. Here speaks a trembling finger.
Tones carry to my ears,
a choir of ten thousand singers.

He securely holds the wheel.
And he—my heart in his palms.
An old Chevy becomes a miracle-city,
his eyes in every brick of the walls.

My head, with all this joy, grows tired,
and rests against sky. Stars come near.
My body sings a quiet solo.
Quiet. The night mustn't hear.

דיינע אָרעמס

דיינע אָרעמס האָבן מיך אַרומגענומען –
טויזנט שטיגן הייבן מיך צו די הימלען.

דיינע העגנט – יונגע, שטיפערישע צווייגן –
נעמען מיט פרילינגדיקער פרייד אַ יונגן בוים אַרום.

איך הער סימפאָניעס אין דיין שווייגן.
איך זע דיך אַ צעשטראָלטן אומעטום.

דיין ברוסט – מיין פרישצעבליטער טאָל –
שמעקט מיט יונגע קאַלאָשינע גראָז.

איך – אַ לאָשעק אויף דער פּאַשע צום ערשטן מאָל –
וויל קיין גרעזעלע ניט איבערלאָזן.

262

Your Arms (1944)

∾ Dora Teitelboim

Your arms have drawn me in,
a thousand steps lift me to heaven.

Your hands (young, playful boughs) embrace
with spring's delight, a youthful tree.

I see you, radiant, everyplace . . .
I hear, in your silence, a symphony.

Your chest (my freshly blooming valley)
smells of newly trampled grass

and I, a foal, first time on the pasture,
dare not let one green blade pass.

סאָנעט און דועט צווישן אַ פלעפער מיט אַ פּאָעט

אַלעקסאַנדער [פּאָמעראַנץ] ‎∽‎

וויפיל שמייכלען וועסטו געבן פאַר אַ מעשה׳לע, צינאַנקע,
פאַר אַ וואונדער־שיינע „סטאָרי", לייכט מיט זונען׳דן?
וויפיל קושן וועסטו געבן פאַר אַ ליד צו דיר, וואָאַקבאַנקע,
פאַר אַ זעלטענער פּאָעמע, וואו כ׳באַזינג דיך, ליבסטע׳קרוין,
וואָס וואיברירט פול מיט דיין שיינקייט, ווי דער גלאָקן׳טורם אויבן,
פול מיט ביינקענדינע טענער פון דעם אָוונט גלעקער׳קלאַנג?

פאַר דער מעשה אָנגעבאָטן האָט די פלעפּערקע רחמנות‏–
אַ קליין קאָפּיטשקע רחמנות און אַ נעניץ פאַר׳ן ליד,
און זי זאָגט אים, אַז זי דאַרף ניט קיין פּאָעזיע, בנאמנות,
אַז נאָך קליידער און ברילאַנטן ביינקט איר גליד נאָר, ביינקט איר גליד!
נאָר פאַר רייכקייטן, טיטולן, וועט זי אירע אוצרות שיקן,
אירע קושן, אירע שמייכלען, אירע פּלאַם׳צינויינער׳בליקן...

264

Sonnet and Duet for Flapper and Poet (1928)

∼ Alexander Pomerantz

How many smiles for a tale, gypsy girl?
For a wonderful sun-golden story?
How many kisses for a song for you, dancer?
A rare poem that sings of you, morning glory,
that echoes your beauty, like bell-towers,
full of yearning peals in the evening hours?

For the song, the flapper-girl offered her pity,
a smidgen of pity, a yawn for the song,
and she tells him she doesn't need poetry,
that clothing and jewels make her body yearn.
And that only for riches will she give her treasures—
her kisses, her smiles, her gypsy-glance-burn.

קאַמף און שפּיל

פֿאַר וועמען לעבן איז אַ קאַמף,
פֿאַר מיר איז עס אַ שפּיל –
מיט צופֿרידנקייט אין האַרצן
דאַרף מען דאָך ניט פֿיל.

„אַ לאָבן ברויט, אַ לידער־בוך,
און דו, מײַן ליבסטער, בײַ דער זײַט" –
איז מײַן לעבן אָנגעפֿילט
מיט טאָפּלט־העלער פֿרייד.

266

Fight and Play (1957)

Sarah Kindman

For some life is a fight,
it is a game for me—
with a heart of happiness
there's little else you need.

"A loaf of bread, a book of verse,
and by my side, love, you"—
my life is all filled up
with a brilliant joy times two.

267

My Heart

מײַן האַרץ

‎‎— משה נאַדיר

מײַן האַרץ האָט מעכטיק ליב,
און איך האָב ליב מײַן האַרץ –
אַ שאָד עס קען ניט אויסהאַלטן
אַ לעבן אַזאַ האַרטס.

מײַן האַרץ האָט מעכטיק פֿײַנט,
איך האַס מײַן האַרץ דערפֿאַר –
און אויף זײַן ווּיסטן סוף
איך זיץ און האַר און האַר.

My Heart

🙢 Moyshe Nadir

My heart has mighty love,
and so I love my heart.
A pity it can't stand
a life so hard.

I hate my heart because
my heart has mighty hate,
and for its gloomy end,
I sit and wait and wait.

מיין בת־שבע

משה נאדיר

מיין בת־שבע,
ווי איבערן ים אַ מעווע,
דעקסטצו די ווילדקייט מיטן פלאַטער
פון איר ריינעם פליגל, נאַכט־צע־צו,
אַזוי אויך דו
דעקסטסטצו די גרויע לייבנ־גריווע פון מיין אומרו
מיט בלאַנדעקייט, מיט פינקעלקייט
פון גאָלדענע לעכט, וואָס וואַקסן אויפן בוים,
פון גרינע סעדער ביים וואַסערס זוים.

ביי די ברעמען פון מיין טרויער האַלטסטו דעם לאַמטער
פון דיין אויג. דיין ווע ציטערט אויף מיינער. ווער
נאָך ווי ווע־עם צווויי זיך ציטערנדיק אַנטקעגן
קענען ווויסן פאַרוואָס לעבן איז לעבן?

בת־שבע,
צום ראַנד פון ים צילט די מידע מעווע,
צום מיטן ים צילט דער זעלם צעבראָכענער פליגל.
עס ברענגט מיין בריוו צו דיר אינ־איינעם מיטן זינל.
דער טריפּאַקס רויט, וואָס רינט און פּלאַמט,
אַ שטיק האַרץ, וואָס איך האַלט אין דער האַנט
איבערן ליכט פון מיין צער היינט־צו־טאָגיש.

פלאַמענדיק מיט ווערטער דור־הפלגה־שע,
דער בריוו איז איינגעזינלט ביז צו אַש
פון הוגנאַריקע הינט – פון ווינטן אויפגענאַשט,
דער גלותדיקער קנוף, דער פייער־קשר
אויפגעבונדן. ער קניפט ניט מער שוין.

My Bas-Sheva

⌒ Moyshe Nadir

My Bas-Sheva,
a seagull over the water
covers the wildness with the flap
of her clean wing for the night, and you,
you do that, too.
You cover the gray lion's mane of my restlessness
with blondness, with the glitter
of golden light grown on a tree
in green orchards at the edge of the sea.

You hold the lantern of your eyes
to the brows of my grief.
Your eyelid quivers on mine. Who
but two eyelids fluttering against one another
can know why life is life?

Bas-Sheva,
the weary seagull heads for the edge of the sea;
the soul's broken wing heads for the sea's center.
It brings you the seal along with my letter.
The red sealing wax drips and flames:
a piece of the heart I hold in my hand
over the candle of my nowaday sorrow.

Flaming with words like the age after Babel,
the letter is sealed unto ash
by hungry hounds. Winds have devoured
the knot of exile, the fire-knot
is untied—a knot no longer.

נאָר מײַן האַרץ און דײַנס – בת־שבֿע,
נאָך אַלץ אויף די שפּיץ־פֿליגל פֿון דער מעװע
מיט איר איבער די שוימען, טרערן־רוימען.
אַ פֿלעכטל רויך איבער אַ שיף־קוימען
שרײַבט צו אונדז, װעבט אונדז אײַן
אין דעם אויפֿגעװינטלטן, פֿינטלדיקן שטערנשײַן.

פּראָװינסטאָן, סעפּ. 1937

But my heart and yours, Bas-Sheva,
are still on the wingtip of the seagull,
over the whitecaps—expanses of tears.
A fleck of smoke atop a ship's smokestack
writes to us, intertwines
us in the windblown, blinking starshine.

א קוש

מלכה לי ﮳

העי, דו זעלנער אויף די הפקר־באַנעַן!
האָסט אויף מײַנע ליפן פאַרפרעסט אַ קוש.
איך בין אַ קינד געווען און ניט פאַרשטאַנען
דו שיקסט דורך מיר דער וועלט דײַן לעצטן קוש...

אין געפּאַקטן צוג פאַר אַזויפיל אויגן
האָסטו מיך ווי אַ באַל געטאָן אַ הויב.
ווי אַ הויכער ריז זיך געבוינען
אַנטקעגן פּראָסט פון קאַלטער שויב.

איך האָב אַ הוט ווי דײַן שוועסטערל געטראָגן;
איך האָב דערמאָנט דיך אָן דײַן היים.
האָסטו אַ לעצטן גרוס געשיקט איר זאָן
און געוואָיעט זיך אין אַ ווילד געוויין...

ווי אַן אָקס וואָס רייסט זיך פון דער שחיטה
וואָס האָט אין חלף דעם טויט דערפילט,
האָבן הענט זיך אַ טראָג געטאָן ווי אויף אַ מיטה,
דײַן געשריי מיט פויסטן אײַנגעשטעלט...

דער צוג האָט געסאָפּעט ווי אַ שוואַרצע חיה
און געלאָכט מיט פונקען רויט...
דו ביסט געפֿאָרן צו דײַן אייגענער לויה
אויפן שלאַכטפעלד האָט געוואָרט דײַן טויט...

דו פרעמדער זעלנער – אינם מאָסקקבר
אויף אַ ראָבןפעלד שוואַרץ ווי קוילן!
עס איז שוין שטויב דײַן יעדער אבר;
דײַן קוש וואונדינט אויף מײַן מויל...

276

A Kiss (1933)

∾ Malka Lee

Hey there, soldier, from the stateless
trains! Once on my lips you pressed a kiss.
I was just a kid, and didn't understand
that you sent, through me, the world your final kiss . . .

In a crowded locomotive, before so many eyes,
you picked me up as if I were a ball.
Opposite the frost from a cold windowpane,
you bent down like a giant toward someone small.

I had a hat, the kind your little sister wore.
I made you think of her, and the home you left behind.
You'd just sent your last good-bye to her
and you burst into a wild kind of crying.

Like an ox, tearing itself from the slaughter,
having smelt death on the knife,
as if, on a bier, you suddenly moved your
hands, bald fists, squelching your cry.

The train—a black beast—laughed with red sparks,
and panted with animal breath.
You were traveling to your own funeral.
There on the battlefield was death.

Hey, foreign soldier, in the cold, mass grave,
on a raven's field, black as pitch,
your limbs have long since gone to dust,
your kiss is a wound on my lips.

In Pencil

〜 Moyshe Nadir

Written in pencil,
rubbed out with eraser:
so has our love
been erased by the years.

Written with a stick,
on sand and in snow,
is a person's fate,
is the love we two know.

Chiseled with a sledgehammer,
burned in, fire-branded, all
the lies of this life
and the shadow on the wall!

The Poet on Poetry

Proletpen was the literary embodiment of the social, political, and human-itarian ideals of a revolutionary movement. It also drew heavily on the Yiddish literary movements that came before it, either adopting or reject-ing past trends. Proletpen's awareness of its literary parentage is apparent throughout the body of its poetry. Tributes such as Ber Grin's to Morris Winchevsky credit the labor poet for inspiring the later movement. Winchevsky's call for social justice, particularly in the workplace, struck a responsive chord with the linke. Indeed, we can view Proletpen as the direct literary descendents of the American Yiddish labor poets.

A number of poems aim to distinguish Proletpen from prior literary movements, namely, from less self-consciously political poets of the early twentieth century. Proletpen strongly aligned itself with the Russian liter-ary tradition. Yosl Kohn's "Sergei Yesenin" reacts to Yesenin's suicide as a betrayal of the social change that the Russian poet might have affected had he been less self-absorbed. Kohn opens with a number of metaphors for Yesenin's unfinished life, speaking of Yesenin's "Woeful, unspoken words" and his "unborn children." Presumably, Kohn considers the unlived por-tion of Yesenin's life to be the portion that would have done service to the Revolution. Kohn was not alone in addressing the late Yesenin. The cele-brated Vladimir Mayakovsky's famous poem to Yesenin was published officially in 1926, a year after Yesenin's death and his own return from New York. Mayakovsky's poem, which criticizes Yesenin for a wanton life, also laments the symbolist poet's unuttered words:

Eternally
   the tongue
      is now
         shut up in teeth.[1]

Kohn suggests that the tragedy might have been avoided, had Yesenin not "run from daylight." Kohn juxtaposes Yesenin's wasted talent with the struggle of the Russian people for a Soviet government.

Shifre Vays in "To Mani Leyb" assumes that her readers will be familiar with the founder of the Yunge movement. Chaim Schwartz alludes to the yet unfulfilled task of the writer when he refers to hands "that ought to have brought light; / which ought to have brought joy." Proletpen's modernist predecessors were not the only poets worthy of commentary, or vulnerable to criticism. Menke Katz, who entered the stage of Yiddish poetry through proletarian publications, was in constant conflict with Proletpen because of his divergence from the party line. His poem "The Brave Coward" reacts to Proletpen's use of poetry to drive the spirit of a political movement. What is curious is not so much that a complex poet like Menke Katz would question the need to fulfill a political ideal in his poetry, but that a political paper like *Frayhayt* would publish it. Katz's "Letter to the Editor of the *Morgn Frayhayt*" accompanied the poem on page three of *Frayhayt*, August 6, 1938, and responds to his fellow poets' accusations of him. Katz begins the letter, in which he addresses Moissaye Olgin as the "esteemed Comrade M. Olgin," "I wrote this poem . . . for the *Morgn Frayhayt*, as a response to two members of Proletpen, who attacked me in speeches at a 'Proletpen' meeting. I am, however *certainly* not aiming for this poem to serve only as a response to these two writers." He goes on to criticize proletarian poetry for its tendency toward "comical, red happy endings. . . . The time has come, Comrade Olgin, that we should learn to tolerate varying styles, directions, genres, so that our proletarian literature should become a rich, deep, suffering symphony."

Katz's poems, as well as others, like Sarah Barkan's "I Have Not Woven My Poems. . ." and Moyshe Nadir's "Out of the Depths," comment on

---

1. Original can be found in Vladimir Mayakovsky, *Sochineniya v dvux tomax* (Moscow: Pravda, 1987), 347.

the uses of poetry, placing the proletarian movement in a wider context. Had a critical mass of Yiddish speakers lived to see a continuity of its poetry throughout and beyond the twentieth century, undoubtedly future movements would have produced important outcroppings of the social poetry of the twentieth century.

דאָס ליד

ל. טור ‎ﮱ

ס׳איז דער טאָן, ניט די האַרף,
וואָס עס קלינגט אַזוי זיס;
ניט דער שטאָל, נאָר דער שאַרף,
מאַכט דער שווערד, וואָס ער איז . . .

ס׳איז דער ווינט, ניט דער מאַסט,
וואָס אין ים טרייבט די שיף;
ניט דער גראַם מאַכט דאָס ליד
נאָר דאָס וואָרט פון דער טיף . . .

איך האָב ניט...

שרה באַרקאַן ⁓

איך האָב ניט געוועבט מײנע לידער
אין קעלערס, וואו ווײן ווערט געטרונקען
ס'האָט לעבן מיט בראָנדיקע פֿונקען
מיר לידער פֿאַרוועבט אין די גלידער.

איך האָב ניט געלערנט אין שולן –
(זאָל זיך דער הײנט מיט דעם שעמען!)
איך האָב שטענדיק געלײענט פֿעלמען,
זײ געוויקלט אין גאָלדענע טולן.

ס'איז הײנט מיר דער יום־טוב דער גרעסטער;
איך שיק מײנע לידער דער וועלט.
דער צער האָט זיך הײנט אויך צעוועלט
ווען איך ווער אַ גליד פֿון אָרקעסטער.

איך פֿיל, ווי אַ וואַלד אַ צענרינטער,
בעת יאָרן פֿלאַכטן זילבער אין לאָקן.
דאָך ווער איך דערפֿון ניט דערשראָקן –
איך גים אָן אַ פֿולינקן טינטער.

286

I Have Not Woven My Poems . . .

~ Sarah Barkan

I haven't woven my poems
in basement taverns.
Life's burning sparks,
weave poems into my limbs.

I have never been to school,
(Our times can answer for this!)
I've always read poems,
wrapped them in gold tulle.

It's the holiest day for me,
I send the world my poetry.
Even grief was beaming
when I joined the symphony.

Years spread silver in my hair
but I'm a wood grown green.
What's there for me to fear?
I'll pour out a well full of ink.

היינט

שפרה ווייס <

איך וועל זיך שבעה ניט זעצן
נאָך מיינע יאָרן, מיינע נעכטנס,
וואָס זיינען פולע אָדער ליידינע אַוועק.
אויף דעם האָבן צײַט אַלטע באָבעס,
איינגעוויקלט אין שרעק,
וואו דער היינט היינגט אויף בײַנערדינע לײַבער,
ווי אַלטע זעק.

מיר איז דער היינט אַ געליבטער,
אין שטאַרקע אָרימס נעמט ער מיך אַרײַן.
טונק איך היינטינן טאָרט
אין פיליאָרינן ווײַן,
מיין זײַן – מיין נאָענטסטער פריינט
איז אַן עדות:
אַז ס'איז מיך מקדש דער היינט.

– ווען איך בלייב מיט מיט היינט אַליין
באַנאַכט,
מאַכט ער ברכה אויף מיין יונגקייט,
איך פאַרנעם געזונט זאַמען פאַר מאָרגן,
וואָס האָט געבראַכט מיר דער היינט.

Today (1922)

꘎ Shifre Vays

I won't be sitting shiva
for my years, my yesterdays
which are gone, full or empty.
Old women have time for that,
wrapped in fear,
they wear today like old sacks,
on bony flesh.

My Today is a lover
who takes me in strong arms.
I dip Today's fresh cake
in well-aged wine,
my I—my soul mate—comes to play
the witness
at my wedding with Today.

When I lie with Today alone
at night,
he blesses my youthful way.
I plant tomorrow's healthy seed:
a present from Today.

סערגיי יעסענין

‮﮼ יאָסל קאָהן

האָסט אַ ניט דערזעטיקט לעבן
אין ווינטיקע מיילער פֿאַרוואָרפֿן.
ווי צוטראָטענע בלעטער –
אומעטיקן דיינע ניט דערזאָנגטע ווערטער.
ערד רויע האָסטו געגעבן אָנצופֿרעסן
מיט זאָפֿטיקע שטימונגען,
און איבער צעלעכערטע וועגן
בלאָנדושען דיינע ניט דערקענטע קינדער.
אויף וועמען לעבט עס אויף דיין זומערדיקע ווילדקייט,
דו גרויס, דאָרפֿיש, קינד דו?
דו האָסט אין דיין ווילדקייט ניט געקענט דערכאַפֿן
די אַרויסשיילונג פֿון אַ נייער וועלט.
ווי דער שרעק פֿון אַ ווילד פֿערד
וואָס דערזעט אָנקומענדע ליכט,
אַזוי ביסטו פֿון קלאָרן טאָג אַנטלאָפֿן,
פֿון גאָלדענעם אויפֿגיין
אויסגעאָטעמט אין וויסע נעכט.
בלויז אַ וויסטער קלויסטער געבעט
האָט נאָכגעצילט אויף דיין פֿאַרפֿלאָנטערטן טראָט.
האָסט אַזאַ בלאָנדע אומרו
מיט איינענער האַנט דערשטיקט.
ניט דערבראַכט האָסטו דיין וואָרט
ביז זין צעצונדענעם צאָרן,
וואָס האָט זיך צעגאָסן אין אַלע ווינקלען
פֿון דיין נאָכטיק לאַנד,
דו, ווילדקרוייזיקער פֿויער דו!
פֿאַרוואָס האָסטו דיין גאַנג ניט דערפֿירט
ביז צו גרענעצן פֿון צעשטראַלטער פֿרייד?
ס'קלאָרט דאָך שוין אויף דיין פֿאָלק
אַזאַ צעטאַנצטער זוניקער יאָנטעוו!
ס'זומערט דאָך שוין איבער בלאָטיקן שניי
אַזאַ רויטצעפֿאָכטער אויפֿקום.
דיין פֿאַרלאָכט פֿאָלק

290

Sergei Yesenin

∼ Yosl Kohn

You've thrown a life still hungry
into windy mouths.
Like trampled leaves—
languish your unuttered words.
You gave raw earth juicy moods
to gorge on,
and on the pot-holed streets
your neglected children lose their way.
Who will your summer wildness bring to life,
you big country boy?
In your wild ways, you haven't managed to catch up
to the newly hatched world.
Like the terror of the wild horse
who glimpses light ahead,
you've run from daylight,
from a golden dawn
only to breathe out into white night.
Only a deserted church prayer
has followed your entangled step.
You've choked this blond agitation
with your own hand.
You haven't carried your word all the way
to the burning anger
that pours itself into every corner
of your nighttime land,
you curly-locked farmer, you!
Why haven't you led your own way
to the limits of radiant joy?
Now it's clearing over your people,
this sunny, dancing holiday!
Now it's summering over filthy snow,
this red-flapping ascent!
Your people, the ones who were laughed at,

האָט מיט יונגקייט זיך באַפרײַדיקט.
דײַן פאַרלאָכט פאָלק
האָט פון שימל זיך אויסגעשניטן;
און דו האָסט דײַן יונג קרעפטיק בלוט
ווי אומרײַן וואַסער אַרויסגעגאָסן,
און דו האָסט מיט דײַן גליענדיק לעבן,
פוילע גופים אָנגעזעטיקט.

ס׳וויינען דאָך פון דאָרפישע קאָטקעס אַרויס
דײַנע צעבליטע יאָרן,
וואָס דו האָסט פון פאָלק פאַלק אַוועקגענעריסן.

have rejoiced with youthfulness.
Your people, the ones who were laughed at,
have shed the mold of olden days,
and you've poured your young, vital blood
out like impure water.
And you've used your radiant life
to satiate the idle.

Your blooming years
still cry out from country huts,
the years you wrenched from your people.

מאָרים ווינטשעווסקי

א. פרינץ (בער גרין) ~

(צו זיין 75-יאָריגן יוביליי)

זיידע טײַערער, יונג און פראָסט
וויל איך צו דיר רײדן:
ס׳איז פאַר אונז אַ הײסער רוף
דאָס וואָרט פון יונגן זיידן.

זיידע טײַערער, יונג און פריי
קלינגען דײַנע יאָר,
מיט קאַמף און וואָר
אין שטאָלצן דאָר,
וואָס שפאַנט
מיט ליכטיקע טריט
צום לאַנד
פון דײַנע טרוימען און דײַן ליד.

זיידע טײַערער, אונזער פּיאָנער,
מיר הויבן הויך דײַן וואָרט
און רויט געווער.
ס׳האָט אופגעשיינט אַף ווײסן קאָפ
דאָס גרויסע ליכט-סאָוועטן,
און ס׳קלינגט דײַן ליד אין ליד
פון פּראָלעט-פּאָעטן.

זיידע טײַערער, שווער און דאָרנדיק
איז געווען דײַן גאַנג—
איצט גייט אויף מיט פרײד און זין
דײַן יונג געזאַנג;
אַף דײַנע וועגן גייען מאַכנעם,

294

Morris Winchevsky (1930)

A. Prints (Ber Grin)

For his seventy-fifth birthday.

Grandfather dear, young and simple,
there's so much we'd discuss:
this young grandfather's spirit
is a warm call for us.

Grandfather dear, young and free,
your years ring out loud,
with your truth and your fight,
to a proud generation
that strides
brightly along
to the land
of your dreams and your song.

Grandfather dear, our pioneer,
we raise up high your words,
and firearms of red.
On your white head
has shone the great light—the Soviet,
and your song rings in the song
of the Prolet Poets.[2]

Grandfather dear, your walk along the way
was difficult and thorny—
now your young song rises
with victory and joy today
and multitudes follow in your steps

2. Prolet Poets: Ber Grin refers to the proletarian-identified poets of his generation who saw themselves as direct descendents of Winchevsky's circle of earlier proletarian or labor poets. See the translator's introduction to this section for more on this.

גייען אין דער שלאַכט;
כאַװוירים פֿון פֿאַבריקן און פֿון שאַכטעס
צינדן מיט די פֿאַקלען
לעצטע, לעצטע נאַכט.

זיידע טײַערער, ס'אַ גרױסער יאָנטעװ
אין טיפֿן שניי מיט ביקס צו װאָכן
אַף די פֿראָנטן,
ס'אַ יאָנטעװ–צו דערשפֿאַנען
פֿון האָסקאָלע ביז סאָװעטן
און מיט אייניקלעך צו לויפֿן
אין די סאָצגעװעטן.

זיידע טײַערער, ס'װעט די פֿאָן פֿון דיינע טעג
װי די זון באַלויכטן אונזער װעג,
ס'װעלן יאָרן דיינע העלפֿן
בויען באַריקאַדעס,
ס'װעלן יאָרן דיינע לויפֿן
אין די שלאָג־בריגאָדעס!

new to the fight;
comrades from factories and from mines
lit torches
the other night.

Grandfather dear, it's a great joy
to guard the front in deep snow
with rifle in hand.
A joy to march
from the *Haskole*[3] to the Soviets,
and to compete for the socialist cause,
running, with grandchildren, forward.

Grandfather dear, the flag of your days will fly,
lighting our way like the sun in the sky,
your years will help
build barricades,
your years, they'll run
in the shock brigades!

3. *Haskole*: Jewish enlightenment movement (Hebrew, *Haskalah*).

מאַני לייבּ'ן

שפרה ווייס ✑

איך וויל מיין ברויט ניט אין טאָרבּעס,
מעג עס האָבּן טויזנט עקן.
פֿון אור־אַלטן בוים און שטאַרקסטן האָלץ
וועל איך טאָקן מיר אַ שטעקן.

מיין וועג וועל איך גיין מיט שטאָלצן קאָפּ
פֿון לאַנד צו לאַנד,
מיט אַנדערע גייאינגע, ווי איך,
זייט בּיי זייט, האַנט אין האַנט.

און אַז קומען וועט אַנטקעגן מיר די צייט
מאָנען מיך אין רוֹלאַנד,
וועל איך מיין געטאָקטן שטעקן
דערלאַנגען גלייך אָן אַנדער האַנט.

To Mani Leyb

∽ Shifre Vays

I don't want a bag of bread,
even with a thousand crusts.
I'll carve myself a walking stick
from an ancient tree, the sturdiest.

I'll go my way, head held high,
from land to land,
with other wayfarers like me.
Side by side. Hand in hand.

And when it comes my time to set,
they'll summon me in dreamland.
And my handcrafted stick will pass
into someone else's hand.

העכט

⋘ חיים שווארץ

האָבן העכט אין פײער זיך געלײטערט
און געצונדן, און געצונדן
אין דער שװאַרצקײט פײערן.. .
האָבן העכט געלײטערטע
גערימען שטיקער נאַכט
און זײ אין פײערן געשלײדערט.
האָבן בײנערדיקע פינגער
פרײדיק זיך געפלאָכטן,
אין דער פינסטער זיך געפלאָכטן
און געבענטשט די העכט,
װאָס האָבן פײערן צעצונדן אין דער נאַכט.. .
האָבן פױסטן זיך געפלאָכטן
אין אַ קלאָלע זיך צעפלאָכטן:
װײ, װײ, טױזנט װײען די,
װאָס לעשן און פאַרלעשן פײערן,
װאָס דאַרפן ברײנגען ליכט;
װאָס דאַרפן ברײנגען פרײד
צו העכט געבײנערטע,
צו העכט מאַזאַליעטע,
אין װענט געשטײנערטע– – –

סעמ. לואים.

Hands (1925)

∾ Chaim Schwartz

Hands were purified in fire
and they kindled, and they kindled
fires in the blackness . . .
Purified hands have
ripped bits of night
and pitched them into fires.
Bony fingers
merrily intertwined
in the dark, intertwined
and blessed the hands
that kindled fires in the night . . .
Fists intertwined
and with a curse came unentwined:
Woe, a thousand woes to the ones
that quelched and squelched the fires,
that ought to have brought light;
that ought to have brought joy
to hands of bone,
to calloused hands,
in walls of stone . . .

דער בראַווער פּאָכדן

מעינקע קאַץ ✑

אייביק וועט דער פּאָכדן,
פֿאַר מײַן שטאָלצער באַבע מײַנע זיך שרעקן –
ס'זאָל מוישעראַבינום צוויבער-שטעקן,
פֿון מאַכיקן שלאָף זי ניט וועקן;
זי זאָל אַ טויטע און אַ לויטערע פֿון אוראַלטן קייוועור ניט קומען:
פֿון זייַן קאָל – צעבוינן דאָס בלעכענע ברומען,
מיט איר אָטעם, די אויפֿגעבלאָזענע שטאָלצן צעבלאָזן,
מיט איר בלוט, דעם וואָסערדיקן רויט פֿאַרמעקן
און נאָר דעם כאַרכל פֿון דעם כאַרקלער לאָזן.

1. ווענן פֿרייד און אומעט

אייביק וועט דער פּאָכדן,
אַף טונקעל שטעגן דעם טרוים באַפֿאַלן
און דרײַען זיך הייליק און ריטשען גערעכט:
„העי, פּאָעט, אָהער גיב פֿרייד,
פֿרייד – פֿאַר אומעטיקע קנעכט;
העי, פּאָעט, אָהער גיב שטראַלן –
ליכט – פֿאַר בלינדע קנעכט.
איך בין אַ היינט מיט טאַמען פֿול, ווי מיט זאַפֿט געשמאַקע סעדער.
דעם נעכטן, האָט שוין די צייַט דערוואָרגן,
דעם מאָרגן – פֿאַר קרענקלעכע באַטלאָנים;
דעם היינט גיב אָהער, אָהער דעם היינט.
פֿון דייַן ליד שיינט בעיסוילעם-שרעק.
דייַן ליד – אַ טוכלער ווענ צום מויזנלאָך;
ניט שטעק דייַן וואָנזין אין אונדזערע מונטערע רעדער."

The Brave Coward (1938)

～ Menke Katz

Ever will the coward[4]
shake before my Grandma Mona—
may the magic staff of Moses never
wake her from her mighty sleep.
May she never return, a poltergeist, from the ancient grave:
he may bend metal beams with his voice alone,
but she can blow away pride, overblown.
Her blood effaces his reddish water,
to leave but a trace of the chatterer's chatter.

I. ON JOY AND SADNESS

Ever will the coward
fear the dark, attack the dream
and wander round, rant righteously,
"Hey, poet, give us some joy,
joy for the ages of night;
hey, poet, give us some sunbeams,
light for a blind slave.
I'm a today with flavor, like orchard-fresh juice.
Time has just choked yesterday,
tomorrow is for sickly idlers;
give us today. Today—give it here.
Your poem shines with cemetery-fear.
Your poem's a stale path to mouseholes.
Stick not your sadness in our sprightly wheels."

---

4. This translation is from the version Katz published in his book *S'hot dos vort mayn bobe Mayne*. However, he also published a version of the poem in the *Frayhayt*, Aug. 4, 1938. In his book, Menke prefaces the poem by writing, "'The Brave Coward' is brought here as a document, which was the focus of 'the discussion'—the attack against me."

303

בראַװאָ, בראַװער פּאַכדן –
דײן פױקנדיקער רוף,
װעט געװיס פֿון דרימל, אַ ציטעריק העזעלע װעקן,
נאָר איך װעל צום שלאַכט ניט פֿירן
מײן ליד, מיט שטרױענעם גוף,
אױב אַפֿילע, טױזנט מאָל רױט צעצונדן.
מיט גװאָרע פֿון שטרױ, װי קען מען בערג רירן?
דעם מעכטיקן פֿײנט, װי װעסטו שרעקן,
אױב אַפֿילע, ער זאָל אַלײן זיך בינדן.

דײן װאָרט – אַ מילב מיט פֿאַנטאַסטישן פּױסט,
מאַנט פֿרײד – אַ פּלאָקן די גרױס,
װאָס קען נאָך אומעטיקער זײן?
פֿון גרױע רײד – אַזאַ שטורעם,
װאָס קען נאָך גרױער זײן?
פֿון גרױע רײד – אַזאַ שטורעם,
װער קען דערהערן?
מיט האַרץ פֿון שטאָל, מיט רואיק בלוט,
װי קען מען שװערן?

2. װען נעכטן, הײנט און מאָרגן

אַי, ברידער פֿון נעכטן – אַי, שװעסטער פֿון מאָרגן:
עס שװערט מײן האַרץ, עס שװערט מײן בלוט,
אײך װעלן ניט בײזע צײן צעקריצן.
אײך װעט ניט גרײכן דעם פּאַכדנס רוט.
איך װעל מיט האַרץ און מיט בלוט אײך שיצן.

אײביק װעט די אומעטיקע אַלטקײט יונג האַלטן די װײנען.
אײביק װעט דער װײטסטער מאָרגן,
געאָרעמט מיט דעם װײטסטן נעכטן,
דורך צױבער פֿון נאָענטסטן הײנט שײנען.

3. און דו ביסט אומעטיק װי טױזנט „קוני אײלאַנד" זונען

דײן צאָרן – אַ פֿײער־רײז,
געניג געװיס דעם אומעט פֿון אַ פֿליגעלע פֿאַרברענען –

Bravo, brave coward,
your drumroll
will surely wake a trembling hare from a snooze,
but I won't drive my poem
off to battle, with its straw body,
even if it's burnt a thousand times.
How do you move mountains with the strength of straw?
How will you frighten the mighty enemy,
even if he ties himself up on his own?

Your word's a mite with fantastic fists,
demanding joy—as big as a cudgel,
what can be gloomier than this?
Such a storm from gray talk,
what can be grayer than this?
Such a storm from gray talk,
who will hear it out, and care,
with a heart of steel, with calm blood,
and how can anyone swear?

2. ON YESTERDAY, TODAY AND TOMORROW

Oh, brothers of yesterday, oh, sisters of tomorrow,
my heart, it swears. My blood, it swears,
evil teeth won't scratch you.
The coward's rod won't catch you.
I, with my heart and blood will defend you.

Ever will gloomy old times cry like the young.
Ever will the furthest tomorrow,
arm in arm with the furthest yesterday,
shine through the charm of the nearest today.

3. AND YOU ARE GLOOMY AS A THOUSAND CONEY ISLAND SUNS

Your fury is a fire-breathing dragon,
which can surely burn the sadness of a fly.

וואָלט נאָר דיין האַס געבן, דעם פיינט אין אויג אַ גראַבל;
וואָלט נאָר דיין פלאַם קענען, אַ פּראָסטיק שטיבעלע באַהייצן.
ס'פּלאַצט דיין וואָרט ווי ליכט אַ מאָבל,
געגונג אַזש – די נעכט פאַרפלייצן,
געגונג מיט שטראַלן – דוירעם שיך צו פוצן –
נאָר מיר ווערט פינצטערער-פינצטער פון אַזויפיל ליכט
און מיר ווערט טרויעריק-טרויעריק פון אַזויפיל פרייד.
און נאָר דיין פרייד קען מיך שרעקן,
ווי אין אַ מאַיסעביכל – אַמאָל-אַמאָל,
אין מיכאַלישעק, באַנאַכט, אַרום בעיסוילעם:
ווען אַ גוילעם מיט אויסגעקלערטן קאָל,
מיט אַ שעד-געוויכט און אַ טאַכריכים-קלייד,
פלעגט די מייסים, מיט אַ פריילעך האָפּקע ווען.

ווייל דו ביסט אומעטיק ווי טויזנט „קוני-איילאַנד" זונען,
איז אומעטיקער פון אַלע אומעטן דיין פרייד;
ווייל פריידיקער פון אַלע פריידן, קען דעם דיכטערס אומעט זיין,
האָבן מיינע טעג, אַזויפיל אומעט געפונען
און ווי ס'קען אויך די פינצטערניש דורך העלסטער פרייד שיינען,
שיינט אויך די פינצטערניש דורך מיין ליד.

איך גיב דיר אַלע טייכן פון רינענדיקע קראָנען,
איך נעם אַ טראָפן – פאַרקלערטן טוי.
איך גיב דיר אַלע רעגנבויגנס פון ווערטערדיקע ראַקעטן,
איך נעם פון אַלע פייערן – אָן אײנציקן פונק
און האַלט האָב איך אַזוי:
אָן אײנציקער פונק, דורך אַלע פינצטערנישן שפּאַנען
און האַלט האָב איך אַזוי:
זיין אַליין דאָס ליכט וואָס העלט דעם כוישעך אַרום מיר.

איך האָב געזען,
אַ פונק – אַלע פייערן פאַרשטעלן;
איך האָב געזען,
אַ בלינדן נעכטן – דעם מאָרגן צעהעלן.

If your hate would only scratch the enemy in the eye,
if your flame could only heat a frosty little house . . .
Your word explodes like lightning to a flood,
even enough to flood the night.
Enough sunbeams to polish generations of shoes,
but it grows so dark for me from so much light,
and I grow so sad from so much joy.
And only your joy can frighten me,
like a storybook, once upon a time,
in Michaleshik, at night, around the cemetery:
when a golem with a made-up voice,
with a ghost face and a shroud for clothes
used to rouse the dead in a happy dance.

Because you're gloomy as a thousand Coney Island suns,
your joy is gloomier than gloom itself;
because a poet's gloom can be more joyful than joy,
my days have found so very much gloom
and as the darkness also shines through the brightest joy,
darkness also shines through my song.

I give you all the rivers of running faucets,
I take a drop to think about the dew.
I give you all the rainbows of wordy rockets,
I take a single spark from all the fires,
and I like it like that,
a single spark spreading through all this darkness,
and I like it like that
to be, myself, this light that brightens the darkness around me.

I've seen
every fire hidden by a spark;
seen
tomorrow lit by blind yesterday's dark.

איך האָב געזען,
דעם אָקטאָבער, ווי טויזנט מאַיען בליִען;
איך האָב געזען,
דעם שענסטן פויגל אויך פון וואָרים זיין יעניקע ציִען
און איך וועל ווי דער פֿאָכדן זיך ניט שרעקן,
מיין וואָרט אויסטאָן נאַקעט, אפילע אין מויזנלאַך.

איך האָב געזען,
אַ נאַכט אָן ענדלאָזע טאָנן;
איך האָב געזען,
אַ שטורעם – דעם פֿאָכדן פֿאַריאָנן.

4. די טפילע פון באַראָבאַן

און ווען פון צופיל בראָזגען ווערט אויך טויב דער וויסטער בראָזגער,
שטומט אַ טפילע אוים, דער איינזאָמער פויק:
קום, אַ בראַווער פויקער, קום –
ווי זאָל איך אויסבענקען די וואָלקנס,
אַז ניט דער רעגן,
נאָר אַ האָגל האַרטע רייד פויקט אין מיר,
קום, אַ בראַווער פויקער, קום;
שטומט אַ טפילע אוים דער איינזאָמער פויק:
קום, אַ בענקשאַפט – קום, אַ ליבסטע, קום,
ווייל אנדערשט איז אַן דיר מיין פֿרייד – פון פֿרייד,
ווי אנדערשט ס'איז אַ דופטיקע פינצטערניש אין פֿרייען פעלד –
פון אַ פאַרמישפעטער פינצטערניש אין טויטנקאַמער;
און קום, אַ, טרויעריקע פֿלייט –
גיב אַ טונקלקייט וואָס נאָגט ביז לויטערסטן שיין,
אַ שיין וואָס נעמט אדורך ביז טונקלקייט.
אַ, גיב אַ פֿרייד וואָס שוידערט אויף ביז טרערן –
אַ פֿרייד, אַ טרויעריקע פֿלייט,
וואָס הויבט די טיפן אויף,
און טראָגט זיי ביז דער בענקענדיקסטער הויך אַרויף –
אַ, גיב אַ פיין וואָס זאָל יאַנטעוון די וואָך.

I've seen
October bloom like a thousand Mays;
seen
the prettiest bird nourished by a worm,
and I won't cower like a coward,
stripping my word to nakedness, even in a mousehole.

I've seen
one night take forever to reach day,
seen
a storm drive the coward away.

4. PRAYER OF THE DRUM

And when the gloomiest drummer grows deaf from too much drumming,
a prayer grows quiet, the lonesome drum:
come, oh brave drummer, come . . .
how should I convince the clouds
that it isn't the rain,
but speech, hard as hail, that drums in me,
come, oh brave drummer, come . . .
a prayer grows quiet, the lonesome drum:
come, oh longing, come oh loved one, come . . .
for my joy without you is other than joy.
How different is a fragrant, pulsing darkness in the free field
from a condemned darkness in a death chamber,
and come, oh sad flute . . .
give us a darkness that gnaws through to the purest kind of shining,
a shining that penetrates through to the darkness.
Oh, give a joy that shivers to tears,
a joy, sad flute,
that lifts the depths,
and carries them to peaks of yearning,
oh, give a pain to make weekdays holy.

ממעמקים

משה נאַדיר ❧

ווער זינגט אין פינצטערניש – פֿון ליכט,
זיצנדיק אין פֿײכטן תהום?
עס איז דער דיכטער, עס איז איך –
דער לעצטער אײנוואוינער פֿון סדום.

פֿון דער גליווערדיקער טיף,
עבֿלאָ, אויסגאָנגלאָ –
איך זינג דער שיינקייטס בלויעם מיף,
ווי דורכגעגילט ווענעציש גלאָז.

אַז באָמבעס קראָכן אין דער נאָכט
און אימה עסט דעם פּחד אויף,
בײ די וואָכפֿיערן עס וואָכט
דער גייסט אַלײן – אָן דעם גוף.

ווען יאוש, ווי אַ צווייג פֿון בלײ,
נעמט אַרום די זעל – אַ רײף,
איך זינג פֿון ליבע אויפֿדאָסניי
אין אַלע בלוטנעפֿלעקטע הייף.

ווען מענטשנשנמאָרכן בליצן אויס
דעם לעצטן פֿונק פֿון כלם פֿאָרב,
איך ברען דעם מוסטער פֿון אַ רויז
אַריין אין איובדיקן שאַרב...

דאָס פֿײער ביז צום האָלדז? די ליפּ
איז פֿרײ פֿאַר לעצטן תהילים-שיר,
זי לאָכט מיט זינגענדיקן כליפּ
פֿון טויט אַלײן, וואָס לאָכט אין מיר...

יאַנואַר 23, 1942

Out of the Depths (1942)

                                                  ~ Moyshe Nadir

Who is singing of light in the dark,
sitting in a damp abyss?
It's the poet, it is I,
Sodom's last dweller. I sing of this

out of the hardened depths,[5]
echoless, exitless,
I sing beauty's blue myth,
like gilding through Venetian glass.

While bombs are cracking in the night
and fear devours terror,
the spirit leaves the body
to keep watch beside the watchfires.

When despair rims round the soul
like a branch of lead,
in all the bloodstained alleyways
I sing of love again.

When the last spark of thought
flashes through the human brain,
I burn the pattern of a rose
into Job's broken shard.

The fire's reached my neck?
For the final psalm, my lips are free,
laughing with melodic sobs,
at death itself, which laughs in me.

---

5. Out of the Depths: a reference to Psalm 130, "Mem hameykim."

טויטע כריזאַנטעמעס

אין זיינע לידער און פּאָעמעס
בלעטלעך פון טויטע כריזאַנטעמעס,
וואָעמס פון קינע,
אָקסן-הערנער פון אַרגענטינע,
שטײנער פון ירושלים,
זאַמדן פון מצרים,
ביינער פון טויטן טאָל, –
נאָר ניט קיין מענטשלעך קול.

312

Dead Chrysanthemums (1964)

∽ Ber Grin

In his songs and poems:
petals of dead chrysanthemums,
vases from China,
bull-horns from Argentina,
stones from Jerusalem,
sands from Egypt,
bones from Death Valley—
    but not a human voice.

Wars to End All Wars

While Proletpen's focus was largely the United States, increasing violence between World War I and World War II made it impossible to ignore the turmoil in Europe. With the outbreak of the Spanish Civil War, Spain became a critical focus for Proletpen. Simultaneously, violence against the Jews of Eastern Europe increased, especially in Germany and Poland, and the Hitler regime began its reign of terror against Jews and leftists. The possibility of a second World War became a growing concern in the Yiddish press in America, particularly in the leftist *Frayhayt*.

For the proletarian poet, the Spanish Civil War embodied the struggle between workers and fascists. Anti-fascists from around the world traveled to Spain to help quell the fascist onslaught personified by Franco and his allies. Twenty percent of the International Brigade were Jews. The Spanish Civil War was also an opportunity to give substance to the call for an international workers' party. Proletarian poets such as Aaron Kurtz devoted entire volumes to those fighting in Spain. Kurtz's book *No Pasarán* intersperses poems written in the form of letters from various worker-partisans with poems about broader war motifs. The title poem, "No Pasarán" (literally "They shall not pass") draws from a phrase that came to stand for worldwide leftist solidarity against Franco's counter-revolution.

History would prove the Spanish Civil War to be a dress rehearsal for a struggle against fascism and Nazism. Long before Theodore Adorno's suggestion that "to write poetry after Auschwitz would be barbaric," Zishe Vaynper writes, in his 1938 "Word," "Now isn't the time for verbal images. We need bandages for our wounds." By the 1930s, Proletpen was almost

315

prophetically aware that atrocities in Europe would change literature for-ever—particularly Yiddish literature. And yet it is poetry that underscores the universality of war, with words, themes, and images that repeat them-selves from the programs to Spain to the rise of Hitler.

שפּאַניש וויגליד

ון אַהרן קורץ

ס׳פֿײַפֿט דער ווינט,
דורך אונזער דאַך,
הימל צינדט
זיך אפֿדערנאַכט.

קינד מײַנס, קינד,
אָפֿגיך שלאָף אײַן.
זאָל דער ווינט
דיר זײַן ווי ווײַן.

וואַלד און פֿעלד
דער טויט פֿאַרהילכט.
מאַמען קװעלט
ניט מער קײַן מילך.

טאַטע איז
אין שלאַכט אַװעק.
מאַמע ווינט
אַ וויג מיט שרעק.

קאָרן, ווייץ
וואַרט אָפֿן שניט.
טאַטע שטײַט
הינטער מאַדריד.

שרעק זיך ניט,
מײַן טײַער קינד:
טאַטע היט
מאַדריד פֿון הינט.

טאַטע היט
דײַן ליבע שטאָט
פֿון פֿאַשיסטס
פֿאַרסמטן טראָט.

318

Spanish Lullaby (1938)

∾ Aaron Kurtz

The wind whistles past
our roof, and light
flickers in
the sky tonight.

Child, *mayn kind,*
sleep, child of mine.
May the wind
be like wine.

Woods and field
resound with death.
There's no more milk
at Mama's breast.

Papa's gone
away to war.
Mama rocks
your crib with fear.

Rye and wheat
should be harvested.
Papa's keeping
the dogs from Madrid.

Don't be frightened,
child of mine.
Papa's watching
Madrid, from behind.

Papa's keeping
your city safe
from the fascists'
poisoned step.

קינד מײַנס, קינד,
אַפֿגיך שלאָף אײַן.
זאָל דער ווינט
דיר זײַן ווי וויין.

Child, *mayn kind,*
sleep, child of mine.
May the wind
be like wine.

אַנדאַלוזיער לאַנדשאַפט

(פון אַ מאָלערס אַ בריוו)

אַהרן קורץ ⮜

שפּאַניע – שײנקײט
פון אַ טױזנט קאָלאָראַדעם, –
איז די טעמע
פאַר אַ בלוטיקער איליאַדע.

גאָלדענע פעלד־בלומען – בלאָנדע עופהלעך
איבערגעפּאָרענע,
קאָפּ אַף קאָפּ, װי די יונגע הײסע מתים –
האַלדזן זיך,
װי פאַראָרטײלטע געליבטע
װאָס שטאַרבן אײנגעקלאַמערט אין ליבעס לעצטער רנע.

אַ װאַלד מיט צװײען הענגען
האַלב־פאַרבראָכענע – אָן אַרמי מיט אָרעמס
אָפּגעשאָסענע –
אַ װאַלד ברענענדיקע צװײען װינט זיך
איבערן טאָג מיט טױט צעלײגט אַף הײסן פעלד,
װאָס אָטעמט
מיטן לעצטן, שװערן פּולס
פון אױסגײענדיקן לעבן.

די זון
שטײט איבערן פעלד
און קוקט
װי גיך
מע װעט אױפקלײבן די טױטע.
אַף יעדן שלאַכטפעלד און בית־עלמין שטעלט די זון זיך אָפּ.
אױב די זון דערװאָרעמט הערצער פון געליבטע
אַף בלוװאַרן און אין סעדער,
איז זי דאָ – דאָס פײערדיקע,
פירנדיקע אױג פון ניהנום:

322

Andalusian Landscape (1938)

Aaron Kurtz

From a painter's letter.

Spain: splendor
of a thousand Colorados—
the theme
for a bloody Iliad.

Golden wildflowers: blonde infants
driven over,
head upon head, how the young, hot corpses,
are kissing
like condemned lovers
who die, embraced in love's last instant.

A forest of branches hangs,
like desperate hands, an army of arms
shot away,
a forest of burning branches that sway
above the day, strewn alongside death across hot fields,
breathing
the last heavy pulse
of leaking life.

The sun
stands over the field
and watches
how fast
the dead will be gathered.
The sun stops at every battlefield and graveyard.
If the sun warms lovers' hearts
on boulevards, in orchards,
then it's here: the blazing,
guiding eye from hell.

„גיכער, גיכער
ליידיקט אָפּ דאָס פֿעלד –
מאַכט אָרט פֿאַר יענע!"

אַ היינטיקן מאָלער אין שפּאַניע
גייט ניט אָן דאָס אַמאָליקע מאָלן.
אַנטיקן
זיינען מער ניט קיין טעמע:
אין חרובֿע טעמפּלען לינט אַשיק צעשאָסן
די אַלטערטום־מאַניע,
די טעמע איז – טויט אַף די בערג, טויט אין די טאָלן,
ברענענדיקע בריקן,
וואָס הימל־פּיַיערן צענעמען
און לעבנס געראַנגל אין די פֿעלד־שפּיטאָלן.

הפקר –
דאָס איז טויט.
פֿאַרזיכט –
דאָס איז לעבן.
געפֿינסטו זיך – צווישן די צוויי,
וווייסטו וואָס צו נעמען,
און וועמען וואָס צו געבן.

איך זע איין בילד פֿאַר איצט פֿאַר זיך שטענדיק:
אַף יעדן נייעם לייוונט
וועט מיַין לייוונג – אין דעם בילד זיך וועגנדן:
אין רויכיקע אַטעליעס, אַף יענער זיַיט פֿון לעבן,
ביז שפּעט באַטאָאָנ – שלאָפֿן אָרעמע עסטעטן.
און – לאַנגזאָם, לאַנגזאָם הייבן זיך קעפּ איבער פֿאַראָפּעטן.
ראַשיק שפּרינגנען ברינאָדעם אַרויף
פֿון טראַנשייען.
די שמעקנדיקע ערד עפֿנט טויזנט ניַיע קבֿרים יעדע נאַכט,
און די זון
קומט יעדן טאָג
צו אַלעמענס לוויה.

"Faster, faster,
empty the field!
Make room for the next!"

A contemporary painter in Spain
doesn't care to depict the past.
Antiques
are no longer a theme.
In temples, shot to ash
is obsession with old times,
the theme is death on the mountains, death in the valleys,
burning bridges
that heaven's fires consume
and life's struggle in field hospitals.

Abandon:
this is death.
Caution:
this is life.
You exist between these two,
you know what to take,
and whom to give what.

I see one image now, always before me:
on every new canvas,
my redemption will depend on this image:
in smoke-filled studios, on the other side of life,
poor aesthetes sleep until late in the day.
And slowly, slowly, heads come up over the mounds.
Brigades will jump hastily
from trenches.
The smelly earth opens a thousand new graves a night,
and the sun
comes every day
to everyone's funeral.

„נאָ פּאַסאַראַן!"

(דאָס שפּאַניש ליד)

‎ אהרן קורץ

דאָס ליד זינגט אַף אַלע ראַדיאָס.
דאָס ליד זינגט דורך דיינע דינסטע אָדערן
און לייכט־אויף אין דיר
דערלעבער פון אַלע פיינסטע אַריעם.

דאָס ליד איז די ליבשאַפט פון גוטן מענטש,
דאָס ליד שמעקט מיט בלומעזון פון אַנדאַלוזיע,
מעלאָדיע – פון לעבנס צעוװייטיקט האַרץ
אַף טויזנטיאַריקע אילוזיעס.

דאָס ליד איז דער טעם פון מאַלאַנער װײן,
פון סעװוילער גאָלדענע אָראַנזשערײַען,
דאָס ליד איז שפּאַניעס פּלאַטערדיקע פרייד,
וואָס זינגט איר טרוים דורך אומעט פון טליענדיקע װײַען.

דאָס ליד זינגט מיטן שװויינן פון מאַדרידס אלמנות,
דאָס ליד זינגט מיט צער פון ליבע אין אַ װעלט פון שנאה,
דאָס ליד זינגט מיט איינגעהאַלטענעם געװוויין
פון זוכנדיקע הענט און אויגן אין אַשיקע רואינעס.

דאָס ליד איז
די טיף פון טיפעניש
פון דורות ראָמאַנצערק,
דאָס ליד איז דער דראַנג
צו די מענטשלעכסטע באַנערן.

דאָס ליד, דאָס ליד: „נאָ פּאַסאַראַן!" –
זינגט איבער דער וועלט דער גאָרער.
װי גליענדיקער מערב־היממל גליט דיין גלויבן אין דעם טאָן.
יעדעם פאָלק האָט אַזאַ ליד.
אַזאַ פאָלק – קען ניט אייביק זיין פאַרלאָרן.

326

No Pasarán (1938)

～ Aaron Kurtz

Spanish Song

They sing this song on all the radios.
They sing this song through your narrowest veins
and it lights you up,
glory of the finest arias.

This song is the love of good people,
this song smells of sunflowers in Andalusia,
melody of life's aching heart
from thousand year illusions.

This song tastes of Malaga wine,
of golden Seville oranges,
this song is the fluttering joy of Spain,
that sings its dream through the sadness of smoldering pain.

This song sings the silence of the widowed of Madrid,
this song sings the sorrow of love in a world of enmity.
This song sings with the stifled cry,
of searching hands, of eyes in ashen ruins.

This song is
the depth of depths
of generations of *romanceros,*
this song is the striving
for the most human of desires.

This song, this song: *"No Pasarán!"*—
sings across the whole wide world.
Your belief glows from its melody like the sky glows in the west.
Every nation has such a song.
Such a nation can't be forever lost.

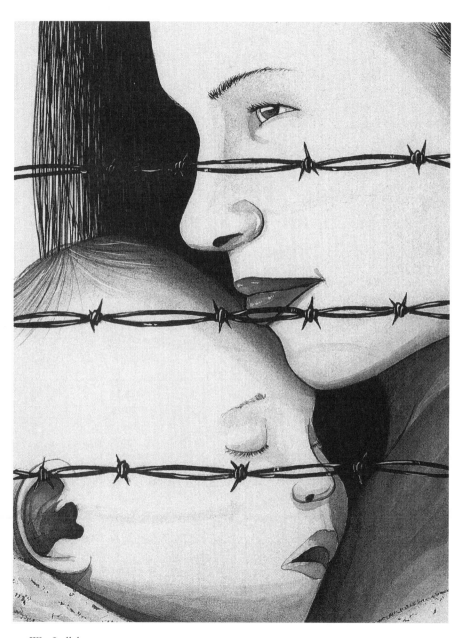

War Lullaby

מלחמה וויגליד

דאָרע טײטלבוים ❧

שלאָף ניט, קינד מיינס, שלאָף ניט איצט,
האַלט די אויגן אָפן,
זע אין הימל ווי עס בליצט,
ס׳האָט אַ בליץ דיין הויז געטראָפן.

ס׳איז דיין בעטל פול מיט ליים,
און דיין צימער פול מיט ציגל,
אַ בית־עולם איז דיין היים,
און אַ קבר איז דיין וויגל.

וויין, מיין קינד, נאָך שטאַרקער וויין,
דיינע אויגן – רויטע קנעפ.
איך וויל הערן דיין געוויין, –
ס׳איז אַ סימן אַז דו לעבסט.

ס׳איז איבער דיר ניטאָ קיין דאַך,
קענסטו זען די שטערן,
זע ווי רויט עס איז דער „מילכשליאַך"
און ווי רויט די „בערן".

אויף דער לבנה, זע, בלוט־טראָפנס,
ווי אין אַ געלבל פון אַן איי,
אַזוי, ביי דיין צוקאָפנס,
דיין מאַמע׳ס האַרץ פאַרגייט.

די לבנה – אַ מאַמע אין געבערן,
וואָס האָט נאָרוואָס אַ קינד געהאַט.
ס׳איז איר קינד דער קליינער שטערן, –
ציטערט ווי אין האַרבסט אַ בלאַט.

שלאָף ניט, קינד מיינס, שלאָף ניט איין,
ס׳וועט באַלד ליכטיק ווערן,
ווי נאָר עס קומען אונדזערע אריין
וועלן זיי אונדז דערהערן.

War Lullaby (1944)

꩜ Dora Teitelboim

Don't sleep, baby, keep your eyes
wide open a moment more,
watch the flashes cross the sky,
a flash has found your door.

Your little bed is full of clay,
bricks fill your room.
A cemetery is your house,
your cradle is a tomb.

Baby, cry. Your eyes are red
buttons, from a hard cry.
Let your sobbing be a sign
for me that you're alive.

You can see the stars out. There's
no roof above your head.
See how red the Milky Way
and the Bears, how red.

How your mother's heart dies
at your bedside. All the while,
the moon, a birthing mother,
has just brought forth a child.

Her child is a tiny star,
like an autumn leaf, it shakes.
And on the moon, look, drops of blood,
like spots of blood in eggs.

Don't sleep, baby, don't drift off,
the sky will soon be pale,
as soon as our allies come marching in,
we will tell our tale.

פֿון מיין שטעטעלע אַ גרוס

(פֿון בריוו פֿון פּוילן)

וצ ≀ חיים פּלאָטקין

.1

כ'שווייג איצט. אַ שווייגן וואָס קען ס'האַרץ אַרויסשלאָגן...
אויף שויבן פֿלאַצן טראָפּנס רעגן.
ס'וואָרנט דער זייגער: באַלד וועט נעמען טאָגן –
זינקט אומרו אין מיר ווי ציין ביים זעגן:

ווי אַן אָפֿענע וואונד לינט פֿאַר מיר דער בריוו,
וואָס אָן אַ שיר מאָל כ'האָב דורכגעלייענט.
כ'האָב דערפֿילט דעם צער פֿון טיפֿסטן טיף –
פֿונם מענטש וואָס האָט ביים שרייבן געוויינט.

דער מענטש פֿון בריוו איז מיר נאָענט און ליב:
זיין נאָמען און שטאָט מ ו ז בלייבן דאָ פֿרעמד...
כ'זע איר פֿנים אין די פֿינטעלעך פֿון מיין ליד:
– די פּוילישע שפּיקעס האָבן לאַנגע הענט...

.2

אין מיין שטעטעלע געווען איז שוין דער דריטער פּאָגראָם:
דעכער האָבן געקראַכט ווי די שויבן.
אין חושך־נאַכט האָט גערעוועט דער פֿירער־כוליגאַן:
– „די זשידעס ברענט אויס מיט בענזין די אויגן!!..."

כ'זע איצט לאָזער דעם קופּער־שמיד,
פֿאַלן ביים שוועל מיט אַ צעבראָכענעם שאַרבן;
און ווי אַ שאָטן, יחיאל־בער, דעם תהילים־איד,
וואָס „פֿון די וואונדן, שמועסט מען, וועט ער שטאַרבן".

כאַסיע לייזער־שלומ'ס, וואָס שטייט מיטן עפֿלסטראָנאָן
מ'פֿלענט איר רופֿן: „די עלנד־ווייסטע יונגע אלמנה"
איבער איר האָט זיך „דערבאַרעמט" אַ זינדל פֿון אַ רייכן „פּאַן"
איז איר יונג לעבן אויך איצט אין אַ סכנה...

332

Greetings from My Shtetl (A Letter from Poland) (1937)

∿ Chaim Plotkin

1.

I'm silent now. A stillness to carry my heart away . . .
raindrops explode on windowpanes.
The clock warns it will soon be day,
unrest sinks into me like the teeth of a saw.

The letter lies before me, an open wound,
I've read through it countless times by now.
I've felt the pain, the most profound,
of the one who, weeping, wrote it down.

The letter's author is near and dear,
I see her face in my punctuation;
her name and town *can't* be mentioned here.
I fear the Poles' retaliation.

2.

It's the third pogrom my shtetl's seen.
Rooftops cracked like windowglass.
In the dark of night the gang leader roared,
"Burn the Yids' eyes out with benzene."

Now I see Lozer the coppersmith, who
falls, skull cracked, in the entryway.
And Yekhiel-Ber, the town's head Jew,
will die from his wounds, they say.

Leyzar-Sholem's Khasye's by the apple stand.
"Lost and lonesome widow" we called her.
A rich Pan's[1] son used a "merciful" hand,
but now her young life's back in danger . . .

1. Pan: Polish for "Mister."

מאָטל'ען, דעם שטעפּער, האָבן זיי ווי אַ שעפּס געבונדן
און צעפּיצלט אין הויז אַלץ, צעבראָכן און צעשטאָכן.
זיי וואָלטן די כאָטע ווי אַ ליכט אָנגעצונדן –
ווען ניט סטעפּאַן, דער שוסטער, זיין פּוילישער שכן...

.3

„געדענקסטו, ברודער, ווי מיר זיינען אין קעלער געזעסן
און ס'לעבן אונזערס איז געהאָנגען אויף אַ האָר...
דאַן איז אויך ניט געווען ווי היינט – וואָס אָפּצועסן –
האָט מען פּאַדאָטקעס כאָטש ניט געדאַרפּט אָפּצאָלן יענעם יאָר...

„דעמאָלט איז דאָך געווען – מלחמה. היינט איז דאָך כּלומר'שט – פֿרידן –
ליינט מען אויף אונזערע רוקנס שטייער נאָך שטייער!..
ז י י שלעפּן פֿון אונזערע הייזער וואָס זיי קענען נאָר קריגן:
אַ ווינקל, אַ קישן, אַ סאָנאָן קאַרטאָפּל פֿון פֿייער...
‎– – – – – – – – – – – – – – – –
‎– – – – – – – – – – – – – – – –

כ'לייען דעם בריוו מיט גריזשענדן פֿיבער,
די געליטענע פֿון מיין שטעטעלע – כ'געדענק זיי נאָך גוט:
כ'וואָלט צום הארץ געדריקט די פֿאַרוואונדעטע גלידער
און מערדערס נאָמען פֿאַרשריבן – מיט טראָפּנס בלוט!..

Motl the quilter was bound like a lamb,
his house broken and slashed—nothing left whole.
They would have lit the hut like a candle
but for Stefan the shoemaker, neighbor and Pole.

3.
"Remember brother, how we cowered
in the cellar? Our lives hung by a hair . . .
Back then, like today, there was nothing to eat—
at least there weren't taxes to pay that year.

"That was war. Now it's supposedly peacetime.
So they lay tax upon tax on our backs.
They've emptied our homes of all they can:
a cradle, a cushion, potato from the pan."
— —— — — — — — — — — — — —

— —— — — — — — — — — — — —

I am reading the letter with gnawing fever.
How well I remember the innocent victims.
I would press their wounded limbs to my heart
and write, in blood, the murderers' names!

שטעטל מיינס ביים דניעסטער

בער גרין ‎⸾

איך האָב אַ גאַנצע נאַכט געוויינט,
שטעטעלע, מיין שטעטעלע, מיין ליבע היים;
טייער איז מיר דיין יעדער שטיין,
טייער יעדעס שטיבעלע פון ליים.

איך האָב קריעה געריסן אויף מיין הויט,
מיט ביטערע טרערן געוויינט;
ניין, דו ביזט ניט טויט,
ליב מיינס, ביין פון מיין געביין.

ניין, איך גלויב ניט – עס לעבט דיין עדה,
שטעטעלע מיינס, היים פון מיין טאַטע און זיידע;
איר לעבט, איר לעבט, בר︌ידער מיינע, שוועסטער,
אין שטעטעלע מיינעם ביים דניעסטער.

טויט? זיכער וועלן מיינע אויערן טויבן
אײדער איך וועל דאָס גלויבן.
ניין, דו ביזט ניט פאַרשוואונדן,
אויף אייביק, וויג מיינע, בין איך מיט דיר פאַרבונדן.

שטעטעלע מיינס פנים פון מיין פנים,
וויי איז מיר פאַר דיין יעדן געסל.
פאַר יעדן טראָפן בלוט וועלן מיר מאָנען,
דיינע קדושים וועלן מיר קיינמאָל ניט פאַרגעסן.

My Shtetl on the Dnestr

∽ Ber Grin

I cried all night, my little shtetl,
my shtetl, beloved hometown. What
a treasure is your every stone,
how precious each mud hut.

I have rent my own skin,
cried with bitter tears;
my flesh, bone of my bones,
you haven't disappeared.

No I don't believe it. Your congregation lives.
You live, you live, brother, sister,
in my shtetl, home of my father and his,
in my little shtetl on the Dnestr.

Dead? My ears will go deaf
before I believe it's true.
No, you haven't disappeared,
my cradle, forever I'm bound to you.

My shtetl, image of my image,
how I cherish every alleyway.
For every drop of your martyrs' blood
we'll demand they pay.

קינד, דו נייער מענטש

מלכה לי ~

דו שלאָפסט, מיין קינד, ביי דיין וויגל איך וואַך.
דער הימל צוקאָפנס – אַ בלוי געשליפענער דאַך.
פון דאָרטן די זון אין נאָלד גייט אַרויס
און קושט דיר דיין ראָזע פּנים'ל אויס.

איך טרוים דיין אויפבלי אין מאָרגן, מיין קינד,
דו צווייג פון מיין לייב, מיט מיין לעבן פאַרשפינט.
די וועלט איז פינצטער – אַ מאָנסטער נאָך רויב.
דו, מענטש פונעם מאָרגן, אין דיין טאָג איך גלויב.

קינד, מיין שוואַרצאַפּל, דו מענטש פון מאָרגן,
איך גיס אין דיר איבער מיין פאַרפייניקטע שטים;
ווי ברויזיקן וויין אין אַ געשליפענעם גלאָז;
טרינק מיין לעבן פון פון ביטערן קום.

עס האָט געוווּנגען אַמאָל מיין פּאָלק אונטער קנוט,
דער טאָל איז פון טרערן און מענטשלעכן בלוט.
מיט טרערן געמישט איז דער בעכער פון פיין,
ביים ווינ ווען דו שלאָפסט, אַזוי זינג איך דיך איין.

דו, מענטש פונעם מאָרגן, ביי דיין וויגל איך וואַך,
איך זע דיך שפּאַנען אויף אַ ליכטיקן שליאַך,
פאַרבריידערט מיט פעלקער איך זע ווי דו שפּרייזט,
פון היינטיקן גרויל וועסטו זיין אויסגעלייזט.

פון דורות צעשרינען עס יאָמערט מיין מויל,
פון ליבער צעפייניקט איך וווייטיק דאָס קול.
און דער הימל איז בלוי, אַלעמאָל בלוי געווען,
עס האָבן דורות פאַר מיר אויך די בלויקייט געזען.

ביים ווינ ווען דו שלאָפסט שרייב איך אָט דאָס ליד,
נעם די שורות אין גאַנג פון דיין יונגלעבן מיט.
מיין קינד פונעם מאָרגן, ווען איך וועל פאַרגיין,
זאָלסט דערמאָנען דיין מאַמעס געביין...

338

Child, You New Man

∽ Malka Lee

Sleep child in your cradle, I'm watching you.
The sky overhead is a roof polished blue.
The golden sun slips down from its place
and kisses your rosy little face.

I dream that tomorrow you bloom, little one,
branch of my flesh, of my life you're spun.
The world is dark as a beast after prey.
Man of tomorrow, I believe in your day.

You, apple of my eye, man of the morn,
I pour into you my voice, pained and worn,
like a long-stemmed goblet of well-brewed wine;
drink a bitter toast of my life, child of mine.

My people sang under a whip long ago . . .
it's a valley of tears and blood, and so
the tears are mixed into the pitcher of pain.
By your cradle I'll sing you a sleepy refrain.

Here, man of tomorrow, I sing your refrain,
as I watch you stride down a bright, unpaved lane,
a brother to nations, you go your own way,
free from the trembling of today.

Generations have turned my mouth down with fear.
My voice aches from those lives and each painful year.
And the sky is clear blue, it's always been blue,
generations have left me this, too.

I'm writing this song by your cradle today.
May your young troubles drift away.
Child of tomorrow, when my life is done,
be there to remember your mother, my son . . .

תוהו ובהו

אסתר שומיאטשער ❧

דער אָוונט אויף מיין פֿענסטער לייגט זיך שווער און מיד.
אַ שלאַכטפֿעלד איז דער טאָג.
עס וויינט מיין יעדער גליד.
אַן אָנגעקלאָנטע שטיי איך שטום:
אַ פֿאָלק גייטאָפּ אין בלוט –
און מיר דאָ
גייען אום
ווי אַלע טעג פֿון יאָר
מיט זאָרג;
אַ שווערער לאַסטוואָגן
די וואָר.

אָ, פֿינסטערניש,
טראָעט אָפּ אַ רגע פֿון מיין שוועל!
דאָס בלוט שרייט פֿון תהום,
איך וואַרט אויף אַ באָפֿעל.
נאָר קיינער רירט זיך ניט,
און קיינער גייט.
מיר גרייטן אונדזער עסן צו דער צייט,
און ריידן ווערטער הייליקע
פֿון קינס רויב,
און דאָס געשריי
פֿון הבלען.

אָ, פֿינסטערניש,
טראָעט אָפּ אַ רגע פֿון מיין שוועל!
צוקאָפֿנס – אַ תליה ברענט,
אַ מאַמע טראָגנט איר שגעון פֿאַר דער גאָם.
עס קלאָנען אין פֿאַרוויסטונג אירע הענט.

Toye-Voye (1938)

∿ Esther Shumyatsher

The evening lies down in my window, heavy and tired.
The day is a battleground.
My every limb cries.
Accused, I keep quiet:
a nation loses blood.
But here, we
go on
as always
with our usual cares.
Reality
is a load to bear.

Oh, darkness
leave my doorway for a while!
My blood is screaming from a pit,
I wait for an order
but no one stirs
and no one goes.
We fix our daily meals
and tell, in sacred words,
of Cain's deceit
and Abel's cry . . .

Oh, darkness
leave my doorway for a while!
Gallows burn into the head of my bed,
a mother wears madness out into the street,
wringing her hands in despair.

ס׳איז נאַכט.

ס׳איז פינסטערניש אין בלוט.

איך הער דעם אָטעם פון מײַן שטאַם:

מיט בלוט פאַרגײַט יעטװידער טאָג,

און צינדט דעם זאַמד װי שׂרפות װאָלטן ברענען.

אינדרוסן איז תשרי־נאָלד,

אױף יעדנס פנים צו דערקענען.

אינדרוסן – אזאַ חושך אין יעדער קלענסטער בריאה.

אינדרוסן איז תשרי־נאָלד

און פינסטערע תוהו ובהו...

It's night.
Darkness pervades my blood.
I can hear my people breathing.
Each day dies away with the draining blood
and sand bursts into a blaze.
Outside it's Tishre-gold.[2]
You see it on everyone's face.
Shadows envelop the tiniest souls.
Outside it's Tishre-gold
and the dark toye-voye.[3]

2. Tishre: month in the Hebrew calendar, usually falling in September/October.
3. Toye-voye: chaos

Word

וואָרט

ז. ווײנפּער ‏

אַזוי פֿיל ליכטיקע ווערטער פֿאַרהילטע
מיט שטויב.
און גיי, גלויב,
אַז דו וועסט מיט דײַנע געזאַנגען
ערגעצוואו הערצער דערלאַנגען.

וואָרט,
נישטאָ קיין אָרט
איצט אין מיר
פֿאַר דיר,
איז וואָסזשע גראָבלסטו זיך, ווי אַ הונט בײַ אַ טיר?

אַ, וואָלסטו געקאָנט זיך פֿאַרוואַנדלען אין אַ גליאיקן שפּיז
אין דער האַנט פֿון אַ ריז, –
מעג ער זײַן אַ ליימענער גולם,
וואָס וויסט נישט דעם חילוק פֿון אַ פּתח ביז אַ חולם,
וואָלט יעדער שרץ
געהאַט פֿאַר דיר דרך־אַרץ.

אָבער אַזוי ווי דו ביסט?
אומזיסט, אוי אומזיסט
איז דײַן מי.

די זון וועט נאָך אויפֿגיין אין גילדענעם גלי?
אַ דאַנק פֿאַר דער טרייסט, –
מען וויסט שוין, מען וויסט!
עס האָט דער נביא געזאָגט, און גערעדט,
אָבער אָנשטאָט אַ טרייסטנדיק קול,
דאַרף מײַן פֿאָלק איצט אַ בעט

346

Word (1938)

~ Zishe Vaynper

So many bright words covered
with dust!
Well then, trust
that you and your songs
will touch someone.

Word,
I haven't got room
any more
for you.
Why do you scratch like a dog at the door?

If only you could turn into a glowing lance
in a giant's hands—
(Even if he's a clay *goylem*,
who can't tell a *pasech* from a *khoylem*.)[4]
Every crawling creature would
bow down and wish you the way of the good.

But as you remain?
In vain. Oh, in vain
is your toil and pain.

Will the golden, glowing sun rise again?
Thanks for your cheer,
but it's finally clear!
The prophet has said what he's said.
But instead of a comforting chord,
my people need a bed

4. *Goylem* (Yiddish pronunciation of golem): the legendary story of a man built of clay
by the rabbi of Prague. *Pasech*: a mark used in the Hebrew alphabet to connote the short
"a" vowel. *Khoylem*: a Hebrew marking which connotes an "o" or "oy" sound.

אין אַ שפּיטאָל, –
עס איז קראַנק
פֿון אייביקן גאַנג,
עס בענקט נאָך אַ דאַך און נאָך רו.

אָ דו,
שליח פֿון האַרץ און פֿון מוח, –
עס איז איצט נישט פֿאַר דיין כּוח
צו טראָגן די מאַסע
פֿון מיין פֿאַרפּייניקטער ראַסע,
איז וואָסזשע רייסטו זיך אַלץ פֿון מיין בלוט?

וואָרט,
נישטאָ קיין אָרט
אין מיר פֿאַר דיינעטװעגן איצט.
צעדונערט און צעבליצט
איז איבער אונדז דער גאַנצער אוניװערז,
און דיר װילט זיך דורך אַ פֿערז
אויסשרייען די געפֿאַר,
דעם צער
פֿון די געליטענע,
די פֿאַרשניטענע?
עס איז איצט נישט קיין צייט פֿאַר קיין װערטער־אימאַזשן,
מיר דאַרפֿן באַנדאָזשן
פֿאַר אונדזערע װאונדן.
היטלער האָט אָנגעצונדן
אַ שריפֿה פֿון האַס,
ברענט אונדזער גאַס,
בלוטיקט אונדזער לייב אונטער דער בייטש
אין דער האַנט פֿון דעם נאַצישן דייטש.

וואָרט מיינס, שטום איין
אין דיין אייגענער פּיין,
און לאָז צעפּירן די פֿאַרמאַטערטע העַנט,
וואָס זוכן שפּאַרונעס אויף װענט
זיך דורכצורייסן,
זיך דורכצובייסן...

in a hospital ward.
They're suffering
from eternal wandering,
they long for a roof and rest.

Oh you,
messenger of heart and of head,
but without the strength
to tear the masses
off my tortured people,
how dare you tear forth from my blood?

Word,
there isn't room
for you in me now.
Flashed past, thundered away
on us is all the universe.
And you want your verse
to herald
the guillotine's peril
and the dread
of the beheaded?
Now isn't the time for verbal images.
We need bandages
for our wounds.
Hitler has lit
a blaze of hate.
Our street is burning,
our flesh is bleeding under the whip
in the Nazi German's hand.

Hush, my word
in your pain
and let those tired hands lead you,
to find crevices in the walls
to attempt to make it through . . .
to gnaw through . . .

Matters of Life and Death

While war may have been the greatest tragedy of the twentieth century, it was far from the only tragedy that was reflected in Proletpen's verse. Poems about accidents at work, suicide, and hopelessness define societal ills that illustrated for them the need for social change. Martin Birnbaum's "The Man Who Hanged Himself" shows a person whom a degrading, monotonous system has robbed of all self-respect. Ber Grin's "A Man Falls at Work" is a terrifying image of the hazards of the workplace.

The theme of life and death also prompted poets to sometimes rupture the proletarian model. Menke Katz's volatile relationship with Proletpen came to the fore once again when he produced a cycle titled *Three Sisters*, which shocked his leftist colleagues and alienated him from the group.[1] It was bad enough that the sensuous stories of the three sisters were laden with descriptions of women's bodies and raw sexual imagery. Menke Katz went a step further by suggesting political slants that were diametrically opposed to the Communist Party. One of the poems in this cycle, "To Her Three Unborn Baby Boys," portrays the self-torture of a woman who cannot live with the abortions she has had. Her inability to accept the reality of abortion neither follows the expected pro-choice line of the Left, nor adopts a typically conservative position.

1. Menke Katz, *Dray Shvester,* 2nd ed. (Rowen, Wales: Farlag "Dray Shvester," 1993). The title echoes Winchevsky's "Three Sisters," published in *Dos Poylishe Yidl* in England at the end of the nineteenth century (William J. Fishman, "Morris Winchevsky's London Yiddish Newspaper, One Hundred Years in Retrospect" [Oxford: Oxford Centre for Postgraduate Hebrew Studies, 1985], 16).

Like Katz's *Three Sisters*, Hershl Miller's "Without God's Blessing" and "Kaddish" fell far from accepted Proletpen orthodoxy. In both poems, Miller refers to God as interminably linked to life and death. "You back away from God and God is tied more closely to you," he writes in the first. In the second, he writes about uttering the traditional kaddish prayer for his deceased father in his sleep, having neglected to say it before. These poems reveal the frustration of an individual who is doing his best to join the secular world but remains nonetheless tied to his faith. While Hershl Miller only occasionally published alongside Proletpen, I include his poems here in contrast to the more forward-thinking and adamantly anti-religious poems of the proletarians. It seems fitting to conclude with Dora Teitelboim's "Gambling," which leaves us waiting for the future, "at the airports of time."

איִרע דריַ ניטגעבאָרענע ייִנגעלעך:

.1

זיַ פּוסטעווען אַרויס פֿון די קלענסטע שיכעלעך
אין די פֿינקלענדיקע פֿענצטער פֿון פֿולע קראָמען,
און שריַבן ניטגעשריבענע לידער
אויף אומבאַרירטע בלעטער פֿון שוואַרצע אַלבאָמען.

זיַ גרויען אַרויס פֿון זונפֿאַרגאַנגען
ווי פֿינטעלעך שרעק קעגן נאַט,
און פֿאַרגרויען מיט די ווידערקלאַנגען
פֿון יעדער שטאָט.

זיַ וואָלטן אַלע ייִנגעלעך געווען,
יעדער שענער פֿונעם שענסטן לומפּ;
דורך בלינדע געפֿאַרן וואָלטן זיַ זען
אַ באָרוויסע מיידל ביַ אַ פֿראָסטן פֿלומפּ.

זיַ וואָלטן אַלע – דו געווען,
היַמלאָזע האַרן פֿון הינטערהויפֿן;
מיט האַר צעפֿאַטלעטער שאַטען
וואָלטן זיַ פֿון טאָג אַנטלויפֿן.

זיַ וואָלטן אַלע – דו געווען,
פֿון נאָס און ווינט די זינגענדיקע שאַרפֿן,
אויסשפּילן זייערע זינד
וואָלט אַ מלאָך אויף האַרפֿן.

האָב איך זיַ צו אַ קברן פֿאַרנאָרט,
און פֿון מיַנע ייִנגעלעך געלאָזן
נאָר מיַן אויפֿגענאָמטע טראָכט,
און פֿון מיַנע ייִנגעלעך געלאָזן
נאָר אַן אייביק מפֿילדיקע נאָכט.

Her Three Unborn Baby Boys (1932)

❧ Menke Katz

They spill from the tiniest shoes
in busy shops' glittering cases,
and write unwritten poems
on black albums' untouched pages.

As dots of fear before God
they dawn out of sundowns,
and dawn out of echoes
in every town.

They would all be baby boys,
each one handsomer than the handsomest bum;
past blind dangers they would gaze
at a barefoot girl at a plain old pump.

They would all be you,
homeless backyard masters. They'd
have light brown, disheveled hair,
and run away from day.

They would all be you,
the scarves that sing of street and wind.
A little angel on a harp
would sing their sins.

I betrayed them to an undertaker,
and all that's left of my baby boys
is my womb, scoured and distorted,
and all that's left of my baby boys
is a night, eternally aborted.

פֿון זייערע זומערן
האָט דער ווינט קיין צוויטן ניט געקליבן,
און ס'האָבן זיי קברים ניט דערווואַרט –
איז פֿון יעדער יינגעלע געבליבן
נאָר אַ סנאָפּ פֿאַרשניטענע יאָרן,
איז פֿון יעדער יינגעלע געבליבן
נאָר קאָשיקלעך מיט פֿאָזימקעס און באָרן
אין די גוידערן פֿון שווערע אָקושאָרן.

האָב איך מײַנע יינגעלעך אויף מיסט געביטן,
ראיען זיך אין זייערע יאָרן
ברעקלעך זון פֿון קאָרנע פֿאַרטאָגן –
זײַנען זיי די פֿורפֿורנע לאַטעס
אויף פּוסטע לעכערדיקע שטיבער,
שפּינלען זיך אויף פֿאַרדריפֿעטע גראָטעס
ווי אויסגעטרוימטע קרינער
מיט אַלטע פֿאַרגעסענע שפֿיזן,
און גייען ווי אַ גאָלדיקער טויט
איינע די אַנדערע אַריבער.

האָב איך מײַנע יינגעלעך אויף מיסט געביטן,
ראיען זיך אין זייערע יאָרן
ברעקלעך זון פֿון קאָרנע פֿאַרטאָגן –
שאָרן זיי זיך אַרוים ווי טאָגנדיקע הענט
פֿון די בלוטיקע שפּאָרעס פֿון אַ שלאַכטהויז,
און נעמען אַרום
די קאָרקלענדיקע קעפּ פֿון קעלבעלעך און שאָף,
און פֿאַרטראָגן
אין מײַן וואַכן שלאָף
פֿון געבונדענע אָקסן אַ לעצטן קלאָנג;
שאָרן זיי זיך אַרוים ווי טאָגנדיקע הענט
פֿון די בלוטיקע שפּאָרעס פֿון אַ שלאַכטהויז,
און רײַסן אויף
די קעלבערנע ווייעס פֿון גליקלעכע בן־בקועות,
און פֿירן מיט זייערע שוואַרצאָפּלען
אַ ניטדערבאָרענעם שמועם.

Their summers
left no blossoms for the wind,
and graves did not await them.
So each baby boy left behind
just a sheaf of shorn years,
and each baby boy left behind
only little baskets of strawberries and pears
in stout midwives' double chins.

I traded in my baby boys for trash,
swarming round their years
shards of sun from miserly dawns:
they are the purple patches
on empty houses overrun
with holes. They mirror muddy grates
like warriors whose dreams are done,
with old forgotten lances;
they walk like golden death,
each one past the next.

I traded in my baby boys for trash,
swarming round their years,
shards of sun from selfish dawns:
they spill as though from uncupped hands
from bloody cracks in a slaughterhouse,
hugging close
the rolling heads of calves and sheep
and carrying away
to my fitful sleep
the last cry of a bound oxen. They
spill as though from uncupped hands
from bloody cracks in a slaughterhouse,
and rip apart
the doe eyelashes of womb-fruits slain in incubation,
and with the pupils of their eyes
have an unborn conversation.

2.

אין שווערער פּאָטינע – אומרואיקע שפּינען
ווינן זייערע געשטאַלטן,
אין שווערער פּאָטינע – אומרואיקע שפּינען
האָבן מיינע יינגעלעך באַהאַלטן.

ביינאַכט – אויף מיין פּינטלענדיקער סטעליע
סאָושעט זיי אַ גאַזערער אויס,
און איך – צום גייענדיקן שלאָף געשמידט
צייל אָן קופּעם טריט,
און וויל מיט די וועגט זיך פּאַרשטיינען
ווען איך פּאַרצייל אַ טראָט;
אין שווערן שטויב – קלייבן זיך
זייערע ניטגעערדטע רייד,
וויל ווערטערדיקער שטויב זיך צערייד,
וויל אַ ניטדערבאַרן קול זיך צעווינען –
פּראָווועט די שטילקייט אַ שטומע קאָפּעליע;
מיט אַ פּאַרצוינן שטריק – ווערג איך
ווי אַ לעבעדיקע מיין שאָטענענע קלייד,
און טויט – מיט ניטדערבאַרענע אויגן
גיי איך אום אין מיין דרויסנדיקער הויז,
און הער,
ווי ס'קערן זיך אין ווינט דריי יינגעלעך,
און קלער –
שוין צייט מיינע יינגעלעך צו זוינן.

אַ שענסטער לומפּ פון גאַסן און פון לידער,
זיי וועלן דיך באַנעגענען אויף דיין לעצטן שוועל,
און קאָפּען ביי דיין צוקאָפּנס
ווי אַ היסער חלבנער טריפּן,
און פּאַרשווינדן –
ווי אַ פּאַקן פון שיידנדיקע הענט
ביים אומעט פון אָפּגייענדיקע שיפן.

2.
In a heavy cobweb, restless spiders
swing and sway,
in a heavy cobweb, restless spiders
hide my baby boys away.

At night on my twinkling ceiling
a gas pipe conjures them in soot
and I, the sleepwalker, I keep
counting piles of steps through sleep
and want to stone myself with the walls
when I miscount a step.
In the heavy dust
their untalked talk collects,
word-filled dust would talk and talk,
an unborn cry would weep and weep.
The silence plays a silent symphony.
Tightening a rope, I choke
my light brown dress, like a living being,
and once I'm dead, I go
round and round my outdoor house
with unborn eyes.
I hear three baby boys turn on the wind,
and know
it's time to nurse my baby boys.

O handsomest pauper from streets and from poems,
they'll greet you at your final door,
and trickle down the headstone of your grave
like hot dripping wax
and disappear
as the wave of parting hands
at the sorrow of departing ships.

זעלבסטמאָרד

מעינקע קאַץ &

ווי ס'וואָלט אַ וואַלד אַ דעמבענער
געבאָרן מיך אין האַלבענאַכט,
בין איך ווי אַ פינצטער דעמב – שטאַרק און מוראדיק,
וואָלט איך גערן ווי אַ וואַלד אַ דעמבענער
אין האַלבענאַכט זיך צעצינדן,
אָדער גאָר אַליין זיך בינדן
און פירן זיך אין שחיטה-הויז קוילען ווי אַ ביק.

כ'וועל אַמאָל מיט זיך אַליין זיך געזעגענען,
צום לעצטן מאָל ווייזן זיך אין שפּיגל,
און מיט מיין איינן פֿגר די וועלט באַגעגענען.

נאָר פינפֿאונצוואָנציק פרילינגס
האָב איך פון אייביקייט דאָ אָנגעקליבן,
און יעדער פרילינג
איז ווי דורך באָבלומטע טרונעם גענאָנגען,
איז וואָס איז פון מיר אַצינד פֿאַרבליבן
אויב ניט די אַלע זונפֿאַרגאַנגען;
שוין וואָלט איך מיין פרילינגדיקן קאָפּ
געביטן אויף ווערימלעך אַ טאָפּ;
שוין וואָלט איך פון יעדער קלייד
פון די דריי שוועסטער – מיינע שענסטע לידער
פלעכטן זיך די שענסטע שטריק,
און ערגעץ אויף אַ בוידעם זיך אויפֿהאַנגען.

צווישן חורבות ליידיקע און שיידימדיקע שויבן
וועל איך זיך אַליין וועון עס איז פֿאַרנאַרן,
און דרייען זיך ווי אַ שליסל אין איבערגעדרייטע שלעסער;
צווישן חורבות ליידיקע און שיידימדיקע שויבן
וועל איך זיין אַליין אַ לעבעדיקער מעסער,
וועל איך מיין איינן האַלדז וועון עס איז באַרויבן.

360

Suicide (1932)

∾ Menke Katz

As if a wood of oaks gave
birth to me at midnight,
I am like a dark oak, strong and frightful.
I'd gladly, like a wood of oaks
at midnight, set myself aflame
or even tie myself up tight
and lead myself to slaughter, to be butchered like an ox.

   Someday I'll bid myself adieu,
   look one last time in the mirror,
   and bring my carcass, world, to you.

   Just twenty-five springs
   have I gathered from eternity
   and every spring
   passed like coffins strewn with flowers,
   so now what is left of me
   if not all the sunset hours;
   I'd already give my springtime head
   and have a pot of worms instead;
   I'd readily take every dress
   of the three sisters—my prettiest
   poem—and braid a pretty rope
   and hang myself somewhere in an attic.

Amid empty ruins and window ghosts
I'll trick myself come time,
like a key in a spring lock;
amid empty ruins and window ghosts
I'll be my own living knife,
come time, I'll steal my own life.

A Third (1929)

∽ Moyshe Nadir

Between life and death, I lie
like a third
between man and wife.

I keep them
from coming together
in love.

Both of them groan,
toss about,
want to get their hands
across me.

I lie awake and cold
between them
and divide them!

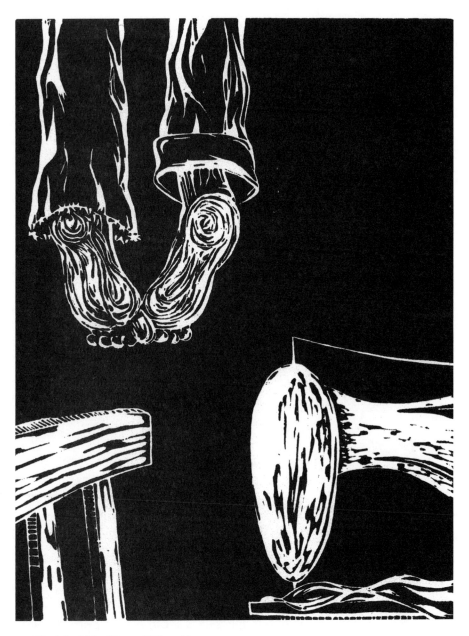

The Man Who Hanged Himself

דער, וואָס האָט זיך אויפגעהאַנגען

◄ מאַרטין בירנבוים

געווײנטלעך העגנט מען קליידער אויף אויף יענע רונדע שטאַנגען.–
אַ וואוילער מענטש געווען דער נאַר, וואָס האָט זיך אויפגעהאַנגען.

אַ וואוילער מענטש געווען–נאָר שטיל, אין מידקייט אײנגעפֿאָרן.–
ס'האָט שנעל, ס'האָט פֿאַר דער צײט דער שאַף באַלאָדן אים מיט יאָרן.

ער האָט בײם לעבן נישט געפֿרעגט קײן ביטערע פֿאַרוואָס–
צוואַנציג יאָר בײ דער מאַשין–און ס'איז די צײט געפֿלאָסן.

זײן ווײב איז אים געווען געטרײ–דערויף איז ער באַשטאַנען–
צום „גליק" האָט בלויז געפֿעלט אַ קינד–ווי ס'שטײט אין די ראָמאַנען.

נאָר אײנמאָל האָט זײן ווײב געזאָגט, געזאָגט אַ ביסל זויער:
„יאַנקל, ווי דו זעסט עם אויס! אַי, ווי דו ווערסט גרויער!"

האָט ער גענומען זיך די מי, זיך גוט באַקוקט אין שפּיגל–
און ס'ערשטע מאָל מיט ביטערקייט געשמייכלט–און געשוויגן.

נישט גרוי אַלײן–די אויגן אויך צעקניטשט און אויפגעשוואָלן...
איז יעדן טאָג, פֿון דעמאָלט אָן–האָט ער זיך שוין געגאָלן.

נאָר יעדער טאָג, פֿון דעמאָלט אָן, האָט מאָדנע אים דערקוטשעט;
און יעדע נאַכט האָט אַ קאָשמאַר אַן אַנדערער געמוטשעט;

אים אויפגעוועקט פֿון שלאָף פֿאַרשוויצט, מיט דראָזש, מיט קאַלטן ציטער...
–הפּנים: ער איז טאָקע אַלט... הפּנים עם איז ביטער...

„יאַנקל, ווי דו זעסט אויס!"–זײן ווײב האָט נישט פֿאַרגעסן.–
איז ער אין שאַף, בײ דער מאַשין, שוין אויך האַלב-טויט געזעסן.

אַ באָם האָט ליב זיך נעמען צײט–צו זען ווי ס'ווערט „געשאָסן".
נאָר דאָם וואָם יאַנקל נעמט זיך צײט, אָט דאָם האָט אים פֿאַרדראָסן.

366

The Man Who Hanged Himself (1937)

∾ Martin Birnbaum

They used to use that circular rack to hang up clothes,
a nice man, the fool who hanged himself was.

A nice man, but silent, and paralyzed by weariness,
weighed down before his time with a life of shop dreariness.

He asked no bitter "why's" throughout his years.
Twenty years at the machine, and time just disappears.

His wife was always true to him; he lived on that alone.
And as in novels, all that was missing was a child of their own.

But once his wife remarked to him, remarked a little sour.
"Yankl, just look at yourself! You're growing grayer by the hour!"

He took himself to be the trouble, looked hard in the mirror.
And smiled for once, and kept quiet. Everything seemed clearer.

His eyes were pinched and swollen—not only was he gray.
From that day forth he scribbled himself out, more every day.

But every day, from that day on, something wasn't right,
and nightmares came to torture him, a new one every night;

He'd wake from sleep, perspiring, with spasms, with cold shivers . . .
It's evident: he's gotten old . . . It's evident: he's bitter . . .

"Yankele, look how you look!" his wife did not forget.
And so he sits by the shop machine, already halfway dead.

A boss, he likes to take time and see who should be "spit."
But the way that Yankl takes his time has him in a fit.

אָון אין אַ פֿרײַטאָנדינן טאָנ איז יאָנקל טיף־נעבױוין

אַרױס פֿון שאָף, מיט בלײַכער ליפֿ־און רעזיגנירטע אױגן...

אַ חודש צײַט זיך אומגעשלעפּט מיט שװערע פֿיס מיט שלאָפֿע–

און אין אַ הײסער זומער־נאָכט זיך אױפֿגעהאָנגען אין שאָפֿע.

אַ בריװל זײַנס האָט קורץ געזאָגט: „מײַן װײַב, דו װעסט מיך פֿאַרגעבן:

איך האָב זיך לעצטנס אומגעקוקט–איך בין צו אַלט צום לעבן"...

– – – – – – – – – –

זעקס און פֿערצינ יאָר געװען איז יאָנקל, אָט־דער זקן–

דער שאָף האָט אים געעלטערט פֿרי; דאָס װײַב האָט אים דערשראָקן...

צװאָנצינ יאָר בײַ דער מאַשין–און ער איז מיד געװאָרן.

אַ מילדער מענטש, אָן גיפֿט, אָן געלט און־אָן אַ בֿרעקל צאָרן...

שטיל געלעבט די אַלע יאָר, װי אין אַ פֿלעט געפֿאַנגען–

אַ װאױלער נאַר געװען–דער מענטש װאָס האָט זיך אױפֿגעהאָנגען.

סאַן פֿראַנציסקאָ, סעפּטעמבער, 1937

And one Friday afternoon, the haggard Yankl left behind
the shop where he had worked, his lips pallid, eyes resigned . . .

A whole month's time he dragged around his heavy feet and head.
But one hot summer night, he hanged himself, out in the shed.

His letter said it briefly: "Forgive me, please, my wife.
I've lately looked into myself. I am too old for life."
— — — — — — — — — — — — — — — — — —
This old man was forty-six. What had brought him there?
The shop had aged him early; his wife had given him a scare . . .

Twenty years at the machine, and he could go no longer.
A mild man, no venom, no money, not a bit of anger.

He lived quiet and chained, the way a prisoner does.
A nice man, the fool who hanged himself was.

געפֿאַלן אַ מענטש ביי דער אַרבעט

בער גרין ⸻

די װאָרעמקייט פֿון פֿינגער
ציטערן נאָך אויף שויבן
און פֿירט־אַריין די זון אין שטוב
װי אַ ליכטיק גלויבן.

אין פֿרעמדע פֿענצטער געצונדן זונען
און פֿרישע טעג;
איצט ליגט ער הענט צעשפּרייט
אינמיטן װעג;
ס׳לעשט די זון זיך אין זיינע אויגן
מיט לעצטן רויט,
און ס׳גייט־אויף װי שקיעה אויף שויבן
אַ בלינדער טויט.
קוליען זיך יונגע יאָרן אין רויטע פֿאַרבן.
די זאָפֿטן פֿון לעבן צענאָסן אויף שטיין—
טריפֿן פֿענצטער אַראָפּ
מיט ליכט און געװיין.

ליגט אויף שטיינער אַ לעבן פֿאַרלאָשן.
אן אַרבעטער געװען. פֿרעמדע פֿענצטער געװאָשן.
ליכטיקייט פֿון הענט
אויף אויסגעפּוצטע שויבן
װאָרעמט נאָך און בלענדט.

370

A Man Falls at Work

~ Ber Grin

Still the warm fingerprints
quiver on the panes, and must
send the sun into the house
like a glowing ray of trust.

Suns shine bright in strangers' windows
even on cold days;
now he lies, in the middle of the street,
arms spread out both ways.
The sun goes out before his eyes
a last red,
a sunset on windowpanes
blinding the dead.
Young years tumble in red hues.
The fallen body's juices stream.
The window trickles
light and scream.

A body lies extinguished, on stone,
once a worker. Strangers' windows shone.
A light touch on the shiny
panes.

זעלבסטבאשרייבונג

משה נאַדיר ~

ווייל איך האָב דיך ליב געהאַט, וועלט,
ווי אַ געליבטע,
האָב איך געוואָלט זאָלסט מיך באַמערקן!
האָב איך מיך געקליידט אין הויכע גאָלדקראַגנס פון ווירדע,
האָב איך מיך געפּלייסט צו זיין קלינער, ווי איך בין –
און בלענדענדער . . .
האָב איך מיך געפּוצט אין גאָלדשוים פון ווערטער,
זיך געצוינען אויפן סדום־בעט פון גלאָריע,
האָב איך אַ האַרץ אָנגעצייכנט –
אויף דער דרויסנזייט פון מיין האַרץ
און עס געלאָזט בלוטן אין בלומיקע טופּלען –
כאָטש מיין ריכטיק האַרץ האָט טאָקע געבלוטיקט.

ווייל איך האָב דיך אַזוי ליב געהאַט, וועלט,
ווייל איך האָב דיך אַזוי ליב־ליב־ליב געהאַט, וועלט,
ווייל איך האָב דיך אַזוי אָן אַ שיעור ליב־ליב־ליב־ליב־ליב געהאַט,
קרומע איקאַנע
אויף דער קרומער וואַנט,
וואָס איז וועלט! –

372

Selfwriting

◠ Moyshe Nadir

World, because I loved you,
as a lover,
I wanted you to notice me!
I dressed myself in fine gold collars,
I tried to be smarter than I am—
and more dazzling . . .
I gussied myself in the gold foam of words,
indulged myself on Sodom's bed of glory,
I've drawn a heart
on the outside of my heart,
and let it bleed in blooming blossoms
though my own heart really bled.

World, because I loved you so,
World, because I love-love-loved you so,
World, because I really love-love-love-love-loved you so,
crooked icon
on the crooked wall
that is World!—

אָן גאָטס ברכה

הערשל מילער ﭏ

אָן גאָטס ברכה גייט אָן אַצינד די וועלט,
דורכגעזאַפט מיט בלוט איז די ערד
צעפּוילט לינט דאָס בלי אויפן חרובן פעלד
ס׳גייט אום דער קראַנקער מענטש נישט דערנערט.

די וועלט איז קראַנק, גאָט אַליין איז מיט וואונדן,
דערווייטערסטו זיך פון גאָט, ווערט גאָט נעענטער צו דיר צוגעבונדן.
ביסטו אין סכנה, בעטסט רחמים מיט אויסגעשטרעקטע הענט
טוט גאָט פון דיר זיך אָפּ, ווערט אַלץ פאַרלעדנט.

אַלץ גייט אויס אין האָפן, גלויבן
נישטאָ ווער ס׳זאָל זאָגן ס׳לעצטע וואָרט.
ס׳האָט קיינער זיך נאָך נישט דערהויבן
אַ טרייסט אונדז ברעננען מיט אַ וואָרט.

374

Without God's Blessing

⌇ Hershl Miller

Without God's blessing, the world goes on for now,
the earth soaked with blood.
The bud lies rotten on the devastated field.
The sick man walks around unfed.

The world is sick, and God is wounded,
you back away from God and God is tied more closely to you.
You're at risk, beg mercy with outstretched hands,
God leaves you and all is destroyed in you.

All hope, all belief goes out.
Nobody's left to say the last word.
No one has sought out exaltation
to bring us comfort in a word.

קדיש

‎<‎ העזשל מילער

איך האָב קיין קדיש נישט געזאָנגט
איז מיין טאַטע מיר צו חלום געקומען,
אַליין דעם קדיש מיט מיר מיר וואָרט ביי וואָרט געזאָנגט.
אז מיין מאַמע האָט זיך אויפגעכאַפּט פון שלאָף
האָבן טרערן נאָס געמאַכט איר אויסגעצערט געזיכט,
מיר אָנגעזאָנגט,
כ׳זאָל אינדערפרי
געבן אַ פונט ליכט אין שול אַריין.
זי האָט געהערט ווי כ׳האָב קדיש געזאָנגט פון שלאָף.

Kaddish

~ Hershl Miller

I hadn't said the *kaddish*[2] prayer
so my father came to see me in a dream,
and said *kaddish* himself word for word with me right there
while mother awoke from her sleep,
tears wet on her wasted face.
She said
I should, come morning,
bring the synagogue a pound of candles.
She'd heard me saying *kaddish* in my sleep.

2. *Kaddish*: prayer recited for the dead.

דערנאָך

משה נאַדיר ﮒ

די ערד וועט פלאַמען און גליִען
אויף מייַנע ביינער.
עס וועלן זייַן אַזויפיל אינדערפריִען,
נאָר איך וועל זייַן – קיינער.

ווי זיס עס איז אין לעבן אַלעם,
אויך ס'ביטערע טראַכטן פון ניט ווערן.
אין ווילדן צוויט שטייט די ערד – די כלה
און שמעקנדיק עס זייַנען אירע טרערן.

אויף כלהס קאָפּ די קרוין פון אייביק דויערן,
דער כלהס האַרץ אין פלאַמען, ווי אַ ווידער.
ווי דאָס אַש פון אויסגעבראַנטע טרויערן,
שפּרייט זיך אויף די ווינטן מייַנע לידער.

עס איז שווער דאָס לעבן אונדזערס שלעפּן
זאַלבעצוווייַען, זאַלבעאיינעם, זאַלבענאַרניט.
און פאַלן פאַלט דאָך יעדער אויף די טרעפן –
און דער ריינער אמת איז דאָך אויכעט וואָר ניט.

שווער איז בלויז, אַז אַלעם איז פאַרגעננגלעך.
און מייַן לעבן ז'דין אַזוי און ברעכלעך.
ווי אויסגעקוועטשטע דאַרע טרויבנהענגלעך,
קופעס טויטע טעג בייַ מייַנע קנעכלעך.

פלאָרידע, 1938

378

Afterwards (1938)

◟ Moyshe Nadir

The earth will flame and glow
above my bones.
So many tomorrows will come and go
and I will be—no one.

How sweet are all life's hours,
even the bitter thought of death.
The earth—the bride—wears wildflowers
and fragrant is her tearful breath.

The bride's head is crowned by eternity.
Her heart, like a ram, is in flames.
I scatter my poems to the wind
like burnt-out sorrow's ash remains.

This life of ours is hard to bear
in a twosome, a onesome, a nonesome.
And it's on the stairs that everyone falls,
and simple truth is also false.

It's only hard because it disappears,
and my thin, fragile life will soon give in.
Piles of days have died beside my heels
like dried and squeezed-out grape-skin.

Gambling (1979)

We all are standing
at the airports of time,
like hungry,
poor folk,
and until the end
we wait,
ever-confident,
for the gambler's
rose.

THE POETS

BIBLIOGRAPHY

The Poets

∾ SARAH BARKAN

1889, Dvinsk/Daugavpils, Russian Empire (now Latvia)[1]–December 15, 1957, Maplewood, New Jersey

A poet for children and adults, Barkan began working at the age of eleven in a button factory. She came to America in 1907 with her husband, a tailor, and child, and published her first poems in the socialist *Forverts* in 1922. Later, Barkan became a member of the Communist Party, and shifted her allegiances to the *Frayhayt*, *Hamer*, and other literary collections put out by Proletpen. She published a number of children's poems, short stories, and one-act plays. Throughout the 1930s, '40s, and into the '50s her work continued to appear in anthologies and periodicals, as well as in several volumes of her own poetry and prose.

Italian Masons 66
Negro Song 136
Bring Me Your Woes 220
I Have Not Woven My Poems . . . 286

∾ MARTIN BIRNBAUM (Birnboym)

October 29, 1904, Gorodenka, Austria-Hungary (now Ukraine)–August 13, 1986, New York

1. For information on borders, see Gary Mokotoff and Sallyann Amdur Sack, *Where Once We Walked: A Guide to the Jewish Communities Destroyed in the Holocaust* (Teaneck, N.J.: Avotaynu, Inc., 1991).

Mordkhe Israel Birnbaum began his education in Hebrew and Polish schools. During World War I he lived in Bukovina and in a children's home in Vienna. He returned to Gorodenka after the war, with hopes of moving to Palestine. By 1923, however, he was on his way to the United States. He began publishing poetry in German-language papers in New York, such as the *Deutscher volkszeitung* and the German Communist Party publication, *Der arbeiter*. By 1929, Birnbaum had switched milieus to Yiddish and was publishing in the communist *Frayhayt*, as well as *Hamer, Yidishe kultur,* and *Signal.* Birnbaum continued to publish volumes of his own work into the 1980s.

ᐁ Yosl Cutler

1896, Troyanov, Tsarist Empire (now Ukraine)–June 11, 1935, U.S.

An acclaimed artist and cartoonist as well as a writer, Yosl Cutler, who immigrated to the United States in 1911, brought an important visual element to Yiddish proletarian literature. He studied, and later taught, painting, and, together with Zuni Maud, created the Yiddish marionette theater Modakut in 1925. Cutler's career was cut short when he was killed in a car accident while on a *Frayhayt*-sponsored marionette tour across the United States in 1935.

ᐁ Sarah Fel-Yelin

1895, Krinik, Russian Empire (now Poland)–June 22, 1962, Los Angeles

A teacher, children's poet, and fiction writer, Fel-Yelin moved to the United States in 1920. Before immigrating, Fel-Yelin taught in the Krinik Y. L. Peretz School, and was active in revolutionary organizations, starting an anti-pogrom self-defense team for women and organizing help for homeless children during World War I. In the United States, she taught in the Workman's Circle schools in Massachusetts, and later, after moving to the West Coast, worked in a Los Angeles shop. She coedited the California Yiddish journal *Kalifornyer shriftn* in 1955 and was active in the Los Angeles YKuF, in addition to organizing the Beverly Hills branch of the Workman's Circle. Fel-Yelin published several volumes of her own poetry in addition to contributing regularly to *Morgn frayhayt, Yidishe kultur, Zamlungen,* and *Kalifornyer shriftn.*

Breath of Spring 186

∾ BETSALEL FRIEDMAN

1897, Brest/Brisk, Russian Empire (now Belarus)–July 12, 1941, New York

A poet who transcended political boundaries, Friedman became a teacher in Poland, as well as an active member of the Left Poale-Zion Party. Friedman debuted with poems in Polish Yiddish journals in 1919. He lived in Palestine from 1920 to 1922, where he did agricultural work and built roads. In 1922 he immigrated to New York, where he taught in the Workman's Circle schools and later in the left-wing Yiddish schools. In the United States his poetry first appeared in *Morgn zhurnal* and *Shriftn,* and, in 1927 he shifted over to the *Frayhayt,* where he edited the "Children's Corner." His work also appeared in *Hamer, Signal, Yidishe kultur,* and several revolutionary oriented European journals. In addition to poems, short stories, pedagogical articles, children's plays, and adult one-acts, Friedman wrote several school textbooks.

Scottsboro 138

∾ BER GRIN

April 18, 1901, Yaruga, Russian Empire (now Ukraine)–1989, New York

A pioneer of Yiddish proletarian poetry in the United States, Itsik Grinberg is best known by his pseudonym, Ber Grin. (He occasionally wrote under other names, such as A. Prints.) As a youth he lived through the Ukrainian civil war and pogroms, and from 1921 until his departure for the United States he worked as a teacher in Rumania. He immigrated to the United States in 1923, studied at Columbia University, and earned a law degree at Brooklyn College in 1929. Ber Grin, who began writing poetry in Hebrew and Russian as a youth, published his first Yiddish poem in *Di feder* in 1924, and later became an important literary figure in Yiddish American leftist publications, such as *Signal, Kamf,* and *Frayhayt.* A co-editor of *Morgn frayhayt* from 1931 to 1981, he published in a wide variety of journals spanning political orientations. These included *Di feder, Oyfkum, Yugnt, Idish-Amerike, Hamer, Signal, Yunyon-skver* and *Yidishe kultur* as well as several Canadian and European publications. Following World War II, Ber Grin also became the editor of the Yiddish *Zamlungen.*

ᲙᲘ YOSL GRINSHPAN

1902, Kletsk, Russian Empire (now Belarus)–June 26, 1934, New York

Grinshpan immigrated to Canada from his hometown outside Minsk during the Polish occupation. He was a member of the Canadian Communist Party from 1922 to 1925, moved to the United States in 1917, and briefly joined the U.S. Communist Party. Although he played an important role in the foundation of the Proletpen organization, Grinshpan soon became one of its internal critics with the publication of *Erev tsayt,* a book of what Alexander Pomerantz termed "antiproletarian" poems. Excluded from the organization, Grinshpan managed to reestablish himself politically with his former colleagues, and reentered Proletpen, continuing thereafter to write and edit. Known as a divergent writer whose poems cover the individualistic as well as the ideological spectrums, Grinshpan left some of the most poignant vignettes behind when he died, probably of starvation, during the Great Depression in New York.

⤳ Kalman Hayzler

March 11, 1899, Komarno, Austria-Hungary (now Ukraine)–January 6, 1966, New York

Hayzler began his studies in a cheder and a Polish school. At the age of nineteen he moved to Prague, where he first read Morris Winchevsky in German translation, and began writing his own poetry before coming to New York in 1921. In New York, Hayzler worked in a woman's clothing factory and later became a union organizer. Hayzler caught the attention of Yakob Glatshteyn, one of the founders of the Inzikh (Introspectivist) movement. He was active in a number of the early incarnations of the American proletarian Yiddish journals, such as *Yung kuznye* and *Proletarisher gedank* (Proletarian Thought), in addition to writing for such varied publications as *Di tsayt, Fraye arbeter shtime, Der tog, Forverts, Der Idisher kemfer, Inzikh,* and *Frayhayt.*

⤳ R. G. Ka

An unknown author, R. G. Ka was an infrequent contributor to the *Morgn frayhayt.* Given the images of pregnancy in "To My Beloved," it is probable that this poet is a woman and that the name "R. G. Ka" is a pseudonym.

⤳ Menke Katz

1906, Svintsyan, Russian Empire (now Belarus)–April 24, 1991, Spring Glen, New York

Menke Katz was one of the younger and more controversial of the Prolet-pen poets. He made his debut in the trilingual *Spartak* (1925). In his earlier period, his nonconformity centered on mystical, erotic, and traditionalist motifs that were unacceptable to the literary chiefs of the movement; his *Three Sisters* (1925, reprinted 1993) got him expelled from Proletpen. These disputes evolved to the point where he became the leading spokesperson for a poetry free of party shackles ("The Brave Coward" of 1938, and his *Grandmother Mona Takes the Floor,* 1939). Despite his 1938–39 break with the Left, Katz continued teaching in New York's leftist schools until the murder of the Yiddish poets in the Soviet Union became known in the early 1950s, when he moved to the non-Communist Arbeter ring and Sholem Aleichem school systems. Bereft of a welcoming literary environment, however, he turned to English and became the only Yiddish poet to become a major poet in English, winning Poet Lore's Stephen Vincent Benét Award among others. For thirty years (1962 to 1991) he edited the English poetry magazine *Bitterroot*. In his lifetime he published eighteen books, nine in Yiddish, nine in English. A translation of the nine Yiddish books titled *The Complete Yiddish Poems of Menke Katz* has been completed by Benjamin and Barbara Harshav and will be published by The Smith of New York in 2005.

ᴄᴠ Sarah Kindman

July 2, 1901, Dzierzgov, Russian Empire (now Poland)–October 1974, New York

A professional actress as well as a poet, Sarah Kindman immigrated to the United States in 1913 and married the Yiddish playwright and director Jacob Mestl. Her first poems appeared in 1919. Kindman also wrote songs and radio sketches.

~ YOSL KOHN

December 21, 1897, Krinik, Russian Empire (now Poland)–March, 1977, New York

Kohn began his studies in a cheder and a Russian folk school before immigrating to the United States in 1909, where he graduated from a Newark public school. Throughout the 1920s and '30s Kohn published articles in the Chicago anarchist journal *Fraye arbeter shtime*, as well as poetry, which appeared in literary journals of varying political and aesthetic orientation, including *Inzikh*, *Yung kuznye*, *Spartak* and *Yunyon-skver*. Kohn returned to Eastern Europe to spend 1931 to 1933 in the Soviet Union.

Sergei Yesenin 290

~ N. D. KORMAN

December 15, 1901, Radom, Russian Empire (now Poland)–June 9, 1981, Philadelphia

Nosen-Dovid Korman, at a young age, was a member of the Paole-Zion organization Yugnt and worked for a haberdashery. At eighteen he was drafted into the Polish army. In 1925, after a brief prison term, Korman left for Cuba, where he was involved in revolutionary political circles and began to publish Yiddish poetry. In 1927, Korman immigrated to the United States and lived in Philadelphia, where he became active in the quiltmakers' union, the International Workers' Order, and other workers' clubs.

Eviction Fight 234

~ SHMUEL KREYTER

December 22, 1899, Zloti-Potok, Russian Empire (now Poland)–February 1978, New York

Shmuel Kreyter, who immigrated to the United States in 1913, studied journalism and became a writer and a Yiddish school teacher. In 1916 he edited the journal *Yugend*, and soon after began publishing his own poems, plays, articles, and translations in both communist and socialist venues. He also translated from Yiddish into English. Beginning in the 1930s, he became a theater and literature critic for both the English-language and Yiddish American press.

Vengeance 232

᠊ᢁ Aaron Kurtz

July 28, 1891, near Vitebsk, Russian Empire (now Belarus)–May 30, 1964, Long Beach, New York

Raised in a small town in a Hassidic family, Aaron-Shmuel Kurtz left home at thirteen to work throughout East European cities as a hairdresser. He immigrated to the United States in 1911, where he became a factory worker. Kurtz debuted with poems in the Philadelphia journal *Di Yidishe velt* (The Yiddish World) in 1916. "Two Songs of a Blacksmith," which appear here, was published in the modernist "Introspectivist" journal *Inzikh*. In 1926 Kurtz joined the Communist Party. Kurtz published three volumes of poetry: *No Pasarán* (1938) is devoted to themes from the Spanish Civil War, *Di Goldene shtot* (1935, The Golden City) includes motifs from New York, and *Chagal* (1947) is a tribute to the title poet.

᠊ᢁ Malka Lee

July 1, 1904, Monasterzisko, Austria-Hungary (now Ukraine)–March 22, 1976, New York

After studying in a Polish school in Galicia, Malka Leopold-Rapaport moved to Hungary during World War I. She later moved to Vienna. She returned to Monasterzisko in 1918, where she began writing poetry in German during the Russian Civil War. In 1921 she immigrated to the United States and began to publish her poems in Yiddish, translating them from the original German. She soon began composing in Yiddish, under her pseudonym Malka Lee, and became increasingly active in New York's leftmost Yiddish literary community.

⌒ SAM LIPTSIN

1893, Lipsk, Russian Empire (now Poland)–September 22, 1980, New York

Also known by a second pseudonym, Uncle Sam, Shabsay Liptser was primarily a humorist and poetic satirist. He was born near Suvalki and immigrated to the United States in 1909. Liptsin soon became a union organizer and wrote lyrics on workers' themes, setting them to popular tunes. He also wrote proletarian vaudeville theater songs. A long-time member of the Revolutionary Needle-factory Union, he became one of the driving forces behind the communist newspaper *Kamf* (Fight), and in 1920 he officially joined the American Communist Party.

⌒ L. MATES

February 16, 1897, Bialistok, Russian Empire (now Poland)–November 2, 1929, Los Angeles

Mates Lumianski immigrated to the United States in 1913, and contributed to several of the early proletarian Yiddish publications in the United States under his pen name, L. Mates. His contributions to Yiddish literature include picturesque scenes, be they in the country or city. His long poem "Colorado" (not included) illustrates the natural landscape of a state that served as a convalescent home to a number of Yiddish poets recovering from tuberculosis and other ailments.

⌒ HERSHL MILLER

May, 1899, Drobnin, Russian Empire (now Poland)–?

Hershl Miller arrived in the United States at the age of fourteen, having been educated in cheders and a Polish school. In the United States, Miller began publishing under the pseudonym H. Maler. His writing appears in a number of workers' literary journals, including *Yung kuznye, Hamer, Morgn frayhayt,* and the anarchist *Fraye artbeter shtime.* He made his living as a garment worker.

∾ L. MILLER

November 10, 1889, Lanovitsy, Russian Empire (now Ukraine)–May, 1967, New York

Eliezer Meler, who would later be known as the poet and prose writer L. Miller, grew up in a rabbinic family and, according to Itche Goldberg, has the distinction of being the first to write a Yiddish poem about tennis. Known for his eclectic American themes, Miller studied both religious and secular subjects before immigrating to the United States in 1906, where he lived in Chicago, Philadelphia, and Detroit before traveling extensively throughout the country. Miller began writing as a youth in Eastern Europe and was first published in 1910. In the United States he was affiliated with Di yunge and, in 1925, helped to found the Chicago journal *Kultur.* Miller began writing for the *Morgn frayhayt* in 1928, along with other communist journals, both in the United States and in the Soviet Union. He would continue to publish his own work in several volumes throughout the 1940s and '50s, as well as a 1940 rendering of Walt Whitman's *Leaves of Grass* into Yiddish.

∾ MOYSHE NADIR

1885, Narayev, Russian Empire (now Ukraine)–June 8, 1943, New York

Born Yitzhok Rayz, Nadir began publishing poems and prose in 1902 in German and Yiddish and would become known by his literary name in 1915 with the publication of his first book, *Vilde royzn* (Wild Roses).

Settling in New York's Lower East Side in 1898 with his wife Khane and children, Nadir continued to publish a number of literary satires, poems, and stories. He became particularly well-known for his plays. In 1916, Nadir coedited the anthology *Fun mentsh tsu mentsh* (From Person to Person) with his close friend Moyshe-Leyb Halpern and, along with Halpern, was among the first regular contributors to the *Frayhayt*. Through his affiliation with the *Frayhayt*, Nadir was seen as a fellow traveler to the Communist Party. Due to his popularity and satirical style, he became a literary role model for the Left. In 1925 Nadir briefly opened a *kinstler kafe* (artists' café), which, though it was quickly closed down, served as one of the many informal meeting places for New York's Yiddish literary scene. Nadir wrote a number of dramas (many of which were never performed) and translated works by Kipling, Tolstoy, and Mark Twain, among others. In 1926 Nadir traveled to the Soviet Union, where he was given a celebrity's reception, and toured the country for several months. Nadir continued to write intermittently for the *Frayhayt* until 1939, while waging, however, ongoing battles with its editorial staff over political and aesthetic questions. With the purges of Soviet writers in the late 1930s and the Hitler-Stalin agreement, Nadir retreated from the paper. He spent the last years of his life writing contemplative and often highly self-critical poems. Nadir's 1940 volume *Confession* includes a tone of apology for his earlier harsh attitude toward his political opponents. He died of a heart attack at the age of fifty-eight.

∿ Y. Nokhem

August 1, 1888, Bober, Russian Empire (now Belarus)–February 19, 1966, New York

Born near Mogilevsk, Nokhem Yerusalimtshik, who would later shorten his literary surname to Y(ud) Nokhem, studied religious subjects at a cheder and secular subjects with tutors until the age of fourteen. He began writing poems in Russian, and later, while living in Warsaw, switched to Yiddish. He began to publish his poems in 1913. In 1916 Nokhem left for the United States where he continued his career as a writer on the pages of New York's leftist Yiddish journals.

The Fly 176
Hounds Howl at the Moon 178

∾ Isaac Platner

November 17, 1895, Sokolow Podlaski, Russian Empire (now Poland)–July 26, 1961, Palanga, Lithuania

Platner studied in traditional Jewish schools, which he left to become an actor. He joined the Viennese branch of the Poale-Zion movement in 1919, and later wrote for the Left Poale-Zion *Arbeter tsaytung* in Kovna. Platner came to the United States in 1921, where he became a teacher in the Workman's Circle schools. Active in both the Union Square writers' union and Proletpen, he maintained his contacts with the American proletarian literary circle despite his departure from the United States for Minsk in 1932. In the Soviet Union, Platner worked for a number of Yiddish literary journals and edited the anthology *In shotn fun tliyes* (In the Shadow of the Gallows), in which he included many of Proletpen's poets. In 1948 he was arrested alongside most of the other Soviet Yiddish writers and spent the next eight years in a work camp in Siberia. In addition to writing Yiddish poetry and satirical sketches, Platner contributed to a number of Russian-language journals and worked as a translator. He passed away in a sanatorium on the Lithuanian coast.

We Are the Heirs 242

∾ Chaim Plotkin

1910, Rozan, Russian Empire (now Poland)–1996, U.S.

Trained as a tailor, Plotkin was a member of the Left Poale-Zion movement in Poland before immigrating to the United States in 1927. He worked in several clothing factories in New York and began publishing his Yiddish poetry in New York periodicals including *Tsuzamen, Morgn frayhayt, Hamer, Idish-Amerike,* and *Yidishe kultur.* Plotkin served in the U.S. Army during World War II, participating in the D-Day invasion of Normandy. A founding member of the journal *Zamlungen,* Plotkin continued to write poetry and prose long after World War II, publishing in the United States and Israel.

Greetings from My Shtetl 332

ᑎ ALEXANDER POMERANTZ

May 1, 1901, Grodno, Russian Empire (now Belarus)–February 19, 1965, New York

Pomerantz's early education was in cheder and yeshiva, as well as in a Russian high school where he took upper-level Hebrew courses. He began writing poetry at the age of fifteen in *Grodner tsaytung,* having become close to a small circle of poets, including the well-known young Yiddish poet Leyb Naydus. At the age of twenty, Pomerantz came to New York, where he studied in the Workmen's Circle Teaching Seminar. He was active in publishing several Yiddish journals, including *Hamer, Signal, Yugnt, Spartak,* and *Yung kuznye.* From 1933 to 1935 he studied at the Kiev Institute for Proletarian Yiddish Studies, where he wrote his doctoral dissertation under the tutelage of Max Erik. This appeared in book form soon after, under the title *Proletpen.* Following the rise in Stalinist atrocities, Pomerantz left the Communist Party. His final book, *Di sovetishe haruge-malkhes,* published in Buenos Aires in 1962, is an exposé of Stalin's murder of the Soviet Yiddish poets. He died in New York following a battle with cancer. Pomerantz occasionally published under the pseudonyms Yehoshua Grodner and P. Aleksander. A few years before his death he catalogued the Hebrew and Yiddish books for Columbia University's Spinoza Collection.

New York 30
My Father the Foundryman 100
Chandeliers 124
Sonnet and Duet for Flapper and Poet 264

❧ AARON RAPOPORT

February 9, 1895, near Minsk, Russian Empire (now Belarus)–September 1, 1964, New York

A poet and storyteller, Rapoport was schooled in both Jewish and Russian subjects before leaving for the United States in 1911. In New York he studied in an English-language school, and became a successful mechanic, patenting several of his inventions. Rapoport fought in the U.S. Army in World War I. He began publishing his writing in the socialist *Forverts,* helped to found Reyzin's *Nay-idish,* and continued to publish poems— particularly on themes of war and the workshop—in *Frayhayt, Signal, Hamer, Oyfkum, Tsukunft,* and other journals.

❧ Y. A. RONTSH

1899, Konin, Russian Empire (now Poland)–June 20, 1985, Los Angeles

Having spent most of his childhood in Konin and Łodz, Isaac Rontsh immigrated to the United States in 1913 and began publishing poetry in 1915 in *Kundes.* He became a regular contributor to the daily *Di Yidishe velt,* publishing stories, essays, and political articles. He attended North-western University, became a teacher in the Yiddish schools, and coeditor of the journal *Yung Chicago.* Rontsh moved to New York in 1924, where he became involved in Communist Party circles, started to focus on workers' themes, and helped to found Proletpen. His verse, in addition to appearing in periodicals throughout the course of the century, has appeared in several original volumes and anthologies. Many of his poems have been set to music.

➤ CHAIM SCHWARTZ

December 25, 1903, Berezino, Russian Empire (now Belarus)–

Schwartz immigrated to the United States at the age of twenty-one and lived in St. Louis, where he began writing and publishing poetry, debuting in *Yung kuznye*. In 1933 he moved to New York, and the move was hailed with an official greeting in the June/July 1933 issue of *Signal*. He was a teacher in both cities' leftist Yiddish schools.

Hands 300

➤ DOVID SELTZER

April 2, 1904, Soroki, Russian Empire (now Moldavia)–198?

Born to a tailor's family, Seltzer studied in a Talmud-Torah until 1917, when he switched to the city high school. In 1920 he became an apprentice at a printing press, shortly before immigrating to the United States with his family. He continued to work as a printer in New York while studying in the leftist Jewish Workers University. After graduating in 1928, he became the cultural director of the leftist Workers Clubs. Seltzer worked for the *Morgn frayhayt,* beginning in 1931, as a writer, correspondent, editor, and poet. He also published in *Yung kuznye, Di feder, Oyfkum,* and completed several original volumes. In 1939 he edited the *Nyu-Yorker shriftn,* a journal of which there would only be one volume. Much of his creative writing consists of children's poems and stories.

A Blessing Over Bread 64

➤ A SHTRIKER

Author unknown. Probably a pseudonym, "A Shtriker" literally means "a knitter."

Figaro 116

➤ ESTHER SHUMYATSHER

December, 1899, Homel, Russian Empire (now Belarus)–December 21, 1985, New York

Widely known as the wife of the famous playwright Perets Hirshbeyn, Esther Shumyatsher began attracting attention with her own poetry with a 1920 debut in *Inzikh*. Born in October of 1900 in Homel, Russia, Shumyatsher moved to Calgary in 1911 and began writing poetry in English. Together with Hirshbeyn, Shumyatsher traveled much of the world before settling in Los Angeles. She published in the central organs of the Communist Party, including *Hamer, Frayhayt,* and *Royte velt,* as well as in *Tsukunft, Almanakh, Di Yidishe velt,* and other journals of varying affiliation.

My New York Street Sings 36
Earth Dream 182
Toye-Voye 340

YURI SUHL

July 30, 1908, Podgaytsy, Austria-Hungary (now Ukraine)–November 1986, Martha's Vineyard

Younger than many of his fellow Proletpen poets, M. A. (Yuri) Suhl came to the United States in 1923 and began to write poetry in English. He soon began publishing his Yiddish poetry widely. Suhl, who graduated from the Jewish Workers University in 1932, studied with Ber Grin, under whose influence he became a well-known contributor to the American leftist press. Suhl worked as an editor and a teacher, as well as a librarian for the foreign language section of the U.S. Army Library. He served in the U.S. Army during World War II. In addition to Yiddish poetry, which he wrote and published into the 1980s, he published fiction and non-fiction in English.

Winter 190
My October Song 230
Kh'hob dikh lib 254

DORA TEITELBOIM

December 17, 1914, Brest/Brisk, Russian Empire (now Belarus)–July 1992, Tel-Aviv

One of the better known younger poets of the American Yiddish Left, Teitelboim began writing poetry as a young girl in Poland. She immigrated to the United States in 1932, where she worked as a milliner while studying at night. In 1942 Teitelboim began publishing verse in the communist *Morgn frayhayt*, as well as in several literary journals, including *Yidishe kultur* and the Buenos Aires–based *Folks-shtime* (People's Voice). Her themes range from American social activism to romance, feminism, and war. Her work appears in numerous volumes, and has been translated into several languages. A posthumous volume of her selected poetry, translated by Aaron Kramer, appeared in 1996.

∾ L. TUR (pseudonym for L. Turetski)

dates unknown

L. Turetski published poetry into the 1980s, his final volume appeared in Israel in 1981.

∾ ZISHE VAYNPER

March 15, 1893, Turiysk, Russian Empire (now Ukraine)–January 27, 1957, New York

Born in Volhynia, Zise Vaynperlikh grew up among the Trisker Chassidim. His father, Yitshok-Leyb, was a cantor. As a youth, Vaynper received a serious religious education. At sixteen he left home and traveled throughout Ukraine and Poland, studying Yiddish and Hebrew literature. In 1910 he lived in Warsaw, where made his poetic debut. Vaynper immigrated to the United States in 1913, worked in New York shops, and later became a teacher in one of the then new secular Yiddish schools. He made his American debut in 1914 in the journal *Dos Idishe folk* (The Jewish People). He would continue to publish poems, stories, and articles on literature and culture for the rest of his life in periodicals such as *Morgn zhurnal*, *Naye velt*, *Tsukunft*, and *Literarishe bleter*. In 1918 he fought in the Palestinian borderlands with the Jewish section of the English army. He made a personal political shift, however, after the 1937 world cultural congress in Paris, from the Poale-Zion to the communist *Morgn frayhayt*. He later became one of the most important voices in the leftist YKuF. His poems and stories are remembered for their lyricism and humor.

Whiteness 164
Word 346

BERESH VAYNSHTEYN

March 18, 1905, Rzeszow, Austria-Hungary (now Poland)–September 27, 1967, New York

Though not an official member of Proletpen, Beresh Vaynshteyn remained close to the Left throughout his life and set many standards for social poetry and for poetry about the United States. Raised by his grandmother in Galicia, Vaynshteyn fled the pogroms during World War I and moved to Reichenberg, Germany, to study. In 1923 he moved on to Vienna, where he remained in hiding from the police for two years. He left for the United States in 1925 and began publishing poetry.

from *America* 38
A Negro Dies 166

SHIFRE VAYS

1889, Kelme, Russian Empire (now Lithuania)–December 12, 1955, en route from Los Angeles to Florida

Shifre Vays, who grew up outside Kovna, Lithuania, immigrated to the United States in 1906 after politically subversive involvement with the Bund. In the United States she first lived Pittsburgh and Chicago and moved to California in 1917, where she helped to organize the Workman's

Circle school in Hollywood. A prolific poet, Vays published in a number of primarily workers' organs, including *Frayhayt, Hamer, Fraye arbeter shtime, Yidishe kultur, Ineynem,* and *Dos vort.* She has been noted for her optimistic tone and for her strong focus on women's and workers' themes. She died in 1955, en route from Los Angeles to Florida.

Today 288
To Mani Leyb 298

∾ NOKHEM VAYSMAN

1894, Russian Empire (now Rumania)–1944, U.S.

Born in a small town in Rumania, Vaysman began writing poems and stories in Yiddish in 1917, often publishing them in Rumanian journals in Latin characters. He served in the Rumanian army until 1919, when he became a teacher. Vaysman taught in the Workman's Circle schools after immigrating to the United States in 1920, and later transferred to the International Workers Order schools. A frequent contributor to the *Frayhayt,* Vaysman wrote for children as well as adults.

 from "On the Hudson" 42
Anna Pauker 238

∾ AVROM VIKTOR

1871, Bereza, Russian Empire (now Belarus)–July 12, 1954, Los Angeles

Born into a religious family, Avrom Vigdorovitsh moved to Ukraine at the age of twenty and became a teacher and a bookkeeper. In 1904 Viktor immigrated to the United States and worked in cigar factories in Chicago, Detroit, and New York. He began publishing Yiddish poetry in Chicago literary journals in 1906. He also was a prolific translator from Russian, German, and English. A member of the Russian Social Democratic Party in 1904, Viktor joined the International Workers Party, and in 1928 he joined the Communist Party. Viktor was one of the initial members of Proletpen at its foundation in 1929.

Shadows 40

Bibliography

LITERARY PERIODICALS

Almanakh [Almanac]. Paris: 1955–1972. Ed. L. Domankyevitsh, Leyb Kurland, B. Kutsher, L. Leneman.

Brikn: A fertl yerlikhe shrift far literatur un konstruktiver kritik [Bridges: A Quarterly of Literature and Constructive Criticism]. Chicago: November 1933–September 1934. Ed. Ben-Sholem, Mates Daytsh, Shloyme Shvarts.

Di feder: Zamlshrift far literatur, kunst un kritik [The Pen: Miscellany of Literature, Art and Criticism]. New York: April 1919–196?. Ed. Leyvi Goldberg, Y. E. Kalushniner, Arn Karlin, A. Lutski, B. Rivkin, Moyshe Shifris, Zishe Vaynper, L. Zislman.

Fraye arbeter shtime [Free Voice of Labor]. New York [briefly in Philadelphia, early years]: July 4, 1890–December 1977. Ed. Herman Frank, Yoysef Kahan, M. Mrotshni, Sh. Yanovski.

Der Idisher kemfer [The Jewish Fighter]. Philadelphia, New York: March 30, 1906–. Ed. Khayim Grinberg, Shloyme Grodzenski, Kalmen Marmor, Mordkhe Shtrigler, A. Sh. Valdshteyn.

Inzikh (In zikh) [In Oneself]. New York: January 1920–February 1930; April 1934–December 1940. Ed. B. Alkvit, Yankev Glatshteyn, Arn Leyeles, Y. A. Vaysman.

Kultur: Ilustrirter vokhnblat far literatur, kunst un algemeyne kultur inyonim [Culture: Illustrated Weekly for Literature, Art and General Cultural Matters]. Chicago: October 2, 1925–February 26, 1926. Ed. L. Miller.

Literarishe bleter. Ilustrirt vokhnshrift far literatur, teater un kunst. [Literary Pages: Illustrated Weekly of Literature, Theater and Art]. Warsaw: 1924–1939. Ed. Moyshe-Mikhl Kitay, Nakhmen Mayzl, Meylekh Ravitsh, Moyshe Zilburg.

Morgn frayhayt [Morning Freedom]. New York: June 1929–Dec 1982.

Di naye velt: A khoydesh zhurnal [The New World: A Monthly Journal]. Vilna: January/February–March 1919. Ed. Shmuel Niger

Nay-idish: Monatshrift far literatur un kunst [New-Yiddish: Monthly of Literature and Art]. New York: July 1922–November 1923. Ed. Avrom Reyzn

Nyu-Yorker shriftn [New York Lines]. New York: 1939. Ed. Dovid Seltzer.

Oyfkum: Vokhnshrift far literatur, publitsistik un visnshaft [Rise: Weekly for Literature, Publicistic Writing and Science]. Lodz: December 24, 1926–1928. Ed. H. Beyzer.

Di royte velt: Politish-gezelshaftlekher literarish-kinstlerisher tsveyvokhntlekher zhurnal [The Red World: Political-Social Literary Artistic Fortnightly]. Kharkov/Kiev: September 1924–January/March 1933. Ed. Shane Epshteyn, D. Feldman, Khayim Gildin, H. Kazakevitsh, M. Levitan, M. Ravitsh-Tsherkaski.

Shikage: Literarisher koydesh zhurnal [Chicago: Literary Monthly Journal]. Chicago: 1930–1939. Ed. Meyer Zolotorov.

Shriftn: A zamlbukh [Writings: A Miscellany]. New York: 1912–1925/1926. Ed. Dovid Ignatov.

Signal: Khoydesh zhurnal far proletarisher literatur un kritik [Signal: Monthly for Proletarian Literature and Criticism]. New York: 1933–1936.

Spartak [Spartacus]. Moscow, New York: October 1925.

Di tsayt: Zhurnal far sotsyale visenshaft un kultur [The Time: Journal for Social Science and Culture]. New York: September/October 1916–? Ed. M. Goldfarb, A. Litvak, M. Olgin, Y. B. Salutski.

Di tsukunft: A monatlekher zhurnal far visnshaft, literatur un sotsyalizm. [The Future: A Monthly Journal for Science, Literature and Socialism]. New York: January 1892–August 1897; January 1901– Ed. Avrom Lyesin.

Dos vort: Vokhnshrift [The World: Weekly]. December 7, 1921–January 11, 1922. Ed. Sh. Ts. Zetser.

Yidishe kultur: Khoydesh-shrift fun dem alveltlekhn Yidishn kultur-farband (YKuF) [Yiddish Culture: Monthly of the World Congress for Jewish Culture]. New York: November 1938–. Ed. Nakhman Mayzl, Itche Goldberg.

Di yugend [The Youth]. New York: 1907–1908.

Yugnt [Youth]. New York: 1926.

Yung kuznye [Young Forge] New York: 1924. Ed. Alexander Pomerantz.

Zamlungen: Fertlyor-shrift far literatur, kritik un kultur-gezelshaftlekhe shtudyes [Miscellanies: Quarterly of Literature, Criticism and Socio-Cultural Studies]. New York: 1954–1965. Ed. Ber Grin, Moyshe Kats.

BOOKS

Aibrams, William, and Kalman Marmor, eds. New York: *Revolutsyonerer deklamator: zamlung fun lider, poemes, dertseylungen, eynakters, tsum forleyenen, shpiln un zingen ba arbiter-farvaylungen* [Revolutionary Reader: Collection of Songs, Poems, Stories and One-acts to Recite, Perform and Sing for Workers' Entertainment]. International Workers Order, 1933.

Cutler, Yosl. *Muntergang*. New York: Signal, 1934.

Idish-Amerike: Zamlbukh [Jewish America: Miscellany]. New York: Lebn, 1929. Ed. Noyekh Shteynberg.

Kats, Moshe, L. Faynberg, and Moshe Shifres, eds. *Hurbn Daytshland* [The Destruction of Germany]. New York: Proletpen, 1938.

Katz, Menke. *Dray shvester* [Three Sisters]. Rowen, Wales: Farlag "Dray Shvester," 1993.

———. *S' hot dos vort mayn bobe Moyne* [My Grandmother Moyne Takes the Floor]. New York, 1939.

———. *Meynke sonetn* [Menke Sonnets]. New York: The Smith, 1993.

Kurtz, Aaron. *No Pasarán.* New York: Kooperative folks-farlag fun Internatsionaln Arbeter Ordn, 1938.

Mayzil, Nokhman. *Amerike in Yidishn vort: An antologye* [America in the Yiddish Word: An Anthology]. New York: YKuF, 1955.

Miller, Lui. *Do iz mayn heym* [My Home Is Here]. New York: Signal, 1939.

Nadir, Moyshe. *A lomp afn fentster* [A Lamp on the Window]. New York: o.fg. 1929

———. *Moyde ani* [Confession]. New York: Narayev, 1944.

Rapaport, Aaron. *Mayse-shop.* New York: Morgn-Frayhayt, 1935.

Rontsh, Y. A. *Hungerike hent* [Hungry Hands]. New York: "Signal" by Proletpen, 1936.

Shtarkman, Moyshe, ed. *Hemshekh: Antologie fun Amerikaner-Yidisher dikhtung, 1918–1943* [Continuity: Anthology of American-Yiddish Poetry, 1918–1943]. New York: Hemshekh Farlag, 1945.

Suhl, Yuri. *Dem tog antkegn* [Towards the Day]. New York: Signal, 1938.

Teitelboim, Dora. *Inmitn velt* [Mid-world]. New York: Shrayber sektsye, Yidisher kultur farband (YKuF), 1944.

Tsuzamen: Zamlbukh far literature, kunst, Yidishe problemen un dokumentatsye [Together: Miscellany of Literature, Art, Jewish Problems and Documentation]. Tel-Aviv: 1974. Ed. Sh. L. shnayderman.

Vaynper, Zishe. *Ratmya.* Philadelphia: Kunst un bukh, 1921.

Vaynshteyn, Beresh. *Amerike (poeme)* [America (An Epic)]. New York: Culture Congress, 1955.

Yunyon-skver: Zamlbukh funem farband fun proletarishe shrayber in Amerike (Proletpen) [Union Square: Miscellany of the Association of Proletarian Writers in America]. New York: Proletpen, 1930.

WORKS CONSULTED

Abtshuk, A. *Etyudn un materyaln tsu der geshikhte fun der Yidisher literatur-bavegung in PSR'R* [Essays and Material on the History of Yiddish Literature in the U.S.S.R.]. Book 1. Kharkov: Literatur un kunst, 1934.

Carter, Dan T. *Scottsboro: A Tragedy of the American South.* 2d ed. Baton Rouge: Louisiana State University Press, 1984.

Daytsh, Mates, Ben Sholem, Shloyme Shvarts, eds. *Antologye mitvest-mayrev* [Anthology Midwest-West]. Chicago: Tseshinski, 1933.

Encyclopaedia Judaica. Jerusalem: Keter Publishing House Ltd., 1971.

Fishman, William J. "Morris Winchevsky's London Yiddish Newspaper, One Hundred Years in Retrospect." Oxford: Oxford Centre for Postgraduate Hebrew Studies, 1985.

Glenn, Susan A. *Daughters of the Shtetl.* Ithaca, N.Y.: Cornell University Press, 2000.

Halpern, Moyshe-Leyb. *Di goldene pave* [The Golden Peacock]. Cleveland: Grupe idish, 1924.

———. *In Nyu York.* New York: Vinkel, 1919.

Harshav, Barbara, and Benjamin Harshav. *American Yiddish Poetry: A Bilingual Anthology.* Berkeley: University of California Press, 1986.

Hellerstein, Kathryn, tr., ed. *In New York: A Selection.* Philadelphia: Jewish Publication Society of America, 1982.

Hood, Thomas. *The Works of Thomas Hood: Comic and Serious, in Prose and Verse, with All the Original Illustrations.* London: Ward, Lock, 1882–84.

Kagan, Berl. *Leksikon fun Yidish-shraybers* [Lexicon of Yiddish Writers]. New York: American Academy for Jewish Research, 1986.

Katz, Dovid. "Dray shvester fun Menke Katz." *Yidishe kultur* 4 (1992): 41–49.

———. "Grodna Atheist's Inspiring Tale." *Forward,* January 8, 1999.

———. "Mayn Tate Menke Katz" [My Father Menke Katz] *Di goldene keyt* 136 (1991).

Katz, Menke. *Burning Village.* New York: The Smith, 1972.

———. *Der mentch in togn* [Dawning Man]. New York: Astoria Press, 1935.

Kaufman, Martin. *Prolet-shtife.* New York: Royte Fedim, 1934.

Kaun, Alexander. *Soviet Poets and Poetry.* Berkeley, Los Angeles: University of California Press, 1943.

Klehr, Harvey, John Earl Haynes, and Kyrill M. Anderson. *The Soviet World of American Communism.* New Haven: Yale University Press, 1998.

Vieviorka, Avraham. *In shotn fun tliyes: Almanakh fun der Yidisher literatur in di kapitalistishe lender* [In the Shadow of the Gallows: Almanac of Yiddish Literature in Capitalist Countries]. Kharkov: Melukhisher Natsmindfarlag, 1932.

Korman, E. *Yidishe dikhterins antologye* [Anthology of Yiddish Women's Poetry]. Chicago: L. M. Stein, 1928.

Kramer, Aaron. *The Last Lullaby: Poetry from the Holocaust.* Syracuse, N.Y.: Syracuse University Press, 1998.

Kronfeld, Chana. *On the Margins of Modernism: Decentering Literary Dynamics.* Berkeley: University of California Press, 1996.

Lee, Guy, tr. *The Poems of Catullus.* Oxford, New York: Oxford University Press, 1989.

Linder, Douglas O. *Famous American Trials: "The Scottsboro Boys" Trials, 1931–1937.* http://www.law.umkc.edu/faculty/projects/ftrials/scottsboro/scottsb.htm.

Marsh, Rosalind. *Images of Dictatorship: Stalin in Literature.* London and New York: Routledge, 1989.

Mayakovsky, Vladimir. *Sochineniya v dvukh tomakh* [Works in Two Volumes]. Moscow: Pravda, 1987.

Mayzil, Nochman, and Jacob Mestel, eds. *Reports, Speeches and Resolutions.* New York: YKuF, 1947.

Minkoff, N. B. *Pionern fun Yidisher poezye in Amerike* [Pioneers of Yiddish Poetry in America]. New York: Grenich Printing Corporation, 1953.

Mokotoff, Gary, and Sallyann Amdur Sack. *Where Once We Walked: A Guide to the Jewish Communities Destroyed in the Holocaust.* Teaneck, N.J.: Avotaynu, Inc., 1991.

Murphy, James R. *The Proletarian Moment: The Controversy over Leftism in American Literature.* Urbana and Chicago: University of Illinois Press, 1991.

Murray, Hugh T. Jr. "The NMCP versus the Communist Party: The Scottsboro Rape Case, 1931–1932." *Phylon* 28 (1967).

Nahshon, Edna. *Yiddish Proletarian Theatre: The Art and Politics of the ARTEF, 1925–1940.* Westport, Conn.: Greenwood Press, 1998.

Olgin, Moyshe. *Folk un kultur* [People and Culture]. New York: YKuF, 1939.

Pomerantz, Alexander. *Proletpen.* Kiev: Farlag fun der alukrainisher visnshaftlekher akademie, 1935.

———. *Di sovetishe haruge-malkes* [The Jewish Writers Martyred by the Soviet]. Buenos Aires: YIVO, 1962.

Prager, Leonard. *Yiddish Literary and Linguistic Periodicals and Miscellanies: A Selective Annotated Bibliography.* Darby, Penn.: Norwood Editions, 1982.

Reyzin, Zalman. *Leksikon fun der nayer Yiddisher literatur* [Lexicon of the New Yiddish Literature]. New York: Martin Press, 1956.

Roback, A. A. *Contemporary Yiddish Literature: A Brief Outline.* London: World Jewish Congress, 1957.

Rontsh, Isaac Elhanan. *Amerike in Yidishe literatur: An interpretatsye* [America in Yiddish Literature: An Interpretation]. New York: Marstin Press, 1945.

Rubin, Ruth. *Voices of a People.* Philadelphia: The Jewish Publication Society of America, 1979.

Shtarkman, Moyshe, ed. *Selected Writings.* Ed. Mordekhai Halamish and Yitshak Yanasovitsh. New York: Cyco-Publishing House, 1979.

Wisse, Ruth R. *A Little Love in Big Manhattan.* Cambridge: Harvard University Press, 1988.